Six Moons in S

Six Moons in Sulawesi

HARRY WILCOX

SINGAPORE
OXFORD UNIVERSITY PRESS
OXFORD   NEW YORK
1989

Oxford University Press

Oxford New York Toronto
Delhi Bombay Calcutta Madras Karachi
Petaling Jaya Singapore Hong Kong Tokyo
Nairobi Dar es Salaam Cape Town
Melbourne Auckland
and associated companies in
Berlin Ibadan

Oxford is a trade mark of Oxford University Press

First published as White Stranger: Six Moons in Celebes by Collins, London 1949
First issued as an Oxford University Press paperback 1989

ISBN 0 19 588919 3

Printed in Malaysia by Peter Chong Printers Sdn. Bhd.
Published by Oxford University Press Pte. Ltd.,
Unit 221, Ubi Avenue 4, Singapore 1440

CONTENTS

CONTENTS

ILLUSTRATIONS

ILLUSTRATIONS

EXPLANATION AND DEDICATION

IN this book I have attempted two things.
   Firstly, I have tried to record the excitement and the satisfaction of a successful experiment in living. Like millions of others, I wanted to escape for a while from the post-war world and the twentieth century; unlike those others, I did escape. In rather poor shape after a collision at Potsdam with the Asiatic conquerors of half Europe, I was sent East, only to become involved in the seedy conflicts left behind them in Island India by the defeated Japanese. Then I escaped and found my way up into a lost, sun-brimmed valley and made my home and my rest there for six happy moons.

   Secondly, I have introduced to the English-reading world the South Toraja highlanders of Celebes, who were my good neighbours during those months of freedom. There has never been a book about the Torajas in English, but I could not attempt the full ethnographical account we ought to have. This is just a portrait-sketch, the result of my idle, amateur exploration of their lives and character. The portrait is not very good, but the subject is so attractive that I believe it may please even those who have never imagined that happiness might be found off the map or sweetness and light among people whom we—with our atom bombs —still call savages.

   I escaped alone into the golden valley of La'bo. This book represents an attempt to share my good fortune, in particular with my father and two old friends, Biddie Kindersley and Robert Riddell.

H.W.

I

PARADISE FOUND

THERE was a new moon, but the rain hid it. There was a new year, though in that land, over the hills and far away, years neither begin nor end. And I was beginning a new life, with the new moon and the new year. Before me, beautiful in the rainy twilight, lay the mountains and valleys of the South Torajalands. Behind me . . . . behind me lay the world and the twentieth century.

A bridegroom riding to his wedding may perhaps muse for a while on the moment of first meeting with his bride. In some such mood of retrospect now, as the Toraja driver braked with a strong naked foot and swung me and my servant and my household goods down the narrow lane to La'bo, I saw again the summer afternoon in 1940 when the earliest inkling of this adventure had visited me.

Out of the brassy haze round the sun a formation of two hundred enemy bombers had appeared with an array of fighters above them. An exquisitely lovely spectacle, like a great diamond tiara in serene progress fifteen thousand feet above Portland Harbour. That was out of range of our gun, so we could do nothing but watch during the early stages of the attack. In the exhilarating enlargement of perception which danger brings I saw my life, which might conceivably end before tea-time, as hitherto altogether too compliant and unenterprising. I ought to have been thinking of my soul in its everlasting peril, but instead I was regretting my failure to push through various plans for blameless adventure that had haunted me since childhood.

If I came out of the war alive and whole, I promised myself that afternoon, I would adopt a tougher attitude to

problems of time and space. As the first bombs fell into
the harbour, sending up great ostrich feathers of blue water,
black mud and silver foam, I made a post-war plan. Its
realisation is what this book is about.

I resolved that as soon as I was free of the Army I would
spend a season in a place, and in company, picked fastidiously
from among all the lands of the world and all the peoples of
mankind. Some time later I went so far as to draw up a
list of features I considered indispensable to my post-war
sanctuary:

    i Good neighbours
   ii Interesting society
  iii Healthy climate
  iv Fine landscape (mountains if possible)
   v Low cost of living

As the war years passed far-travelled friends volunteered
suggestions. For some time the main area under discussion
was the region where Burma, China, Indo-China and Siam
meet. The Seychelles Islands were investigated. I was able
to visit Bali and considered a kind invitation from one of
the rajahs there. Then I went to Celebes, only six months
before my twice-postponed release from the Army was due,
and I came across the Torajas and their country.

It was like this.

After several months of unrefreshing tropical nights I
longed to sleep for once under blankets. So when I had
finished inspecting the concentration of Japanese prisoners
of war near Pare Pare on the west coast of Celebes I gave
myself thirty-six hours' leave and turned my jeep towards
the mountains that glimmered so beguilingly in the far
northern sky.

To my dying day I shall be glad I surrendered to that
impulse. With time so short, it was on the face of it rash
to turn my back upon the lovely, island-studded bay of

Pare Pare, in which I had so nearly drowned when the engine of a small Japanese boat failed just as darkness and a wildly hysterical thunderstorm descended together. I had, moreover, fallen in love with a Malay opera company which was also visiting the town.

Incidentally, I shall not for some time forget that company's performance of *Ali Baba*, my first experience of Oriental opera. For one thing, it was as long as *Tristan* in its incredible entirety which I once saw from the gallery of the Vienna Opera, with devotees on either side of me fanning me with the fast-turning leaves of full conductor's scores. The fanning would have been more welcome in my sweltering front stall at the flimsy opera house, built in two days, beside the moonlit bay that evening.

It is no use claiming that I could follow the Malay libretto, except in rough outline, but individual scenes and players come vividly to mind. The leading man's stalwart limbs and mouthful of gold teeth rendered him only a moderately convincing beggar to the eye, stamping him a brother, in fact, of what somebody called the buxom *tuberculeuse* so often seen in *Traviata*; but he contrived a creditable evocation of pathos in his lengthy arias. (The real beggar who was allowed to enjoy the performance from the floor in front of the stalls was, by contrast, jaunty and self-assured. Though he had no arms at all he accepted cigarettes from me with graceful gestures of his accomplished feet, holding them between his toes and puffing away with the easy languor of a boulevardier.) Between her appearances the *prima donna*, a Carmen Miranda type from Sumatra, her gauzy skirts girdled by a Boy Scout belt, refreshed her baby from a shapely breast in the wings, visible from most parts of the house. I was fascinated, too, by a girl in the chorus who yawned frankly during every pause in her numbers. Having succeeded to riches, Ali Baba looked very like Dr. Sukarno and was provided with Johnny Walker whisky, invalid port and six wives; the seven of them, after somebody's death by the sword, knelt in devotional attitudes and sang a long requiem in waltz-time. A vast black moth drifted over the jars from which screams echoed as the boiling oil was poured in, and there was a dreadful moment when a lovely half-caste girl tripped up and the head of the thieves' leader almost rolled off the Chateaubriand steak dish she carried. "I am sorry, sir," said the manager in careful English, bending over me in an interval, "I am sorry that the young lady who sings the English songs is still in hospital with her venereal disease."

So, you see, there were attractions in Pare Pare, but not the morning shiver I hankered after. That, I was told, could be found at the rest-house of Kalosi in the northern mountains; so I went to Kalosi. And there I met Arung-allah, the kindly Aru, who introduced me to the Torajas and their country.

The Aru of Kalosi is a small, ugly, soft-spoken man who bears one of the highest reputations among the rulers of Celebes. When in 1942 the invading Japanese approached the Duri Country he lowered his tricolour Dutch flag and cut it into three narrow pennons, a red one, a white one and a blue one. He flew the red in the north of his province, the blue in the south and the white in Kalosi, his capital village. To Japanese inquiries he replied that the pennons flew in accordance with the *adat* of the Duri people, and they remained flying apart until he had them sewn together again on the return of the Dutch in 1945.

"Tuan will surely not return to his country without seeing the lands of the Torajas," he said, when I went to pay my respects to him.

I explained that I must go back to Pare Pare next day.

"But there is time, Tuan, if you rise early," he urged. "I will come with Tuan in his *oto*."

Such temptations are best surrendered to. Next morning I luxuriated in a whole hour of unaccustomed shivers as

14

my jeep soared at sunrise through the glory of mountains
that cut the South Torajalands off from the world. For
three hours I saw a corner of the Toraja Country and I met
half a dozen Toraja people. Before we turned south again
my mind was made up.

"I shall come back, Tuan Aru," I said. "When I am
no more a soldier I shall come and live here for three
moons."

And now, half a year later, I was covering the last few
miles to my Toraja home.

Getting so far hadn't been easy. Despite the friendly
interest of Dr. van Mook, at that time Lieutenant Governor-
General of the Netherlands East Indies ("Couldn't we
change places?" he suggested with a weary smile when
first I told him of my project), the necessary permits and
formalities had taken all the six months to secure. At the
last moment an outbreak of unrest in South Celebes had
almost brought about a cancellation of my permit to reside,
and I was eventually allowed access to the Toraja country
only on condition that I travelled the two hundred miles up
country from Makassar in a military convoy. In the end
the journey was performed without incident, apart from a
few shots fired by a fool on a crag which enlivened an evening
hour.

Once over the wall of mountains that shuts in the
Torajalands, my difficulties vanished. The Controleur of
Makale made a choice of rest-houses available, found me a
servant and provided transport from his inadequate resources
to convey me to my chosen place of residence. This was
the *baruga*, or rest-house, at Pintu, a hamlet of the village
of Karatuan, four miles from the largest and most important
of Toraja villages, Rantepao. It was usually known,
however, as the *baruga* of La'bo, that being the name of
the village complex of which it was roughly the central point.

15

And now, as darkness fell, cool and rainy, in the last hours of the year the lumbering truck turned into a gateway and I had arrived. . . .

I felt young. In moments of deep personal emotion I usually feel about twelve years old. Perhaps everybody does. Certainly my mates on the ack-ack gun in the Battle of Britain seemed always to look years younger while the bombs were falling near, and in Normandy I often saw tough Irish Guardsmen lose all their facial ruggedness as H-hour approached, and look about them with the eyes of young boys.

With me I think it is largely humility. Such happiness, such privilege, such tragedy can surely not be the rôle assigned to so nondescript a personality as mine . . . that, perhaps, is the way my subconscious argues. At any rate, a bitter-sweet complex of awe, joy, apprehension and unbelief nibbled at my self-assurance as I climbed down from the truck to meet my new neighbours in the dusk.

A problem confronted me instantly. On the bungalow veranda a group of individuals was drawn up to receive me. I peered uncertainly through the gloom and waited for a leader to come forward, but they all merely smiled expectantly and left the ball at my feet. I decided to advance with a hand outstretched and see who grasped it first.

With a bow the ugliest old man I had seen for a very long time took it and shook it and addressed me in Toraja. I was soon to know him with affection as Pong 'Masa'aga, chief of the neighbouring village of Marante, but now as I smiled into his deeply pock-marked, broken-nosed face under its dusty mat of incredible curls I merely wondered how many heads he might have taken in his youth, before the coming of the Dutch put an end to such local enterprises.

Interrupting his direction of the unloading of my goods, my servant Salu explained to the company that I was unversed in the Toraja language and, moreover, only a moderate hand at Malay. He went on to call forward a younger man who removed his hat, which was of white straw and of a kind viscountesses were apt to wear at English garden parties before the war, and approached with the information that he was Deppa, Chief of Karatuan.

" My chief, then," I said.

He laughed over our handshake and the company joined in appreciatively. I began to feel a little at home. Handing round cigarettes, I expressed formal pleasure with the bungalow of which, in fact, I had so far seen practically nothing.

" Three hundred men of La'bo prepared it for Tuan," Chief Deppa told me. " We did not know until this morning that Tuan was coming."

An uneasy conviction of unworthiness overcame me at that and I decided on a short tour of inspection. By torch-light I found three small rooms, walled with plaited bamboo, two veranda rooms with two walls apiece, and at the back a detached stable, cookhouse and lavatory. A thatched way led from the house to the cookhouse, where a powerful young gentleman in a loincloth tended a blazing fire set on a big table while two naked little boys cut a chicken's throat in a corner.

Outside, in the softly raining darkness, I saw two coconut palms marking corners of a new and gleaming fence of split bamboo which enclosed the square of grass surrounding the bungalow. Deppa, now wearing his garden-party hat, told me that the new fence and gates, the new bathing pavilion, the lavatory and two new ceilings had all been constructed in an afternoon by his three hundred men.

I said thank you. Bull frogs were croaking in their ridiculous fashion down the slopes beneath the bungalow. It was seven o'clock and quite dark, for we were only two degrees from the Equator, where the sun rises and sets at six o'clock all the year round.

" How long will Tuan stay? " Deppa asked me.

" Maybe two moons, maybe three, Chief," I told him.
" After two moons I may go to Pangala."

" It is better here, Tuan," he said simply.

" It is good here," I granted.

" Better than Pangala, Tuan," he insisted.

A serious-faced child looked up at me, and said, " Wicked
men in Pangala, Tuan. They will kill you with witchcraft,
and you won't know why you die."

The literal translation of " We shall see " was unlikely,
I thought, to convey the gentle scepticism I wished to
express, so instead of replying I opened the tin of cigarettes
again. The child who had uttered the warning and the
two chicken-slaughtermen were among those who accepted
the offer. They smoked with assurance, commenting to
each other on the choiceness of the aroma.

Back on the large front veranda I found a smiling, boyish
young man muffled from head to foot in a sky-blue sarong,
his hair and eyebrows still wet and glistening from his bath
at my gate. He came forward to introduce himself as
Palinggi.

The name was familiar. Palinggi. Palinggi. The local
prince? I shook hands, offered him a cigarette, openly
drew out my notebook and held it near the guttering
candle Salu had set on a bracket. There was a note on
the flyleaf:

PALINGGI. Toraja evangelist. Lives near the rest-house.
Dr. van Dijk recommends as likely to be helpful in
" contacts with the natives " !

Dr. van Dijk was the missionary at Rantepao. He and
his wife had assisted the Controleur in the task of finding
a servant for me and recommending a village for my
experiment in living. When he had spoken of a Toraja
evangelist I had pictured a Toraja Mr. Chadband and not
looked forward to the acquaintanceship. But here was

18

Palinggi, soon to be a close friend and tireless helper, and obviously in this first encounter a delightful neighbour.

" I live at the Ghosts' Market up the hill, Tuan," he said. " I come to help you."

Help is not hard to come by in the Torajalands.

By the light of wavering flames from twists of paper half-submerged in saucers of coconut oil some of my boxes were being unpacked. Salu—I could see already that he was a gem among servants—divided his time between the cookhouse and the veranda on which the unpacking was in progress. With wry resignation I told myself that a proportion, at any rate, of the stores and chattels I had been busy gathering together for six months would surely go astray in their passage through so many curious brown fingers (only to be painfully ashamed of my suspicions when I found next morning, as on all subsequent occasions, that not a thing had been taken).

" *Wah!* "

Repeatedly this exclamation of wonder arose from amid the welter of boxes. Moving forward to see how things were going, I found an awestruck group gazing at my film developing tank which a shock-headed youth held up in the manner of a Sotheby's auctioneer displaying a goldsmith's masterpiece. A schoolboy read out in phonetic Malay the wording from the label of a toilet roll and in a dim corner two small boys sniffed reverently at a tube of shaving cream.

Followed by a dozen pairs of handsome eyes I descended the three steps and moved out into the gentle rain and the darkness of the garden.

" This," I told myself, and I believe I actually uttered the words; " this is Adventure." Around me a hundred tiny waterfalls sang unseen. A hundred frogs croaked like beings from some eldritch underworld. Far, far below me a wildly flickering torch moved slowly through the abyss of darkness, now and then reflected in a sheet of black water. The fronds of the young coconut palm stirred above me with an idle, metallic rustle. This was the Act of Adventure, to step out of your world and your century into the darkness, ready to accept whatever the morning brought. . . .

A naked figure crossed the wet grass and stood silently at a little distance. Others, men and children, came up behind him. Light from the cookhouse fire glistened on brilliant teeth. They were smiling.

I was moved. I turned to them, and said, " *Sangmaneh*," one of the few words I had learned from a Toraja house-boy in Makassar. Friend.

A child cooed delightedly and took my hand. They all repeated *sangmaneh* in heartfelt tones, laughing with good-natured encouragement. When I moved back to the house it was as the centre-piece of a group, mincing along for fear lest my heavy field-boots should tread on the bare toes of my new neighbours.

Deppa and Palinggi looked slightly taken aback at this spectacle of *bonhomie*. Deppa, with a fine white cock under his left arm, was primed for a ceremony demanding more dignity and formality.

" I give Tuan this cock," he said, handing me the bird with a bow. The snowy feathers were wet with raindrops and the creature's unfriendly eyes blinked as I took it with all the gingerly caution of a curate receiving a baby for baptism.

" *Kurre sumanga, Kepala*," I said, and his approval of my returning thanks in his own language tempted me into showing off two more of my fifty Toraja words. " *Manuk melo!* " A beautiful chicken. Alternatively, a good chicken, for the Torajas have but one word for our two.

This vain display had an inevitable consequence. All assumed that my command of their language was more extensive than Salu had led them to suppose. Deppa made a short speech not one word of which I understood and my ignorance was promptly laid bare.

"But Tuan will learn quickly," Deppa declared. "All will help him. And if Tuan wants anything he may always ask me."

Thanking him, I expressed my wish to hear some music as soon as a recital could be arranged. The chief said at once that he would *panggil* musicians to attend me on the following evening and repeated that I should *panggil* for anything I might require at any time. Just let Tuan *panggil* and all would be arranged.

Here Salu approached to *panggil* me for supper. Ignoring my proposal of a tinned snack in the exceptional circumstances, he and his helpers had produced a fried chicken, green beans, a sauce with little green tomatoes, a great smoking volcano of rice, a dish of fruit and even a finger-bowl. Under orders from Palinggi the crowd withdrew a little while I sat down in isolation. From the gloom many pairs of eyes, very gentle for ex-headhunters', watched attentively.

The open shutters revealed only a square of blackness across which fireflies looped, flashing their intermittent golden lights. I asked the watchers their name for firefly.

"*Silly-silly*, Tuan," answered a dozen voices in chorus.

I liked that. I had already decided that Toraja was a language of pleasant sounds. *Silly-silly*, with the liquids lingered over and the accent on the third syllable, was surely a charming name for rather a charming creature.

Supper over, Palinggi came forward and we chatted for a while, he graciously stripping down his elegant Malay to basic in order to put me at my ease. He invited me to a ceremony in one of his rice-fields a few days later and went on to mention that the death-feast for his father, who had been dead for a year, would be held shortly in the sacred grove of longstones a little way up the road.

"But Tuan is a Christian," I said uncertainly. Death-feasts were, I already knew, the supreme occasions of Toraja cultural life; but a Christian death-feast had a cheerless ring about it.

"Yes, Tuan, but my father was not," said Palinggi. I took that to mean that no alien austerity would be permitted to cast a gloom over the pageantry and festival of the old man's final obsequies and accepted the invitation.

The rain had stopped. The two chiefs and Palinggi bade me a ceremonial good night, saluting me in Malay; but that was one occasion for which I knew the Toraja.

"*Bongi melo*," I answered.

"*Bongi melo, Tuan!*" A chorus of staunch, deep voices filled the little basket-bungalow. Long torches of bamboo cane were drawn from the cookhouse fire and carried, flickering wildly in the gentle monsoon, out through the gate and along diverging homeward paths. Some of the boys split the darkness with wild cries that echoed violently from the cliffs I had not yet seen. Torajas do not much like the darkness, in which so many souls and ghosts linger, to say nothing of *batitongs* waiting to steal the hearts of night wayfarers.

A young man who wore a fillet round his hair at a care-free angle closed the big gates when the last visitor had left. He was, said Salu, the *ronda*, our night watchman, hewer of wood and drawer of water.

I asked him his name.

"Barrrra, Tuan," he said, rolling the r's extravagantly.

"*Bongi melo*, Barra," I said.

He returned the greeting, took off his fillet and balanced it on the veranda rail, stretched himself out on the floorboards and muffled himself in his white sarong until nothing of him but one lock of hair and one toe was visible.

Salu had spread his soft, finely woven straw sleeping mat on a bedstead of stout wooden planks in one of the inner rooms. There he was to sleep, surrounded by my half unpacked boxes, supplies of fruit, vegetables and eggs, two cases of whisky and Deppa's gift cock.

My own little Hounsfield bed had been set up in the opposite room and a mosquito net draped round it. A candle revealed handsomely carved and painted shutters and woven walls. I wished Salu good night and secured the door with a huge wooden bolt.

In the world I had left behind we wound our watches every night before getting into bed, meek slaves of our galloping master, Time. " How goes the Enemy? " certain deplorable individuals would ask when they were afraid of what the time might be, uttering the truth which most of us preferred to hide.

But now, with my thumb and finger on the winding knob, I realised that I had escaped. Most of mankind were still serving life sentences in the Prison of the Clock, but I had broken out.

With a feeling of freedom I threw the watch into the bottom of an old kitbag. When I took it out a month later to time the development of some films I saw that it had died, as the Torajas say, soon after that first midnight.

II

NEW TO THE PARISH

WHEN I woke at sunrise and strode straight out of doors, blinking in the young sunshine, I felt a little like a Muslim bridegroom in the moment of his bride's unveiling. Quite what had I let myself in for?

Bridal, without overworking the analogy, was the picture I found unveiled. The sky was all a delicate flush and the light itself was flushed so that the white egrets flying indolently through the upper air seemed to wear cyclamen plumage. Like veils the dawn mist trembled about peaks that rose above gaps in the eddying bamboo groves. The air was sweet. Clean and sweet as though it blew out of a far and innocent antiquity.

Our bungalow stood, I saw now, at the head of a sort of fjord, a fjord of which the walls and floor had been wrought by my neighbours' forefathers into a great system of terraces. Except for some of the highest and narrowest ledges near the bungalow, all these terraces were flooded and so reflected the blushing sky and the delicate birds that wavered across it. Hundreds of tiny waterfalls connected the rice-terraces in an exquisite system of adjustment and balance that was a masterpiece of soil architecture. The music of those waterfalls was to be one of the abiding enchantments of my days and nights in La'bo.

From the shining lakes of the fjord floor, criss-crossed by narrow bridge-like paths, rose promontories and hillocks edged with cliffs of red soil and crowned with bamboo groves that were restless currents of fresh green foliage, ceaselessly ebbing and flowing like gently troubled waters. Here and there I could see the golden gable of a high,

24

boat-like roof as the bamboos swung dreamily apart in the
dawn breezes.

I was musing that long ago a great lake must surely have
brimmed the valley, or else the headwaters of an immense
river flowing out of sight to the east, when Salu advanced
from the cookhouse with a mug of coffee.

" *Ma'siang melo*, Salu," I said.

" *Ma'siang melo*, Tuan," he answered, smiling.

I was not always patient with the word *melo*, which
means, indiscriminately, " good " or " beautiful." It
described that morning well enough, though I reflected as
I sipped the choice Arabica coffee that had grown in the
highlands of Pangala, thirty miles north-west of La'bo.

" In two moons we shall see the rice planting, Tuan,"
Salu said. " First they will plant the big fields at the
bottom, the rich men's fields. Afterwards, the poor men's
fields up here." He spoke of the rice planting, as all
Torajas speak of anything concerning rice, in a tone of
quiet affection. Rice is their kinsman.

" It is a good house, Tuan." Now he was gesturing
towards the *baruga* that was our new home. I turned my
back on the valley and saw a brown bungalow, raised on
stout wooden piles a yard off the ground. The walls were
of split bamboo basketwork, the shutters decorated with
traditional designs in scarlet, ochre, black and white, the
roof of shaggy atap. The whole structure was neat, its
squareness relieved here at the back by a small arcaded
veranda on one side of the ladder entrance and a covered
way leading to the detached, pavilion-like cookhouse. The
giant fringes of atap roofing sloped so far beyond the walls
that shelter for two hundred people was provided (and, as
I was to discover, quite frequently used). Slender wooden
pillars supported the wide-flung roof's edge.

Moving to the front of the bungalow, which faced the
lane to Rantepao and the wooded cliffs of a handsome crag,
I found myself approving of the large veranda room with

its two outer walls no more than a yard high. Two steps, the lower a boulder of quartz, the upper of wood, led up to a pair of carved and painted doors four feet high. Our front doors.

The level square of emerald turf surrounding the bungalow was bound by the new bamboo fence, two coco-nut palms, three of the absurd kapok trees that look like children's drawings, a jackfruit tree and a few pineapples. Near the front door a small hole had been cut in the turf which, filling with rain-water every day, was handy as a rinse for the bare feet of my visitors. Double doors of chequer-board plaited bamboo nine feet high opened on to the narrow grass-grown track, part of the old road from Rantepao down to the sea at Palopo, forty-five miles away.

During my time in the Army I had developed a faculty for summing up new billets at a glance. This was a good one.

It was little enough that I knew, on that first fine morning, of the land I had entered as a stranger or of the people who were now my neighbours. The library shelves of Batavia and Singapore had offered only the most meagre shreds of information and in England my family and friends had been able to find out very little more for me.

Celebes is, of course, that island shaped like a mutilated octopus which throws its longest tentacle across the Equator a thousand miles east of Singapore and a thousand miles north of West Australia. The Toraja country is the heart of the octopus.

"Where exactly are they?" certain friends had inquired, when told I was going to Celebes, sharing the misconception of the Portuguese navigators who in the early years of the sixteenth century so frequently sighted narrow points of land in those seas that they assumed an archipelago where there is actually a single large rococoform island, and gave

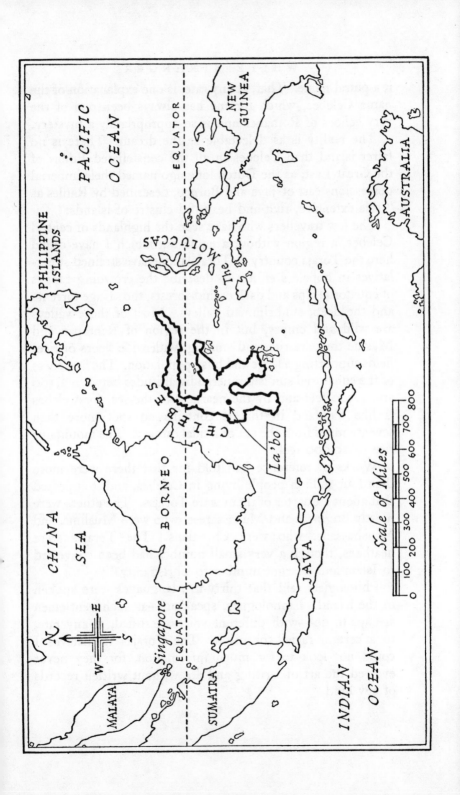

it a plural name. That, at any rate, is one explanation of the
name Celebes, which for me has always been one of the
very echoes of Romance and is so appropriately a mystery.

The reality is as delectable as the dream. There is no
fairer island than Celebes in all the constellated Edens of
the Great East, as the Dutch long ago named their imperial
possessions east of Java and Borneo, described by Raffles as
" this extensive, rich and beautiful clustre of islands."

The few travellers who have seen the highlands of central
Celebes, a region without a name but which I have called
here the Toraja country or Torajalands, have strained super-
latives in hopeless efforts to describe the crowding ranges
of equatorial alps and dark orchid-forests, the savage torrents
and the deep, sunbrimmed valleys. Most of those valleys
are wild and empty, but in the region of Rantepao and
Makale they are rich and smiling, with wide floors of rice-
fields supporting a large and busy population. The fierceness
of the equatorial sun is tempered by altitudes between 2,500
and 4,500 feet and by the nearness of the sea, for Celebes
is like England in that it contains no spot more than
seventy miles from the sea or a tidal estuary. The mountains
rise to 10,000 feet.

Works of reference had told me that there were more
than four million people living in Celebes, and it appeared
that about a quarter of them were Torajas. The others were
mostly Buginese and Makassarese, who were Muslims, and
Minahassans, who were Christians. The Torajas were
heathens, though a very small number had been converted
to Islam and a larger number to Christianity.

Philologists said that thirty-five languages were spoken
in the island. Ethnologists, speaking—as such gentlemen
are apt to do—with different voices, testified, at any rate,
to a certain racial confusion. The Torajas themselves I
could not look to for much information, for they never
evolved the art of writing and are without written records
of any kind.

The forefathers of the Torajas, it seems, came to Celebes before the ancestors of the other races now living on the island. The Torajas are therefore called Proto-Malaysians, to distinguish them from the later-coming Buginese and others, who are Deutero-Malaysians and do not seem to share the proportion of Caucasian blood attributed to the Torajas. At some time within the second and third millennia B.C. the prahus of the Torajas' ancestors beached on the Celebesian coasts at the end of many centuries of wandering that had brought them from the cradle of the race in Central Asia over the Himalayas, through Further India, down the peninsulas of the south-east Asian mainland and across the sea to Sumatra and Borneo. At many points along those immigration trails relatives of the Torajas are found to-day, islanded on the high hills while the younger races who have sometimes driven them there occupy the plains and seashores. In Assam, for instance, the staunch Naga tribesmen, who are also head-hunters and raisers of megaliths, may be recognised as the Torajas' kin. So may some of the head-hunting Dyaks of Borneo and the hill tribesmen of Sumatra.

But the ethnologists, as I said, do not speak with one voice upon any but the broadest outlines of Toraja race-history. I could understand that already, for the first twenty Torajas I had seen convinced me that Salu's race was almost as much a mixture as my own. There is, I realised, no typical Toraja face, any more than there is any typical English face. Or rather, there are a dozen widely different but equally typical Toraja faces, just as there are a dozen or score of different and equally typical English faces. Links between Salu and me are few and immensely remote, though his ancestors and mine may well have been contemporaries in early India or Central Asia. There are one or two ancient language links: his word for " god " is *deata* and one of mine is " deity."

The name *Toraja* merely means " highlander " or

29

" yokel " in the Buginese language. (The name *Dyak*, incidentally, given to the inland dwellers of Borneo by the coastal Malays, has a precisely similar meaning.) It is a scornful name, for the Muslim races despise their heathen neighbours and for many centuries the Torajas, being infidels, were hunted and captured as slaves by the clever, treacherous and venturesome Buginese.

It was only yesterday that the Torajas were drawn for the first time into our world. Celebes lay off the great trade routes first developed by the Portuguese in the sixteenth century and though Makassar has been held by European powers for more than three hundred years, the interior of the island is still incompletely known to white men.

The central highlands were the last large region to remain unknown. In 1902 the Sarasin cousins, Swiss explorers, made the first crossing of the Toraja territories from coast to coast; but more than ten years earlier the pioneer Dutch Protestant missionary and philologist, Adriani, had made contacts with the Torajas of the north-eastern area near Lake Posso. To him and his colleague Kruijt is owed the only comprehensive study of Toraja culture yet available; but this work, which has not been translated into English, is of limited relevance only to the Torajas I looked forward to knowing, for it is concerned with the so-called Barée-speaking tribes whose homeland is a hundred miles of roadless mountain ranges north-east of La'bo, and whose culture is in many ways different. The observations of the Swedish ethnographer Kaudern, confined to the even more distant tribes of the extreme north-west, are also only of oblique relevance.

In 1905 the Netherlands Indies Government abandoned its policy of non-intervention in Central Celebes. Some tribes, led by resolute war-chiefs, resisted the advance of the Dutch colonial troops, but in less than two years the last withstanding force was starved into surrender in the mountains of Pangala. During the ensuing years the

Torajas have suffered what Dr. Kruijt has called a violent collision with the West. Christian missions and the enlightened imperialism represented by the District Officer at Makale have for forty years been in conflict with the faith and culture of the Torajas. The inevitable victory impends.

There has never been a book about the Torajas in English. One might say that Celebes itself is almost an unknown island to Anglo-Saxon readers. I do not know whether the roaring falsehood that distinguishes the few pages devoted to the Torajas out of all the books of the English language is the cause of this or the result. Certainly if I had believed the *Encyclopædia Britannica's* description of the Torajas (whom for some reason they call Toradjas, using the Dutch romanisation of the Malay spelling), I should have gone out of my way to avoid them. That illustrious fount of knowledge, which passes no general strictures on the English or the Americans, does not hesitate to denounce the Torajas as lazy, unclean, short-lived and weakly.

Why so august an authority should want to calumniate a humble and kindly people I cannot tell. If I had had any respect for authorities and experts, I should have been perplexed and distressed to find the *Encyclopædia Britannica's* information on the simple facts of Toraja life in such strong disagreement with the daily evidence of my senses. We all know that experts are sometimes people who wouldn't, in fact, recognise the subjects of their pronouncements if confronted with them; but I, at any rate, would not expect to find any of them contributing to the international oracle.

The " authoritative " *Peoples of South-East Asia*, prepared by Bruno Lasker under the auspices of the American Council of the Institute of Pacific Relations, misled me just as wildly. In order that the Torajas should fit into a theory badly needing additional evidence, they are again slandered right and left. Under a heading, NOT ALL WILD FRUITS ARE SWEET, this highly-coloured authority informed me that some of the Torajas are still believed to be head-hunters, and that they are feared by the coastal Malays. The exact reverse is, of course, the truth, and one wonders where on earth the author could have come by his " evidence." The answer is illuminating.

He quotes from a tourist book by Sir Robert Bruce Lockhart, who visited Makassar for a few days before the war and found round the town evidence of the well-known quick temper of the Buginese and Makassarese and their light-hearted attitude to murder. The Scottish tourist was never within 150 miles of the Torajas and does not even mention them, but Mr. Lasker has to prove the blood-thirstiness of the Torajas to fit in with his theories; so the warlike character attributed by Sir Robert to the Buginese oppressors of the Torajas is calmly transferred to the victims! It is rather as though an authority should prove the dishonest character of the Scottish Highlanders by the report of somebody's pocket being picked in Plymouth.

It must be admitted that the one or two travellers who have briefly visited the Torajas and written a few pages about them have been guilty of a little nonsense, too. They do not, however, pose as authorities and ought not, I think, to be scorned (any more than I should be) for a small proportion of error.

That, then, was practically all I knew about the South Toraja folk on that first morning when I awoke to find myself their guest.

At once I saw how well chosen my basket bungalow had been as a window open on to the Toraja scene.

The lane by which it stood, its surface reminiscent of the lanes connecting the smallest Dorset hamlets in my child-hood days, was one of the great Toraja highways. Even at six-thirty in the morning a score of strong, naked feet were treading the rise past our gate. I took the sponge,

A Rice Barn

Housefront

soap and towel Salu brought me, and crossed the track to the bathing pavilion Chief Deppa's men had erected the previous day. It was a square, roofless compartment, a little bigger than a telephone kiosk, with walls of split bamboo fencing over five feet high, a door of the same and a floor of stout, shining bamboo logs bridging a ditch. A bamboo aqueduct, propped at intervals on trestles, brought water down from a torrent under the cliffs of Buntu Assa, pierced the booth wall at waist level and discharged a strong jet of deliciously cool water. As I approached the door to inaugurate this amenity, as I thought, I glimpsed through the semi-transparent wall expanses of rich brown flesh and heard ablutionary splashing.

I turned away, anxious not to create a bad first impression in the village by intruding upon a nude female parishioner; but as I did so I was reassured by the sight of the circlet of a fillet and the folds of a small pair of cotton shorts hung over the corner-post. Simultaneously Salu's voice, raised imperiously, woke an echo from the cliffs above, causing a pair of startled black eyes to appear above the wall of the enclosure.

I made a reassuring gesture, but the young man snatched his shorts from the wall and almost at once appeared through the hastily opened door, adjusting the fillet on his dripping hair while the shorts clung in what must have been a chilly manner to his wet flesh.

I studied him.

He was an average young Toraja: that is to say, he stood under five feet three inches, though neither he nor most of his fellow-tribesmen were ever to strike me as short, I suppose on account of their good physical proportions. His skin was of a rich dark golden brown, fairer than that of many a sunbather on the beach at Blackpool or Atlantic City. His hastily adjusted shorts revealed an area of his loins, normally concealed, that was fairer still. (I was always slightly surprised at the discovery that the bodies of brown-skinned people show sunburn as conspicuously as our own.) The smooth skin was almost entirely hairless.

The scanty recorded comments on the Torajas from white travellers tend to suggest an unhandsome race. I cannot agree. The chewing of tobacco and *sireh* is a habit which admittedly disfigures a large percentage of both sexes after youth; but any group of young Torajas will include at least as high a proportion of beautiful girls and handsome youths as would be found in a corresponding Anglo-Saxon group. Higher, I think.

This youngster, besides modest good looks, manifested the good nature, simplicity and wholesomeness that I was to find so characteristic of Torajas young and old. The candour of his eyes, even in a moment of some confusion, was striking. His hair, as with all the races who use coconut oil as a hair dressing, had beauty, vigour and lustre. It was quite straight and worn much longer than is usual at home. The fillet, a stiff narrow ribbon of pristine bamboo bark tied in a jaunty, fly-away bow in front, was largely an ornament, however, and not the necessity it is to older-fashioned Torajas who never cut their hair.

The head, round rather than long, was well poised on strong but not massive shoulders. Faces I find difficult to describe: I would say that his was rather broad and certainly flatter than most Anglo-Saxon faces, more on one plane, with small, well-marked features. The outer corners of his eyes, which were dark brown and not black, showed a very slight tilt; so did the clean black brows. Utterly guileless, those eyes. High cheekbones flanked a nose smaller in profile and larger in full-face than most Anglo-Saxon noses; but though wide, it was delicate, not with the flaring nostrils of some Indonesian noses that remind you of a winded war-horse. The lips were finely drawn, bold and very slightly everted. The smile that answered my greeting was brilliant and handsome, for Torajas of both sexes, like some Holly-wood actresses, have their vivid white teeth filed to a straight

34

edge. The line of the jaw was delicate rather than powerful.

On one sturdy, well-carved arm he wore a bracelet of black horn. His hands were broad, but deft looking. His bare torso—for he was twisting his blue sarong into a girdle—was supple, well muscled and shapely. His legs were particularly fine, the powerfully-muscled legs of a mountain dweller. There were many small scars on his strong, broad feet and his toes were parted. As he walked away his gait was strong and free. Altogether a wholesome and well-made creature, I thought, clean and graceful. I was less pleased with my own Nordic proportions as I unveiled them in the semi-privacy of the booth.

I say semi-privacy because the gaps between the upright bamboo strips of the fencing were almost as wide as the strips, so that the occupier was far from invisible from without. What was more, the ground sloped steeply up from the track to the foot of the cliffs of Buntu Assa, so that the lack of a roof disclosed a bather almost in his entirety to observers on the path up to the cliff-foot hamlet of Pintu. As it was, during my first experiments in search of a technique for bathing in a water supply that took the form of a powerful gush aimed below the belt, two girls began to descend that path with long bamboo water-containers balanced over their shoulders.

Talking together, they came carefully down the path that was slippery with mud from the night rains to within a few yards of the booth before they saw me. They halted abruptly then, and the ends of the long pipes slid down to strike the path with two thuds. I thought it best to smile. So far I knew nothing of the disposition of Toraja girls beyond the stories of the prahu sailors in Makassar, which I had taken with a grain of salt. The consternation of these two was considerable, I could see. They did not return my smile, but glanced at each other with nervous whispers. Then abruptly they abandoned the water-pipes and scampered off up the slippery path to vanish into the first bamboo grove.

In the moment of their discovery of the white stranger in their path they had made a charming picture, those two typical South Toraja girls. They were in their middle or late teens, at the height of their beauty, and the eastern sun glorified their delectable freshness. Their glossy hair was parted in the middle, not very tidily, and drawn back into a knot at the nape. Their skin, miraculously smooth and unblemished, was lighter than that of the young man now out of sight along the road to Rantepao. Like his, their faces were more on one plane than may be seen in the Western world, and their profiles, with full young lips and enchantingly small noses, were childlike. There was a feminity in their soft shyness that was exciting by contrast with the prosaic tendency towards the neuter among the emancipated women of our world.

Both wore gold earrings and necklaces of small beads, but their eyes were their jewels, large and shy, of a soft, dreaming brown. Their clothes, though, were a sad story; ragged and shapeless, they were the curse of a puritan ogre, concealing, distorting and cheating the young bodies from shoulder to calf. One wore a black, bag-like tunic having a round-cut neck with a slit below the throat and very tight elbow-length sleeves and a sarong of oatmeal-coloured fabric that reminded me of sandbags, most unbecomingly bunched at the waist. The other had merely a white sarong, the thick, clumsy folds tucked in tightly a little above the breasts. Why this garment did not fall off at every few steps was a mystery I never solved during all my months in La'bo.

Those girls had good legs, but the racial massiveness of lower limb, so handsome in their brothers, comes out now and again in Toraja girls and unbalances their proportions. Their arms were lovely. I was to find that the beautifully sculptured arms and hands of Toraja girls are the chief ornament of Toraja dance.

Not that I was able to note all this in that first short encounter, slightly confused as I was; but they were the first girls I saw in La'bo and those first impressions were confirmed in the days and weeks that followed.

To face the water-spout I had turned my back on the lane, which passed no more than a yard behind me. The rush of water had drowned the approach of many small bare feet and I was startled a few moments later by a snapped-out military command at my back.

" *Berdiri betul! Satu . . . dua . . . tiga . . .* "

A frowning boy of twelve or so, at the head of a mixed group of school children, had given the order. (" Stand still! One, two, three——") In a milder voice he joined the group in the chorused greeting.

" *Tabe, Tuan!* "

It was the first of many hundreds of such formal salutes, the customary compliment paid by Toraja school children to a *Tuang kapua* (literally, " Big Sir ") or person of consequence. I soon got used to the forbidding intonation, which at first I mistakenly attributed to Japanese influence, and took pleasure in the succession of groups, large and small, that waylaid me everywhere and everywhen to repeat the formula.

" Greeting, children," I said now, and straightway the stiff, frowning faces were transformed. Not even in Bali had I seen smiles so sweetly dazzling. They cooed like doves and laughed musically at my accent. The handful of little girls stood shyly grouped together, as though only that solidarity prevailed on them to hold their ground; but the boys came easily forward to examine with eloquent admiration the green army towel and nondescript pyjamas I had thrown over the door, the Indian sandals left outside and my soap and its foam.

The small girls, even the tiniest of them, were dressed exactly like the elder of the two girls who had just withdrawn in such confusion, except that the little tunics were all white or oatmeal colour. Each head of hair was parted in the middle and drawn back into a tiny bun. Several wore gold

37

or silver earrings and most had bead necklaces. Mud-splashes dappled the little bare feet and legs, and they had been quick to see that the new bathing pavilion was a convenient place for rinsing them before going down to the school, a hundred yards along the road to Sangalla. Their eyes were lovely. One eleven-year-old, soon to be my constant visitor, was surely destined to become the belle of La'bo.

Tunics and sarongs were pathetically ragged and patched in most cases, for the world scarcity of cotton goods, which had reduced even the dress of Bali to tattered monochrome, was being acutely felt in La'bo. Each schoolgirl carried on a string round her neck a wooden setsquare and a carved bamboo tube to hold slate-pencils. The moment I pushed open the booth door they turned with murmurs of alarm and raced off down the road, setsquares and pencil-holders swinging and clattering together.

Most of the boys were slender little things, and I wondered momentarily how well fed they might be. As schoolboys they were better dressed than the majority of the village boys, the younger of whom usually wear nothing but a horn bracelet or a sheathed knife lying on the right buttock and secured by a single string knotted round the waist. All wore cotton shorts, for the loincloth is seldom worn now by " modern " Torajas, among whom boys who go to school must be counted. Each had a sarong as well, which was furled and slung diagonally over one shoulder and the opposite hip. Some had short-sleeved tunics, striped or patterned. All carried setsquares and beautifully made pencil-cases; a few had belts with knives and cages of bamboo containing fighting cicadas tied to them. Their hair was short and some were temporarily bald from a recent shave ordered by the schoolmaster so that I could see how extraordinarily flat were the backs of their heads. I thought at first that this flatness must be a deliberately induced deformity, but it is, in fact, a racial feature.

As they danced round me on my progress to the bungalow I noticed how ankle-loose they were, how graceful altogether. I noticed, too, the tender pink of the soles of their washed feet. Only the colour was tender, though; the skin was like leather, no more ticklish than the shell of a tortoise. The sweet tones of their naïve voices delighted me then, as always later. One of them carried a flute on which he played a flourish to give an air of festival to my crossing of the lane.

It might be wondered why children should be on their way to school soon after half-past six in the morning. The road was dotted with them, the older ones moving purposefully northwards. As I dressed I asked Salu why.

The schools opened at half-past seven, he told me.

" But how do they know when it's half-past seven? " I asked.

" The *guru* knows, because he has a watch," he answered. " And if all the children are not there when he opens the school he is angry. So the children come early." He pointed to a group of fifteen-year-olds striding up the rise. " Those boys learn in the high school at Rantepao. More than six kilometres they must walk."

I asked when the school closed.

" At half-past one, Tuan," Salu told me, as though Toraja life was regulated by hours and minutes, even as our own. " The *guru* knows, because he has a watch."

The morning's unpacking and distribution of my few goods was interrupted by several visitors. One of these was Mr. van Lijf, the Controleur of Makale, what we should call the District Officer in charge of the administration of the 220,000 South Torajas.

The crowd which was helping with the unpacking, or looking on and smoking my cigarettes, fell back in some awe as the car came slowly along the lane and nosed cautiously through the gateway. The children had heard the car two minutes earlier, their shouts of " *Oto!* " long before I could hear the faintest engine-murmur introducing me to the astonishing quickness of Toraja ears. When the tall, distinguished figure in the shining gold and black shoulder-flashes saluted me on the steps of the veranda, almost over-powering testimony to my social eminence was communicated to my neighbours.

It was mainly with the kindly object of demonstrating to the local chiefs the fact that I was acceptable to the " government " that Mr. van Lijf had called. La'bo folks, who seldom saw white men and knew them only as government officers, missionaries or doctors, might well be puzzled by one who appeared not to work at all and stayed in their village for several months. The Controleur's call dispelled any doubts there may have been as to my legitimacy as a parishioner of La'bo.

" They are good people," he said, sitting himself opposite me at my rickety work-table. He held his fair head high and spoke deliberate English with an air of fatigued distinction. The fatigue was easily accounted for; it was more than twelve years since he had had leave and three of those years he had spent in Japanese prison camps. There was no very early prospect of leave yet, for the recent unrest in South Celebes had involved the murder of several district officers and the administration was short-handed.

All the same, he was one of the luckiest administrators in the Netherlands Indies. The Torajas had produced not a single terrorist in all the ugly months that followed the Japanese surrender. They, or rather the very small sophisticated minority, were content with the degree of autonomy granted them and their accession to the new dominion of East Indonesia. If he had to be overworked and rather ill in the Indies there could be no better place than the temperate, friendly Torajalands for the ordeal.

Salu brought in a bottle of Scotch and two army mugs.

I could not offer whisky to the large number of neighbours present so I went round them offering cigarettes.

"I should suggest," said the Controleur as I returned to my chair, "that when you offer cigarettes you might stay on your chair and let them come forward to take them. We are not so very democratic here yet."

He was right, of course. Right for himself. If he permitted too free an access and adopted too informal a manner he would, for one thing, never have any time to do his job. As it is, he avoids stopping his car unnecessarily because almost invariably at least one petitioner comes forward to press a claim or plead a favour or denounce a rival. The right of appeal to the Controleur is normally allowed only as a last resort after certain preliminaries, and the public dismissal of humble suppliants, however gently done, is not from any point of view a desirable or comfortable feature of a district officer's programme.

But although I nodded in vague acquiescence I had no intention of keeping my neighbours at a distance. I had come a long way to make their acquaintance, after all. As for the suggestion, which I had heard from certain types of Englishman and Dutchman in the East, that " natives " do not respect a white man unless he keeps them at a distance and maintains a *Herrenvolk* attitude of superiority among them . . . there were too many good answers to such nonsense. (In any case, a man who can use the term " natives " without being aware of its absurdity seems to me mildly a case for a psychiatrist.)

I had not found in the East any reason to change my opinion that in most parts of the world a man will normally receive from his fellows the respect he deserves. " Natives " are seldom so stupid that they will class a distant attitude as a virtue and accord it the respect that virtue merits; nor are they so lacking in acumen that they fail to discern in white men the qualities that deserve respect or contempt.

It depends, I suppose, on what sort of respect you

41

consider desirable. If it is the insincere servility which waiters and lackeys in general accord to those who appear to enjoy it, then I say you are welcome to it, for it will degrade you more than it degrades them. Respect worth having, which is not artificial and cannot be inspired by artificial behaviour, obviously cannot be fostered by distance.

But though I determined not to yield to that friendly recommendation of the Controleur's, I surrendered in the matter of lighting for the bungalow.

" No lamp! " he exclaimed upon my confession that I had proposed to rely on the few candles I had brought and some coconut-oil dips. " But you must have a lamp! The doctor will give you oil. There is a good lamp in a Chinese *toko* in Rantepao. I will take your servant in my car now, and he can bring it back. A good American pressure lamp. Only forty-five guilders." To Salu he gave the news in Malay.

Now one evening in the bungalow had persuaded me that I should, after all, have to buy a lamp. But I had determined to seek one of those Victorian oil lamps of the kind that had still lighted my childhood's home in Dorset. They worked on a simple principle of a wick, or two wicks, immersed in oil and drawn through metal apertures above which they burned, protected by a glass chimney. These lamps give out a fairly strong smell of paraffin and a gentle golden light. They burn for twenty years without once going out of action.

Pressure lamps I knew only too well. In the army and before the war I had been acquainted with all the leading makes. In my experience they all break down persistently, even though treated like the fragile things they are. For the short intervals in which they will work they make a nasty hissing noise and throw a ghastly, merciless light in which everybody looks ill and bad-tempered.

" An ordinary oil lamp is what I want," I said. " Those pressure things never——"

" It is lucky I saw it," said the Controleur.

" I'd sooner——" I began, but Salu was now at my elbow, all agog at the twin prospect of a ride in the Controleur's car and a shiny new gadget to play with. For the Torajas, like most Far Eastern peoples, are drawn as though by irresistible magnets towards all the uglier and shoddier mass-productions of our gadget civilisation.

In Malay too fast for me to follow properly, the nice Dutchman and the nice Toraja plotted away four of my few guineas in order to introduce a curse into my new home.

On my walk that morning I was alone. It was almost the only solitary walk I took during all my time there. The Controleur's visit had left an aftermath of awe, and nobody lined up to accompany me as I crossed the lane and climbed the path beyond the bathing-booth. Within two minutes I had entered the homestead of my next-door neighbour, Pong' Rantebambam.

I didn't like Pong' Rantebambam much. Already I had distinguished him among my visitors, a yellow, sick old figure in his tattered basket cap and stained geranium sarong. His cough was a terrible and exasperating sound that froze the smiles on the lips of the company whenever he performed it from his apparently wellnigh permanent position in the corner just inside my front door. That death-rattle of a cough and the lavish skin disease of his dog marked Pong' Rantebambam as my one less-than-welcome caller.

I was ashamed of myself for disliking him so, because he was a very sick old man. I have no idea what was wrong with him, and since he refused to see the doctor at Rantepao, preferring the treatment of the village wizard, neither did he; but I think he was dying. I also kept telling myself he was poor, not understanding the reason for his stained and tattered clothes, till I realised—some weeks later—that he was one of the richest men in La'bo, owner of the finest piebald bull in the district and related to most of the influential families.

I had no idea now as I reached the top of the path that he was the owner of the compound I found there, an elevated ledge with a swept earth floor surrounded by bamboo groves and several coconut palms, supporting two houses, sundry sheds, two rice-barns and, on a higher ledge in the cliffs overhanging the homestead, a death-house.

I had gone so far as to compose in readiness a phrase of mild banter in case I should see either of the girls who had fled from me a few hours earlier. This showed how unfamiliar I was as yet with the timid habits of Toraja females, most of whom flee or hide themselves on the approach of a stranger. There was a scurry of retreating female ankles now as I walked on to the compound, and the fact that Pong' Rantebambam's wife stood her ground and answered my greeting proved both her upper-class origin and the power of her curiosity.

" Lady, it is hot," I said in tentative Toraja.

" Yes, Tuan, hot," she answered, nodding and smiling with her ruined mouth. Not only does the chewing of *sireh* stain teeth, lips and gums a raw and bloody red, but some older Torajas also file their teeth almost to the gums. This gives them the look of victims of some appalling disease.

Three old men, one of them the village wizard, Sapondama, laughed appreciatively over my use of the Toraja words like old women crowing over a precocious baby. They wore rather voluminous sarongs and tight drawers like those dreadfully disillusioning women's combinations sometimes pictured in advertisements. Two of them held tobacco quids between their lips, a habit I found unattractive until I got used to it and realised that it was no more and no less freakish than the smoking of pipes or cigarettes. Their faces were deeply lined, with no trace of

44

beard, and their heads were held proudly, with fillets of plaited rice-stems binding their vigorous hair. There was nothing shaky about their thin, lavishly wrinkled limbs and their spines were erect. All carried bags or boxes divided into compartments for the various ingredients of *sireh* chewing.

They invited me to sit with them on the platform of the larger rice-barn, where they were resting. That is always the seat of honour for callers, who are never invited to enter the house. A slave brought me a soft woven mat to sit on— another sign of welcome.

It was cool in the shade of the rice-barn and that was a feature of the Toraja climate that was to strike me daily during my stay. The temperature contrast between sunshine and shade was always strong, as though emanations of coolness rose from any object not actually exposed to the sun.

A young man with a gold tooth and a silver ring came to entertain me with conversation in Malay.

" How long will Tuan stay in La'bo? " he asked. He was a well-set-up specimen with a head held high and a wide cloth fillet round his wild locks. Only the smooth skin of his fine gold legs was marred by subcutaneous discs of dull crimson, the scars of former boils. But it was the transparent gaze that was so arresting. " They are all like that," I said to myself. " That's what is so different about them. *They have nothing to hide.*"

I told him I expected to stay for three moons.

" What is Tuan's work? " was his next question.

I tried to explain that I had been seven years in the army and that I had now left the army and was enjoying three months' release leave. My Malay was not quite equal to the task, however, and what with that and the incomprehensibility to a Toraja of three months' holiday, it was not surprising that the young man, bidden by his elders to translate, managed only a halting flow of uncertainties.

45

" Tuan killed many Nippons? " he asked a moment later with friendly confidence.

Since I had arrived in the Far Eastern theatre of war after the Japanese surrender and had had few dealings with the Japanese beyond employing a temporary batman by the name of Signora, I was obliged to disappoint him.

" Tuan is not of the Dutch breed? " he asked then. A white man who was not Dutch was an unfamiliar conception, though a few Australian soldiers had been seen in the district when the surrendered Japanese were being rounded up.

I told them I was English and took a letter from my pocket to show them the stamp. " That is my *maharajah besar*," I said. " The King of England."

After he had studied the stamp for a moment the wizard asked a question which the young man translated.

" How many wives has he got? "

Plainly geared to ejaculate resounding *Wahs!* at my reply, they received my testimony to the King's strict monogamy in deflated silence. As some consolation, I mentioned that eight million people lived in the King's chief village. I have no idea whether they believed me, but they gave exclamations of wonder.

The oldest of the ancients, who had a fastidious, imperial profile, asked how many people lived in my own village. To purify his enunciation he had previously removed the quid of tobacco from his mouth and accommodated it in the knot of his fillet.

" Six hundred and seventy, old man," I told him, an answer which was received with satisfaction since several villages of La'bo boasted a larger population. There was silence then while a number of hens, altogether more self-reliant and less groomed than the hens of my home village, searched round my feet for grains of rice that might have fallen when the night's ration had been taken from the barn above my head.

A Toraja rice-barn, or *alang*, is not easy to describe, but I must try. It is a thing of unique beauty, the supreme achievement of Toraja art.

The essential part of an *alang*, the part in which the rice is stored, is an oblong chamber, surprisingly small having regard to the comprehensive proportions of the structure. It has a small door and a sort of doorstep at one end and the whole surface of the walls, the high gables and even the outer floor, are usually covered with lavish decoration. The chamber is raised from six to eight feet above the ground on four smooth columns of *banga* wood, up the polished surfaces of which marauding rats cannot climb. At about two feet from the ground a platform of heavy wood is stretched between the pillars.

The roof is the most astonishing feature. It is a gigantic superstructure, sheltering an area more than double that of the rice-chamber, rising at each end to a steep, prow-like peak and so enormous that one must stand far back to get a complete view of it.

One thought comes instantly to mind on seeing a Toraja roof for the first time. *A ship!* These people must be seafarers, an ignorant newcomer might decide, and they build their houses on the lines of their ships.

But the Torajas have not sailed the seas for thousands of years. The coasts of Celebes have long been populated by stronger enemy races, the Buginese and other Deutero-Malaysians. They are redoubtable mariners, but the Torajas show no inclination for the sea. I do not know, in fact, whether there is such a being as a Toraja sailor in existence.

It is, I suppose, possible that the houses and barns of the South Toraja tribes are indeed modelled on the war prahus that carried their forefathers from the Asiatic mainland long before the birth of Christ. It seems unlikely, though again and again I was drawn back to the notion by the spectacle of their graceful roofs floating among the

47

eddying bamboo groves as though waiting for a favourable breeze to carry them out amid the blue oceans and gleaming white archipelagos of the noon sky.

The photograph must serve to convey a more detailed impression of an *alang*. The structure of the immensely thick roof is of large bamboo canes split endwise and laid in rows upon each other with the convex and concave faces alternately upwards. Poles, carved and richly painted for the finer barns and plain giant bamboos for poorer men's barns, support the gable peaks. The decoration of the main chamber consists of a series of panels and borders of thin wood which have first been painted black, then engraved with a selection of some hundreds of traditional designs, the motifs later being picked out in white, scarlet and ochre paint. All the designs are representational, though they are so severely formalised that most of them appear abstract even after patient scrutiny. The figure of the sun and the cock surmounting it, which invariably appears high on the gable, is, however, easily distinguished; so, rather less easily, is the mask of the bull, the supreme motif of Toraja art.

I was happy in the shadow of Pong' Rantebambam's *alang*. The affection and respect with which the Torajas treat rice, even giving it a dwelling-place at least as fine as their own houses and often finer, gives to the shade of the ark-like barns an atmosphere of peace comparable to that of an ancient English parish church. By contrast with the barn, Pong' Rantebambam's house, opposite us, was a thing of only shabby splendour. In structure it was basically the same, with the chamber proportionately much larger and nearer the ground. Similar panels and borders of traditional design covered the walls. On the front gable there was a carved bull's head with real horns and above it the head and neck of a stylised cock. The high, fly-away roof was identical in construction with the barn roof.

A small hut of yellow bamboo stood near. It had

Bull, Megalith, Death Tower and Bier

A Tao-Tao

developed a startling list, which was to grow steadily more extreme during my stay down the hill. By now it must, I think, have reached the horizontal. Some kinsfolk of Pong' Rantebambam lived in it.

When I rose to go and turned up the unkind path of rock I passed the resting-place of some of Pong' Rantebambam's most recent ancestors. This was a small pavilion with an ample atap roof in the shade of which sat three life-size wooden dolls, the images of former dwellers in the compound whose mortal remains mouldered in coffins behind them. Their white eyes stared vividly at me and their stiff wooden fingers were held out as though in greeting. Their sarongs were in rags and fixed to the railing of their gallery were the horns of a great bull, which I already realised were the supreme symbols of magical strength to the villagers of La'bo. I passed the place without venturing on too close a scrutiny which might, I feared, have been construed as a lack of respect.

On fringed black wings a superb butterfly came wavering down the path towards me. He was so big that I half expected to hear his wing-beats as he passed. No birds were singing. A few humble close-to-the-ground flowers starred the coarse herbage between the wild path and the cliffs that overhung it and there were many handsome ferns. I stood a moment watching a beautiful aristocratic bird like a large wagtail, blue-grey, black and white with a long black tail and brilliant eyes. It was delicately feminine, its head all the time inclining graciously and turning on its flexible neck like a queen acknowledging acclamations.

Soon I passed through a thicket of bamboo and came upon a new landscape: an expanse of flooded rice-fields flashing in the noon sun and beyond it a narrow belt of green from which a range of half-naked mountains rose abruptly. I did not know then that this range was Sarira, the ruins of a rock staircase which in former times climbed from these valleys into heaven itself until the day when the Toraja Almighty threw it down in a fit of dudgeon. It is also the only mountain of the Toraja country in which the thieving dog-faced baboons make their homes.

Teetering along banks nine inches wide between deep paddy-fields, I crossed the valley floor. The sun was hot, but the air was not heavy with the muffling enervation of noontide in Batavia or Makassar. White egrets rose on reluctant wings as I drew near them, and when two other white birds went screaming overhead I saw that they were cockatoos. The sun, blazing on their pale-lemon crests, blinded me, and I was forced to pause unsteadily on the narrow bank.

"I was right to come," I told myself, stroking my happiness as though it were a sleek, warm cat in my arms. Farther down the valley two big bulls progressed in pomp along a similar bank. The tiny naked boys perched on their backs rose to their knees when they saw me and made the whole landscape ring with loud cries that throbbed wildly as they hammered their Adam's apples with small brown knuckles.

It was cool among the palms and bamboos of Sarira's green fringe, but my path was difficult among so many waterways. A single stout cane of polished bamboo is a good enough bridge for most Torajas and two such canes suffice for the oldest dames and the youngest toddlers. Their stout, handsome feet pass lightly across, but mine in their field-boots advanced with despicable timidity or not at all. And I had not climbed more than fifty feet into Sarira's foothill crags before I was marvelling afresh at the toughness of the Toraja foot, for the rock of Sarira is cruel stuff, fretted into tiny savage spikes and ridges that made the going slow even in my nailed boots. I had already abandoned my presumptuous idea of climbing the mountain alone that day.

Pausing to look back, I saw what appeared to be an almost uninhabited landscape, dominated by the fine abrupt crag of Buntu Assa, which faced our bungalow across the lane. A man in a huge straw hat fishing in a rice-field, two boys on bulls, the sound of an axe on wood and an occasional wild yodelling cry—there was little more to betray the homesteads and hamlets that hid in the surrounding groves. From most standpoints the only visible dwellings were the two houses and rice-barns of Palimbong, Chief of Menke'pe, which stood boldly on a naked slope above his fields.

But already I was discovering that even the cruel rocks of Sarira were the homes of many hundreds of wild Toraja folk. Several times I struggled up a gully to find a poor little cabin at the top of it with a few vegetables or rows of maize growing in carefully tended pockets of earth in the rocks. They always looked deserted, except by the noisy Toraja dogs, that were almost as unpleasant as the dogs of Bali, but mercifully fewer. I did not realise then that women and children and indeed many men in those hills run to hide in the houses or the rocks when they see a stranger.

I think I had already decided to turn back when I emerged from a sort of chimney to find a ledge on which a small garden of beans and taros had been planted. The woman who was weeding it and her two little children had not heard me climbing up to them, and I saw them a second before they saw me.

What happened then is one of the most vivid memories of my six moons in the Toraja country.

The mother saw me first and stiffened with an appalling shock, but did not move. From her lips came a sharp, low note of alarm and her eyes darted for a split second towards her children. They, when they heard her, went rigid, but did not move either. Like their mother they were utterly still, frozen rigid, crouched with their eyes on the ground at their feet.

I had seen it all before, of course; but always it had been

51

wild birds or beasts. Never before wild creatures of my own kind.

The crisis of emotion this roused in me I find it impossible to describe. It was partly that desperate pity one feels for a terrified wild creature that is in one's power. It was something else as well. At once it seemed to me of first importance to dispel that wild and false-founded fear.

I spoke to the woman without moving nearer. " *Sangmaneh,*" I said, and though I spoke from the heart she did not answer. I was smiling, but her eyes were on the ground and she did not see me. Her dark golden body was naked to the waist, her black hair in disarray. She was so still that even the frail silver of her hanging earrings betrayed no sparkling quiver of movement.

The children were nearer me, a plump little girl of three or four and a boy half her age. His round head was shaven except for a thick lock of straight black hair falling down the middle of his forehead. Both remained frozen in their golden nakedness.

I bent down and lifted up the boy. His warm gold limbs made no movement, not even the opening of the thighs that is instinctive with Toraja babies and small children when they are taken up to sit astride an elder's hip. He was rigid and heavy, and would not look up. I said *sangmaneh* softly and laughed in a coaxing way. To the woman I said, " *Pia melo,*" a beautiful child. But she did not stir.

A strange tenderness disturbed me. *This* was the primitive; this little boy was *me* five thousand years ago. To have won any sign of confidence or friendliness from him would have overjoyed me. But he crouched in my arms, a stiff, cataleptic thing, immeasurably remote, while his mother waited, wondering what my magic was and afraid. Afraid not of murder or rape or the loss of her children; just afraid. Afraid with the black, primitive fear of the strange and the stranger.

I raised the child in my arms so that his downcast glance

should rest on my reassuring smile; but as I shifted my hold on him, one hand slid across his ribs and my fingers felt the appalling heaviness of his heart-beat. It was the beat of a dying thing, slow almost to paralysis, I suppose for want of breath, for he seemed not to be breathing at all. With regret that was mingled with horror I set him down beside his sister and did the only thing I could do in kindness for them. I went away.

Writing this even now, I find myself tense and chill with the memory of the distress of discovering an impassable gulf between me and those wild creatures to whom I had felt so poignantly near.

Back at the bungalow I found Salu displaying the new lamp to a crowd of Torajas who had left their primitive fear of the stranger behind them. Squatting on their hunkers, they made a picturesque dado round the veranda room. Now and then one would pause in his *sireh*-chewing, raise himself and spit over the veranda rail, which accounted for the bloody splashes all over the steps and flagstones. I thought it looked like a home for consumptives that day, but I soon got used to it.

Pong' Masa'aga's pock-marked, broken-nosed face grinned a greeting with blackened teeth filed almost to the carmine gums. He had brought me a gift of small live fish, which he offered delicately on a string. I was glad to see Palinggi there, looking—as always—like a nice schoolboy whose mother had just washed his face instead of a leading citizen several years older than myself, for he had been born in the year the Dutch conquered La'bo. I made the acquaintance of Palimbong, the headman of Menke'pe village, whose boldly situated homestead I had admired on my walk. He looked a youngish forty, but was, I discovered later, well over fifty. Torajas usually look younger than their years to Europeans. Deppa was there in a different hat and, of course, Pong' Rantebambam, whose cough would chill us all in a moment or two. His dog, I was glad to see, had been crowded out.

" Why have no ladies come to see me? " I asked.

This evoked a general laugh.

" Ladies, Tuan? " several exclaimed in astonishment.

" Are they shy? " I asked.

" Ladies—in the daytime? " Palimbong interjected.

Assuming the occasional primness with which his Christian training had succeeded in infecting him, Salu took charge of the conversation. I was unable to follow his rapid Toraja, but his manner and the words I did understand made it clear that he was pointing out to the company that, however strange it might seem to them, in the Tuan's country ladies might visit gentlemen by daylight with perfect propriety and decorum. From the gathering primsiness that marked his closing words I deduced that he was impressing upon them the lofty standards of sexual morality observed by me and the rest of my race. At any rate, he succeeded in lowering the spirits of the company with a bump.

In an effort to brighten the gloom I brought out a camera and took photographs of the assemblage. This move was taken with calm, but when I gave the Rolleicord to Palimbong's little son for him to gaze at his father through the large reflex viewfinder, his delight precipitated a scene in which a good deal of Toraja dignity was thrown to the winds. For ten minutes or more they passed the camera round and stared into the ground glass screen to a chorus of explosive *Wahs!*

While this was going on I took Palinggi aside and confided my wish to throw a small dinner party.

" And cut a pig? " he asked at once.

To kill a pig is the most popular form of private celebration among the Torajas. Pork is their favourite food, but the expropriations of the Japanese during the occupation had reduced the swine population to a point at which prices were beyond the reach of all but rich folk.

"Yes, cut a pig," I agreed. "The chiefs and you, Palinggi. I ask you to tell them and say which day would be best."

I authorised invitations to Deppa, Chief of Karatuan; Pong' Masa'aga, Chief of Marante; Poi' Bunga, Chief of Tambunan, and Palimbong, Chief of Menke'pe. According to Palinggi, the paramount chief of the La'bo complex, old Tandilolock, was not in the habit of attending routs or junketings, so he was not favoured with an invitation. (Actually, the old man was not too popular in our end of the complex, I found out later, and I suppose that was why I was advised to exclude him.) Five guests in all.

Salu was summoned and I instructed him to buy a pig for six at Rantepao market. An evening four days later was fixed and sunset was the hour appointed.

Soon after dark that evening, so it must have been between six-thirty and seven o'clock, Chief Deppa returned with a long flute under his arm.

"Music, Tuan," he said, and cleared his pipe with an unearthly rush of harmonics. "Here is Rante, the best musician in Kesu."

This testimonial was endorsed by Salu, who was greeting Rante warmly and telling me that he was a child of Angin-Angin, the village which is Salu's married home. Rante, a lean and remote-looking man in a tattered sarong, sat on his hunkers in a corner and began to make noises on his flute which I trusted were merely a form of tuning-up. The long wooden instrument was played vertically, like the flutes of the ancients.

"Call the others," Deppa ordered, and a dozen throats on the veranda set up a chorus of cries that chilled the blood and suggested the voices of creatures from another planet.

They echoed from the storm-washed cliffs of Buntu Assa and soon there were answering cries, and torch flames flickered and plunged in the upper darkness, climbing down at last to our gate and heralding Lai'Lobo, the woman singer, and Kappa, another flautist. Besides myself the minstrels had an audience of about thirty men and children, thronging the veranda floor.

" What is Tuan's wish? " Deppa asked, his flute at the ready. " What shall we play? "

I said, " I ask each one to choose his favourite music and let me hear that."

The chief raised the pipe to his lips and began to play, the two other men joining him after the first phrase. Soft rain was still falling and the hundred little waterfalls of the valley, whose voices were stronger now after the storm, sang with the flutes. The new lamp, surrounded by a cloud of flying insects, hissed and cast its horrible glare upon rows of black heads and dark-gold limbs. Under the wide eaves silly-sillies traced intermittent lines of glimmering light.

After the first few phrases Deppa, who was a less accomplished player than the others, lowered his flute and joined the audience. Kappa and Rante played with eyes poetically upturned, squatting on their hunkers in Pong' Rantebambam's corner with their flutes between their raised knees. I listened in growing happiness and excitement.

The melodies were elaborate and of haunting beauty. I am unable to give any technical description of them, for I could not even determine in what mode they were set, if indeed they could be assigned to any known mode. A visual image which they irresistibly suggested to me was that of those tiny iridescent wasps or hover-flies which in English summer meadows are seen hovering for motionless seconds in the sunshine and then darting almost invisibly to another stance in the air to hover again. The melody, which Kappa and Rante played in quite astonishing unison, was a series of sweet, long-sustained notes interspersed with short passages of wild *fioritura*, most brilliantly played. It hovered and darted, hovered and darted and hovered again. The tone of the instruments was rich and remote, a little like a *cor anglais*.

What did it express? For a while I thought that if one could believe in the Golden Age then this might well have been the music of that time. But then I thought not. Those long, long notes so powerfully suggested yearning, an ache or sorrow for something lost or unattainable. Not the Golden Age. But possibly the reality of which the Golden Age was an idealisation. The young and tender morning of antiquity, when man had more the voice of a bird and he was sinless like the birds and beasts, and all our vileness had not yet risen to make our selves a prison and our world a slum.

The music yearned, yearned, then flickered giddily to yearn again on another sweet, persistent note, persistent as the flow of the blood. . . . At the end I asked its name and was told *pa'suling to'dolo*, the Music of the Men of Before. It has no name.

Lai'Lobo tore us back from the far-off centuries almost to the present with her chosen song, *Pa'kandope*. It is a very popular Marakka song, one of the many that form the body of light music for the South Torajas. The long series of elegaic chants for the death-feast dances are the most intimately and universally loved music in La'bo, sung and hummed by young and old in idle moments every day; the Marakka songs are the modern favourites, entertaining songs for lighter hours.

Lai'Lobo had prepared herself for song by chewing a mouthful of *sireh* and other pungent horrors. These she now spat deftly over the veranda rail and afterwards sank back into the darkest corner she could find. As she began to sing, she raised one lovely braceleted arm and covered her face, which, like the faces of all Toraja dancers and singers,

was set in lines of rigid impassivity. Her knees, drawn up
and broad under the tight sarong, rocked a little with the
song.

> *" Da mutunai kandope,*
> *Da'o tapai-tapai*
> *Matia kandope ma'pa siruarua . . ."*

There is no exact English translation for *kandope*. It
means a woman who is mature, who has had children.
" Middle-aged " would be wrong. The old phrase " a
woman in bloom " is nearer. In the song the blooming lady
reproves a youth who has disdained her. " Do not mock
the woman in bloom," she says, " for I am still more
beautiful than you and better at making love . . ."

The opening phrase of the melody was a beguiling one:

Alas, the voice of Lai'Lobo was not beguiling! Not to
me, that is, for the rest of her audience were delighted. Up
to the end of my stay, although I heard several of the most
famous Toraja *divas* and could admire their virtuosity, I
could never find pleasure in their voices. Toraja men have
voices instantly pleasing to the Anglo-Saxon ear, but the
harsh and tightly forced timbre of the female singers made
listening something of an ordeal for a Western ear that had
easily learned to enjoy the unfamiliar song of Java and Bali.

I had mentioned to Palinggi my plan of engaging a
resident minstrel. Not Lai'Lobo, I soon decided.

More flute music followed. Rante chose to play *Sailo*,
a most lovely elegaic melody which I asked to be repeated.
Kappa's choice was the opening of the invocation to the

Spirit Bugi, a baffling Toraja divinity whose identity I tried in vain for six months to establish. It was lovely, too. Dutifully, then, I begged Lai'Lobo to sing again and endured another Marakka song which seemed to be a tribute to the women of Kesu. Last of all, more of the Music of the Men of Before.

The evening ended with a group of young men dancing on the sodden lawn while lightning flickered hysterically over the northern mountains. It was a dance I was never to see again, a *marok* dance, one in which the dancers simulate an insane frenzy in a crescendo of short phrases a hundred times repeated in deep baritones, the two rows of youths facing each other, each dancer with one hand on the shoulder of his neighbour and the free hand gesturing before him. The beat of the chant was accented by a heavy step that jerked a sort of hiccup into the melody. After a somewhat Dionysian climax several dancers fell down, rejoining the company as muddy and breathless as rugger players on a wet Saturday afternoon in February.

When they had gone, I discovered with pleasure that Rante had been appointed as a second night watchman for six days. I asked him to play *Sailo* once more after I'd blown out the candle and got into bed.

From the market Salu returned two days later with a slave who carried a half-grown black pig on a shoulder-pole. When I saw him shivering in the small enclosure arranged for him in the stable I was not impressed. He was rather lissom for a table pig, I thought.

" He isn't very fat," I said.

" He's tired," said Salu.

Next day he was killed and his carcase dismembered, to be cooked in several manners for the chiefs' supper. Long green bamboo pipes of *tuak*, the local palm wine, had been bought and stood in a corner of Salu's room, a lively froth breaking through the bunch of aromatic leaves that plugged the mouth of each pipe. I took out a bottle of Scotch and delighted a little boy who had assisted with the pig by presenting him with the moulded cardboard case of the bottle—the bottle's sarong, he called it. (It is strange for the Westerner, with his restricted and not quite accurate idea of the word *sarong*, to note its frequent use by the Malay peoples in names for European articles which they do not generally use. A glove is a hand's sarong, a sock a foot's sarong, and an envelope either an *emplop*—they cannot pronounce a " v "—or a letter's sarong. The most familiar of Malthusian appliances has also been named in that way.)

The first thing that went wrong with the party was the arrival of Palimbong, with two companions, at what must have been about four-thirty. The companions, who were introduced as his eldest son and his writer, he appeared to have invited to the party, for after half an hour he asked bluntly when we were going to eat, since the writer could not return to his home in the mountains after dark. Another arrival, who had announced himself as the chief-elect of Tandung and had brought with him his little son, made a similar representation. When I went out to seek Salu's support in this early complication he met me with the news that Palinggi had sent down word to say that he had invited three local schoolmasters, but that they would bring their own rice. While I hoped that Palinggi would quickly come and take charge, Salu informed Palimbong that the invitation had been for sunset and that any guest unable to go home in the dark could sleep at the bungalow.

I was reluctant to produce the whisky and other sophisticated *bonnes bouches* which had been prepared as a gesture of Western hospitality until all of the invited guests, at any rate, had assembled. With half an hour to go before sunset Pong' Masa'aga arrived in an indigo sarong with a son so handsome that I could not help wondering about the virtue of Mrs. Pong' Masa'aga. Deppa followed him, attended by his writer.

My efforts to lead the conversation soon flagged. I was not yet on terms of familiarity with any of my guests, nor with the Malay language. I still made ridiculous errors and that very morning, anxious to show Deppa honour before a crowd of his men, I had shaken him by the hand with the words, " Peace, O Coconut! " (The Malay for " chief " is *kepala*, for " coconut " *kelapa*; some demon kept changing them round on my tongue.)

The shades of night were falling fast, and I felt rather naked and lonely and hopelessly miscast as host. The arrangement had been that I should provide the meal and grace it with my presence, but that Palinggi should relieve me of most of the graces and leadership of the party. After a time I rose despairingly and said I was going up to the Ghosts' Market to meet Palinggi.

As I turned up the narrow track to Palinggi's house I was breathing more easily. From now on I could lie down and let the party run over me, with Palinggi in charge. But all at once I halted. From the Ghosts' Market the plodding drone of a Dutch Calvinist hymn echoed across the twilit valley in the laboured voices of La'bo's little group of Christians. Palinggi was holding a prayer meeting.

Brevity, I knew already, found no place among the ceremonies of the Dutch Protestant Church. To ears accustomed to the normal tempo of English Church services, every prayer, hymn and sermon seems to drag grimly on like a forceful symbol of eternity. I could only hope that this was the concluding hymn, but even at that I could hardly forsake my guests for so long to await my evangelist friend.

On reaching the bungalow again I was met by Salu with more ill tidings, but at least those were not unexpected. The new lamp had broken down. As it happened, this characteristic performance was an advantage in that it attracted the wandering attention of the company, and my unhopeful efforts to bring the thing to life enlisted the sympathy of my guests, who now included the young chief of Tambunan and his brother.

A slave of Palinggi's announced at length that his master had just such a lamp and he would go and fetch it. He did, but it was, in fact, just such a lamp and wouldn't light either. Already we had borrowed quantities of cooking pots and drinking vessels from Palinggi's wife, as well as chairs and a table. Forms had been brought over from the school. Two candles guttered obscurely on the airy veranda so that the faces of the company were only intermittently visible.

I suddenly said to myself, " To hell with it," a device which I have found will often dissipate a complicated situation into thin air. I poured out Scotch for all and sundry, and got Palimbong's little son Torri to hand round the dishes of buttered biscuits garnished with cheese and sardine. I drank three doubles myself and didn't care what happened.

My guests sniffed at the whisky and made jokes in the manner of bathers at the edge of a very cold pool. They popped the sardine and cheese delights into their mouths and a moment later turned with one accord and spat them out over the veranda rail. Not in the least abashed, they said in a chorus, to put me at my ease, " *Tida biasa*, Tuan."

Tida biassa, not accustomed. It is the watchword of a preliterate people, the diehard answer to the smallest proposal for change. *Tida biasa*. They were the world's bluest Tories, I told myself, and the next moment pulled myself up sharply. These people had seen as much change in one generation as my people had in twenty centuries. . . .

The whisky fared better. They didn't like it, but a single nip, taken in sips, made them mildly and gaily tipsy; all, that is, except the chief-elect, who sat aloof and uncomfortable on his unaccustomed chair. He even refused *tuak*, to which the others turned in relief after the fireworks of the Scotch. One or two poured whisky into the mild, milky *tuak* while I tried not to shudder.

Now the conversation was light and easy. Pong' Rantebambam was not there with his cough to sour our gaiety, and we took no notice of the echoes of the hymns that came floating down from the Ghosts' Market with all the warmth and spirituality of slices of suet pudding recovered from the bottom of an orphanage swill-bin.

Pong' Massa'aga gave me an awkward moment when he asked me whether, in fact, I was a Christian, his tone clearly implying that, at any rate, I had more sense than to be singing hymns that seemed to wail of endless suffering when I could be getting tipsy with a crowd of heathens. I said there were good and bad Christians, and I was a bad one.

At last Palinggi arrived, accompanied by the schoolmasters. When he had swallowed a nip of Scotch that brought astonished tears to his eyes, we sat down sixteen at table.

Naturally, I had wondered how a pig of a size judged suitable for six diners would work out among sixteen; but my preoccupation was diverted by Salu, who appeared to be trying to dispel the genial atmosphere by setting up at my end of the table an intimidating display of cutlery and ware, including the finger-bowl and a plate of red-hot soup, just to show how different I was from my guests even if I did sit down at table with them. Four huge volcanic cones of rice were then brought in by helpers, bowls of vegetables and dishes of eggs, besides roast and fried pork. There was also a plate of corrosive spices.

Just as we pulled forward the forms and took our seats Pong' Rantebambam came out of the night and collapsed with a loud groan into his accustomed corner.

While the pork assigned to me got cold I toyed with the scalding soup, watched with interest by the others. They ate

63

with their fingers, whisking small balls of rice and meat together and tossing them with dainty dexterity into their mouths. Mastication was less dainty, but I concentrated on the main impression, which was one of sober appreciation. Round the cookhouse door I could see a crowd of children gnawing bones.

Not knowing how much they may have expected, I could not tell whether, in fact, they found the meal satisfying or not. It took a long time to eat, at all events, and everybody had three helpings. I think there was plenty and that Salu had been less taken aback than I by the number of gate-crashers. When I remarked to him afterwards that I couldn't recall inviting most of the guests, he said with calm, " *Biasa*, Tuan." That, I realised, was another of the phrases with which one never argued, " It is usual."

Conversation after supper ranged widely, from my military career and my travels to the character of the English race, from Indonesian independence to the noble families of the district, and led finally to the marvels of modern science. I wished then, and several times subsequently, that I had had with me some such volume as the *Boy's Wonder Book of Science*, for the Torajas take the same naïve delight in scientific " progress " as did our Victorian ancestors.

It was established that evening that the two subjects on which I could discourse to the maximum appreciation of a Toraja audience were the photo-electric cell and artificial insemination. I know very little about either, but a sort of *Reader's Digest* report on one or the other never failed to grip. I was pleased to notice that while they shared my childish pleasure in the former, which they could see mildly at work in my photographic light meter, they shared my horror at the latter.

The schoolmasters talked too much. The chief-elect's little son was sick. Pong' Rantebambam, of course, coughed. The veranda grew chilly. It was a relief when an anxious slave came in to beg my assistance in destroying a rabid dog which, he said, had been wounded but was still prowling round a hamlet of Marante.

"Make a festival of everything," is the Toraja motto, and the whole company set out with bamboo torches as an escort to me and my revolver. It struck me as something less than festive, for I knew that the doctor in Rantepao had no anti-rabies serum. Not that a mad dog's bite was fun even within reach of full medical assistance; a friend who had once been bitten assured me that the massive rabies injections were worse than rape.

We all got wet, for the rain had not quite stopped. Deppa's writer fell into a rice-field and got wetter still. The torches dazzled the eyes without shedding much light on the narrow paths. The slave went ahead, talking ceaselessly in an awed voice.

We found the dog under the piles of a house, making a ghastly shuddering noise. The party came to a standstill and looked at me. It was my cue to impersonate a resolute white man taking charge of an emergency, but I was affected by a slight attack of stage fright. Like a fool I had not brought my electric torch and most of the bamboo ones had now gone out; those still alight shed not the faintest gleam under the house.

I was still wearing my field-boots. A wounded dog, rabid or not, should be unable to bite above knee height, I told myself as I took a torch in my left hand and went down the slope to the house, trying not to think of Pasteur and the Russian peasants.

My guess is that the wretched beast was hardly capable of movement, much less attack, though I did not wait to find out. The moment I glimpsed him in the red torchlight, his intent eyes alarmingly near me and some distance from the corner into which I had been peering, I gave him two rounds. He rolled over and I give him another from a range of half a yard. There were loud shouts as the echo of the shots died and sudden light radiated above my head. Inadvertently I had held the torch under a large basket hanging from the wall of the house, and this was going up in cheerful flames.

An old woman screamed, and it looked as though the bamboo house would go up, too; but three or four of us tore down the basket and another that had begun to burn and peace returned.

It made a nice end to the evening.

66

III

A SUPERIOR TYPE OF FUNERAL

HAD I kept an engagement book during my time in La'bo most of the dates noted in it would have been funerals. The most frequent occasions of entertainment, song and dance in the Toraja country are the death feasts, which survive while the other great festivals and ceremonies are lapsing into oblivion.

It is difficult to believe that there remains in existence anywhere in the world a pagan festival so exciting, so colourful or so impressive as a great Toraja *tomate*. To take part in one is to voyage for a few brilliant hours far back along the track down which our ancestors made their way from the silver mists of the antique world. An adventure.

When a prominent Toraja dies his last breath is the starting signal for a succession of festivals, offerings and rituals that may cover three or even four years and culminate in a final feast lasting more than a week, at the end of which the body is at last carried to the tomb. The period for a poor man is short and the ceremonies few and simple; but whether rich or poor a Toraja is of greater importance during that period than ever he was in life.

However gentle and indulgent a man may have been while living, after death his soul is jealous and exacting. If his family fail to carry out most meticulously the proper sequence of ritual over his mortal remains he will be revenged on them with all manner of misfortune. This fear of the stern spirits of the dead the Torajas share, of course, with almost all communities of earlier man.

It does not, however, cast the slightest gloom over the

WHITE STRANGER

final feast. By that time grief over their loss has run its course and the chief mourners, their duty well done, join with their guests in days and nights of entertainment, with the dead person (as the Torajas say) presiding over the feast field in his high-roofed death-tower, a beneficent presence so long as the ancient forms are faithfully observed.

Until the final feast the body remains in the house in which it died. Respect for the dead is so great that the presence of the decaying body in an open coffin is endured with patience and without disgust. Death and the corruption of the body are familiar processes to the smallest Toraja children. Food is cooked and offered to the dead person and the high-born dead have attendants and a vestal who must stay in their immediate presence from the hour of death to the day of the final progress to the tomb.

It is for the final death-feasts that well-to-do Torajas invite large numbers of guests. I received four such invitations during my first week in La'bo.

The first was for the *tomate* of the brother of the Puang of Menkendek. I went with the Controleur and Mrs. van Lijf for the three midday hours of the opening day, the time during which the dead person arrives on the feast-field to mark the most exciting climax of the whole feast. Our car turned south from Makale, and after climbing a rocky track brought us to the arena in which the death-feasts for members of the royal family of Menkendek are held.

"Walk slowly," said the Controleur as we alighted and entered the arena, for I was moving forward eagerly. "They will send out someone to meet us, you see. It would embarrass them if we were to reach the pavilion before we had been greeted."

A handsome son of the Puang approached and welcomed us formally, leading us then to the large pavilion reserved for more exalted guests where the Puang received us, big, fleshy and assertive in a robe of black satin. Over neat

68

whisky in a port-wine glass I chatted with the old Aru of
Kalosi, renewing the acquaintance made almost a year
earlier when he had led me into the Toraja country for the
first time. Most of the prominent figures in Toraja life
were there and several of the tiny white community, including the officer commanding the troops in Rantepao
and Makale and the senior Roman Catholic missionary.
We sat at ease in rattan arm-chairs looking out upon the
rante, or feast-field.

It was a little larger than Piccadilly Circus, with a double
row of megaliths across the middle. The great stones were
unworked and unmatched, some of them leaning at weary
angles. To each a fine bull was tethered. The western arc
of the circle was marked by a crescent of fifty large yellow
guest-houses of bamboo with a very tall boat-roofed tower
in the middle. Each house was crowded with invited guests,
more than a thousand of them, and spectators from miles
around thronged the banks below the guest-houses and the
eastern slopes of the *rante*.

Tree-clad bluffs rose behind the death-tower and the
horseshoe of yellow lodges, but the eastern arc of the field
fell into a narrow valley, on the far side of which rose a
noble mountain. This was Buntu Kandora, all that now
remains of the former rock staircase to heaven down which
the Puang's ancestor Tamborolangi, who was a god,
descended to found the royal families of Menkendek,
Sangalla and Makale. Seen from the Menkendek *rante* it
was a fine cone, with prodigious faces of sheer rock; seen
from the track by our bungalow at La'bo it was a table
mountain, more suggestive of the broken-off base of the
column that had once risen beyond the sight of man and
thrown its morning and evening shadows to the edges of
the world.

It irked me to sit in the seats of the mighty drinking
whisky when I might have been mingling with the vivid
crowds below, taking photographs and tasting more of the

excitement and colour that ran in swift currents round the circular field. Through my field-glasses I could see in the distance an excited crowd on a small hillock, with the horns of a small Toraja roof and shining horns, too, on the helmets of dancers whose spears blazed in the sunshine. I wanted badly to go down there, but instead I had to head one of the many tables in the luncheon pavilion, with the Puang on my right.

There was a great deal of food: pork, buffalo meat, spiced chicken, rice and strange vegetables, served by the Puang's kinswomen in heavy gold necklaces and earrings. The prince himself ate very little, for the cares of a host weighed heavily on him. Several times he broke off conversation with me to shout new orders across my face in a drill-sergeant's voice, and when it became obvious that through faulty synchronisation the procession of the dead person to the *rante* had begun while we were still eating he was obliged to blow his nose on his satin skirts in consternation. (The Puang was the only upper-class Toraja I met whose manners I considered inferior to my own.)

I escaped at last just as the head of the procession approached the feast-field in an intoxicating crescendo of the wild cries that had not ceased from the moment it set out. Ahead of the dead person twenty youths carried the *belotedung*, the flag or emblem of the bull. Only at the death-feasts of those of Puang rank is the *belotedung* seen, a high fan-like structure of bamboo and scarlet and white cloth with plumes and streamers, and a long train of festooned cane. From it radiates the strongest magic known to the Torajas.

A hundred slaves bore the coffin, which was a scarlet cylinder richly ornamented with gold leaf and mounted on an elaborate bier with a high, golden ark-like roof, the whole erected on a wide platform. The slaves who carried it shouted like madmen wild with joy, and jigged the heavy platform frantically up and down whenever they paused in their progress. The dead man's sons, travelling on the bier, clung uneasily to the pillars of the roof. War dancers with spears and plumes, bull-hide shields and silver-horned helmets covered with large silver coins were in attendance, and danced every time the procession halted.

Close behind the dead person travelled his *tao-tao*, his wooden effigy that would later stand outside the door of his tomb. It was life-size and mounted on a horse. Out of the brown wooden face white eyes stared vividly. It wore a tunic of black cloth and a rich tartan sarong, with many gold stars and necklaces and a magnificent turban of indigo and gold silk with plumes. Even the richly caparisoned wooden horse wore a turban, with brooches of beaten gold. The structure on which the models were mounted was decorated with dozens of fine gold swords and rich cloths, with several beaded, bell-shaped emblems of royal rank swinging above it. Sixty slaves bore it along.

In the wake of the *tao-tao* lurched two small black tents on the shoulders of slaves. The two widows of the departed were doubled up inside these; their loud ceremonial weeping could be heard above the exultant shouts of the throng if you got near enough. And finally, plunging along in the rear, came the bulls, scores of them stampeding towards their place of sacrifice. These were immortal creatures, destined after their sacrifice to live in eternal content as the dead prince's herd in the pastures of paradise.

As the procession climbed up to the *rante* the yelling rose to a climax that strained something in one's ear or brain to its utmost limit. If Caruso could shatter a wine-glass with the resonance of one of his notes, I reflected, then surely the whole edifice of the death-tower and Buntu Kandora itself could be in danger of collapse now. Only when the coffin, extracted from the bier, had been hoisted up the high, steep ramp into its commanding station in the top story of the death-tower did the clamour fall, so that the sobbing of the women and the remote consolation of the flutes could be heard.

The famished brown buzzards that had veered away when the shouting started returned now to swing and drift above the platform under which several bulls had already been ceremonially slaughtered. The high, branching tree of bamboo poles, flying flags and pennons of fine cloth was dismantled. The dancers retired. A gong was beaten in the ground floor of the death-tower and then there was silence.

And then the bullfights.

The delirium of the dead person's arrival and the new uprush of excitement among the crowd as the bulls were brought forward prepared me for a spectacle of blood and perhaps horror; but Toraja bullfights are curiously unspectacular as a rule. Pairs of bulls, many of them awaiting the sacrificial knife, fight each other for a few moments or minutes, often without bloodshed, very seldom inflicting more than light flesh wounds and practically never *à outrance*.

To an outsider there is something ridiculous about the preliminaries to a fight. The two noble, supermasculine beasts lumber up to each other and then, instead of coming to grips, elevate their noses, turn sideways and gaze at each other in oblique disdain, like bad actresses in *grande dame* rôles. This goes on for minutes in some cases, with one beast now and then appearing to lose interest and walking away, only to whirl round at speed if the other makes a lunge at his exposed flank.

When at last they engage, head-on, with a loud clash of horns, the crowd sets up a yell of frantic hero-worship and delight. The bulls lay their noses along the ground and push. You expect their heaving necks, bent into semi-circles, to snap. The massive rear hooves are straddled, the great nostrils flaring as they breathe stertorously back between their legs. Their attendants urge them on with frenzied shouts. Then one pair of hooves begins to slide and all at once the weaker bull disengages and lumbers off, with the victor in half-hearted pursuit for a few yards.

Only one pair put up a good show that day. They clinched three times, once in a flooded paddy-field, scattering mud and bubbles in all directions. Finally, the mud-drenched loser stampeded across the *rante* to the delighted alarm of everybody.

After that the white guests left. I determined as I went that at the death-feast for the Puang of Sangalla's mother, to which I had also been invited, I would make arrangements with the Puang whereby I could take more part in the proceedings.

A few days after that Palinggi asked whether I would like to see a *simbuang* erected. A *simbuang*, though the word means strictly no more than " stone," is a megalith or longstone of the kind standing in arcs on each funeral feast-field or *rante* (a word in its turn meaning strictly no more than " place," just as *tomate* means merely " dead person ").

" To-day we will raise my father's *simbuang*," he said.

So I went along to the feast-field of his family, which was no more than two hundred yards from our gate, smaller than the one at Menkendek, with a less elaborate death-tower flanked by no more than a dozen guest-houses. Little cliffs and bamboo groves shut it in except on the north side, which faced, across a deep rice-field, the rocky islet on which Pong' Masa'aga's fine new house was being built. In the bottom of the field the great stone had been found, and when I got there a dozen men were working knee-deep in the water attaching ropes of twisted bamboo bark to it.

By now I had seen many feast-fields and was aware of the practice of raising at least one new longstone for the feast of each prominent dead person; but always the great stones suggested antiquity to me. Because of Stonehenge and the few examples of megalithic erections I had seen, of course. It was pleasant, I told myself freakishly, to be entering the strictly limited company of white men who have seen a megalith erected.

Near the water's edge my small friend Lindung's father and a dozen others were setting up what looked at first like a gallows. As the morning went on it became a windlass or winch, with rough cross-pieces fixed as spokes to the high axle. There was not a nail in the whole erection. On the far side of the field other men were digging a hole near the end of one of the two arcs of longstones, while others erected over it a simple goalpost kind of scaffolding.

It took two days to get the big stone into position. Dragging it out of the bed of the rice-field and across the *rante* took eighty men five hours. The stout, ten-feet-long rock gouged a deep scar across the field in its slow progress. Tandilolock and Pong' Masa'aga acted as foremen, shouting encouragement and taunts as the mass of stone crept forward, or, more often, lay still despite the straining of the best muscles in the district.

" Girls you are! " old Tandilolock would cry, marching up and down in a strange pair of tight cream drawers and an elaborate fillet of plaited rice-straw. " Old women! Must I, the aged one, show you the way? "

I lent a hand myself, throwing my jacket over a longstone that was already draped with a dozen sarongs. I was glad, however, when one of the ropes of raw, twisted bamboo snapped and I could withdraw inconspicuously.

When the great stone lay at last with its foot close beside the grave dug for it, the long pulling ropes were passed over the cross-piece of the goal posts above the hole, carried twenty-five yards across the *rante* to the tall winch and passed many times round the axle. The fourscore men held other ropes attached to the stone's head and on a signal from

Pong' Masa'aga they began pulling, while men hanging on to the spokes of the windlass threw themselves kicking in mid-air in efforts to pull it round. Nothing happened for a moment, and then the tall windlass tottered and collapsed, throwing slaves in all directions.

" We will try again to-morrow," said Palinggi, apparently unperturbed in the face of the necessity to pay (with food, not wages) a hundred extra men for two days instead of one. He had already slaughtered a cow for their morning meal.

The windlass built next day and an extra score of men succeeded at last in raising the head of the stone until its foot slipped heavily into the little grave dug for it. With a rush, in which several might have been crushed to death, a circle of men surrounded the megalith, ready to resist any dangerous leaning before its foot was wedged tightly with stones and sods. It looked strangely unimpressive as a climax to such sweat and perseverance. The field was silent upon the dying of the wild choruses with which the men had stimulated their effort on the ropes.

The mud-splashed, sweat-drenched labourers filed off to the bathing-pool in a corner of the paddy-field, and boys brought bamboos of water and climbed the goal posts to pour them over the muddy, ill-shaped menhir. Palinggi and I watched until it was clean, its wet, tawny facets blazing in the afternoon sun; seeing the sun for the first time, maybe, in a million years.

I had been told that the *simbuangs* were phallic symbols, but that I doubt very much. Certainly the columns standing in the rice-fields of Pangala and Bituang, which I saw later in my stay, must be fertility symbols, but the megaliths on the fields of funeral feasts are surely commemorative. " My father's *simbuang*," Palinggi had said. Torajas are careful to keep separate the two distinct compartments of their religion, named by them the Religion of the Rising Sun, symbolised by rice and concerned with the affairs of the living; and the Religion of the Setting Sun, connected exclusively with death and the many ceremonies for the souls of the dead. Certain principal mourners, for instance, are forbidden to eat rice from the day of their kinsman's death until the death-feast has passed its climax. I would not expect them to raise emblems of the life force in that place.

" They are building a pavilion for Tuan," Palinggi said, pointing to a group of men who were swiftly plaiting walls for a neat shelter by the entrance to the field. " I have ordered it. I will put a table and a chair in there and Tuan may see all at his ease."

It was a kindly thought for which I was grateful during the leisurely hours of the feast, which opened a few days later. It lasted five days and nights, and Palinggi made it most pleasantly clear that I was welcome at any time.

On this occasion I had a few glimpses behind the scenes. I saw Palinggi's wife and the dead man's kinswomen baking huge mounds of biscuits and cakes on the eve of the opening. I often helped to find Palinggi's frequently mislaid sheaf of papers with names and numbers of the various ceremonial delegations and their agreed times of arrival and contributions, lists of bulls given outright for sacrifice or lent only for fighting, lists of borrowed crockery and finery for the dead man's effigy and many other memoranda. I was a sympathetic witness of Palinggi's growing exhaustion as days and nights passed with sometimes no more than a single hour's sleep, till on the last day he fell suddenly asleep on my shoulder in the guest-house next to the death-tower, from which everything that went on in the field of stones could be observed through a yellow grill of baby bamboo canes.

My only contributions were a gift of cigarettes, the typing of the invitations and the loan of the beastly lamp, which contrived to break down no more than once in five nights and shed its sick, blinding beams through a lattice on to the circles of dancers chanting and tracing their slow rings from midnight to dawn.

The thrill of the dead person's arrival on the feast-field was every bit as heart-warming as at the Menkendek feast, though less elaborate. The bulls fought better and the smaller *rante* and restricted outlook gave the feast a feeling of greater intimacy. The megaliths were muffled in the various branches and giant fronds that local custom decreed must be tied to them. To each stone was tethered a bull, and the field became so crowded with stones, trees, bulls and grooms that you couldn't see across it. Buffaloes were slaughtered under the *balaka'an*, the platform from which the wizard subsequently threw the joints of bull-meat to the guests in turn, and the buzzards circled endlessly, descending now and again on small pieces of carrion in daring, ravenous swoops. In so small a sacred grove the crowds of hundreds seemed larger than the thousands at Menkendek.

The heat on the first day was intense. Kopeh, one of the little boys who had slaughtered and plucked the chicken for my first supper in La'bo, was spending his last hours with his bull, which was tied to one of the longstones and due to be sacrificed at sunset. He lay spreadeagled on his face across the great beast's back like a cavalryman killed in action, while his brother brought a bamboo of cool water from the bathing-pool to pour over their doomed hero's head and shoulders. The gilded dragonflies shone in companies over the flooded field below, and languor affected every moving thing until my drowsy eyes might have been watching a slow-motion film.

In the days that followed there were many such hours of tranced indolence. My short visit to the Menkendek feast had, in fact, given me a misleading impression of a *tomate*, which had seemed then an occasion of sustained and titanic excitement. So it is during the climax of the dead person's arrival and to a lesser extent while the bulls are fighting;

but there are many days and nights to a death-feast, and the more clamorous thrills occupy at most an hour or two. The main activities are the arrival and reception of ceremonial delegations by day and the dancing by night.

About a dozen delegations arrived during the five days, big ones from districts like Sangalla, small ones from villages like Menke'pe. I took most pleasure in the delegation from our own village, Karatuan, so I will tell you about that.

The sound of a gong, beaten at intervals of about twenty seconds, was always the first intimation of an embassy's approach. I would leave my chair and move into the sunshine outside my pavilion, for the entrance to the field was behind the pavilion and it was always pleasant to watch the long procession file up the path, with its reflection advancing through the blue waters of the field below. The seer Pong' Sakuru carried the gong at the head of Karatuan's delegation, his face grave, setting a slow pace. Behind him trod six bulls, each led by an adult attendant, and Barra's uncle carrying a glittering lantern-shaped device of beads on a high cane like a banner. Twenty men came next, carrying ten large pigs, each slung on a pole resting on the shoulders of two men moving in single file. One of these bearers was a droll youth of my acquaintance whom I called Oberammergau, on account of the sculptured saintliness of his face and his own quite unpronounceable name; but he gave no sign of recognition as he passed me, and when his pig kicked and squealed his apostolic features remained gravely impassive.

There followed a number of men and boys carrying chickens in wicker globes, succeeded by slaves bearing firewood and buffalo fodder and a dozen boys with green, frothing pipes of *tuak* over their shoulders. Fruit and vegetables were carried by women and the tail of the procession was brought up by Pong' Rantebambam's wife, empty handed, with a group of other village ladies in long black veils, for black is the mourning colour of the Torajas.

I think the school band may have been intended to form part of the procession, but it had somehow got delayed and arrived at a brisk trot shortly afterwards, playing a rudimentary march in European style. My appreciation of their performance was sentimental rather than musical.

The musicians were, of course, the boys who came to greet me every morning and spent a good deal of their days at the bungalow, improving my Malay and giving me all the village gossip—Bombai, Sampekanan, Karrak, Masulo, Bongga, So'lipan and the rest. They frowned prodigiously as they puffed out the rubbishy sub-Sousa harmonies, each one playing the instrument he had himself made. Over and over again the dreadful tune was thrown upon the hot noon air, with two recurring chords of refreshing atonality due to the fact that the immense bass instruments, the *pompangs*, were capable of only one sort of rum-tee-tum, which sometimes only approximated to what was wanted.

As soon as the whole procession had paced the northern border of the field and filed into the large reception pavilion, an equally grave train of Palinggi's kinsmen, the reception party, issued in double file from the lodge next the death-tower, slowly circumnavigated the field and went in to receive them. A moment or two later the refreshment party, eighteen strong, of girls and youths chosen for their beauty, made their appearance, circling the *rante* at a sober pace with silver trays and bowls and boxes filled with *sireh*, coffee, biscuits, cigarettes, matches and so on. Most delightfully the slow dignity of all these embassies accorded with the rich, indolent peace of the noontide and the stillness of the green bamboo plumes overhanging the *rante*.

Not all the beasts in the procession were destined for sacrifice and the feeding of the guests. Some of the bulls were brought for show and good will only. Each delegation stayed for one night, and its offerings served to relieve the host of the greater part of the expense of their entertainment. But do not think on that account that a death-feast is not a heavy expense to the heirs of the dead. In the course of the feasts for his father, Palinggi sacrificed more than fifty buffaloes, most of them his own, representing an expenditure of about £1,000, an immense amount by Toraja standards.

All night they danced. Four hours or so after sunset, when the hundreds of shares of meat had been cooked over scores of fires and eaten in silence, the first *ma'badong* circle started and the first notes of the long elegiac chants tolled through the darkness:

> " *Mariorio kangkami*
> *Malena tampe ambe'ki,*
> *Naboko to'minda dianki*
> *Ankila ma'pamotu. . . ."*

They sang their desolation at the loss of the dead person and praised his memory. Men and women danced together in the ring, that was sometimes large enough to encircle all the longstones and their tethered, couching bulls; but only the men sang. They had resonant baritones and the unison singing (there is no sterner test for a choir) of the casually formed ensemble was impressive.

The whole series of the *ma'badong* choral dances takes several hours to perform and comprises an extensive succession of variations, subtle and initially baffling. As I watched the first ring slowly turning I was perplexed and disappointed; the severe classicism of dance and song was the last thing I had been prepared for. Loose white men's talk, which represents the nights of death-feasts as prolonged orgies, had prepared me for Dionysian frenzies and corybantic fireworks. Instead, here was the subtle fall of the naked heel, the enduring pressure of strong, simple cadences repeated and repeated and repeated,

Our End
of La'bo

Village Cemetery

rhythms as strong and insistent as heart-beats and the flow of the blood.

Nothing further removed from the sophisticated display dance of the West could be imagined. The ballerina of our world spurns the earth, in a glare of lights her feet leap constantly to escape it; when she is most birdlike, least earthbound, she delights us best. But in the darkness of the *rante* the dancers' staunch, faithful feet were in love with the earth, pressing their nakedness upon the dew and the grass and warming the smooth patches of unveiled soil. There was no conflict, no romantic straining or longing. There was peace and massive strength.

The dark stones that stood inside the circle of dancers and the ponderous nobility of the bulls drowsing in their shadow were all of a piece with the monumental strength of the death-dances. The memory of that and many another midnight on fields of giant stones in the mountains of Celebes is more dear and exciting, even, than those nights of dancing under the stars of Bali, the only other memory with which it can be compared.

Each dancer bent his right elbow and rested his right hand on his neighbour's left shoulder. His left hand gestured simply before his breast. The circle moved slowly to the right with the rise and fall of the right heel, the fall jerking an accent into the chant. There was nothing picturesque or visually exciting about it, but I think that only a curiously insensitive Westerner would have been slow to realise its beauty. Anyone who would seriously deny the spiritual value of such an experience to those taking part in it must be, in my opinion, a madman.

"To-morrow, Tuan, we will carry my mother to her tomb," said Palimbong. "I ask Tuan to walk with us."

The death-feast for the Lady Lai' Sappa had ended the

day before my arrival in La'bo. I had climbed one day up to the top of the death-tower on the *rante* behind Palimbong's home and seen her scarlet coffin, and the great wooden doll sitting below with chestnut brow and mother-of-pearl eyes. Naturally I was glad to join the company of kinsfolk and friends that accompanied her to her tomb.

I walked with old Pong' Masa'aga over the hard, rock-strewn path to Menke'pe village next noon and found the big ark-roofed bier and coffin standing outside the death-tower, with the effigy seated grandly in its travelling booth close by. Palimbong's sisters, their heads muffled in black veils, were kneeling beside the coffin and wailing, their fingers clawing at the red silk, their dusty bare feet convulsed by their sobbing. A large crowd was present and nine youths were dancing round the dead person when I arrived.

In those early days I suppose I puzzled my neighbours with my diffidence and rather breathless reverence in the presence of their dead and during the performance of any detail of their ritual. I sat there on a chair that somebody had brought, replying to greetings in a low voice as though I had been at an English funeral. I was wondering whether at some point on the progress to the tomb I might snatch a photograph of the coffin and the *tao-tao* without affronting or grieving the mourners.

"Isn't Tuan going to take photographs of the dead person?" Palimbong asked at last, his tone making it clear that he had been wondering for some time.

"May I?" I asked discreetly.

His gesture confirmed unlimited photographic freedom. I felt uncomfortable over my intrusion upon the ceremonial weeping of the ladies and made a hurried exposure. When I turned to the effigy I was shocked to see Masak, one of the dancers, pull the plumed head off unceremoniously while Palimbong's wife threw yet another gold necklace over the

silk-clad shoulders and bosom. The head was coolly re-
placed and the circle of youths resumed their dance, this
time round the effigy.

Focusing on the ground-glass view-finder, I frowned
with renewed shock at the sight of the cigarette I had given
Tira a few minutes earlier still hanging from a corner of his
mouth as he linked arms with his inseparable friends Masak
and Manga to begin the slow, tranced treading and chanting
of homage to the dead. It was like seeing an archbishop
enjoying a cigar at the high altar.

As a matter of fact, the youngster was pulled up for his
absent-mindedness and removed the cigarette hurriedly. I
took a photograph and immediately preparations for departure were made. My diffidence had held up the move
for half an hour or more.

Two men with a gong led us down the hill and along
narrow paths between the fields of flood towards the north.
The eleven men who shouldered the coffin pushed forward
with deep, throbbing cries that rose at intervals to frenzied
yelling as they jigged the bier up and down. Immediately
before them paced several young men with dog-toothed
pennons of white and scarlet on tall canes and the dancers
chanted starkly on two notes a tone apart. The path was
very narrow, and more than once the massive, sweating
legs of the pall-bearers slipped and plunged into two feet
of water while the high, horn-roofed bier rocked giddily;
but disaster was always averted in a storm of deafening
cries. The *tao-tao*, too, almost capsized once just ahead
of me; a crisis of insane yells, wild splashing and dipping
plumes.

The sun, reflected from the waters on both sides of us,
seemed to scorch our bones; but as soon as we passed into
the woods at the valley head it was as though we were
walking through jets of cool fountain water. After nearly
three miles we paused beside Tandilolock's house at Ke'te
for a rest. When we moved on again we were climbing, for

Lai' Sappa's tomb was high in the great black precipice above Ke'te village.

Little Torri, the dead person's grandchild, grew tired and rode the last half-mile on my shoulder. When we came close to the cliff the gold necklaces and fine silk sarongs were taken off the great doll, revealing a plain white sarong underneath, and an ordinary straw hat was substituted for the high headdress and feathers. A bag of *sireh* and chewing tobacco was thrown over one shoulder, and a little girl climbed into the booth to hold the image in her arms as it was jolted over the last rough paths. But almost at once the slaves fell, and the head and hat came rolling off, horrifyingly. At this Palimbong's eldest son dragged out the decapitated body and carried it easily on his shoulder, while a slave carried the head by the neck.

I do not think that many members of the Alpine Club would have tried the ascent to Lai' Sappa's tomb unroped. The three hundred feet of precipice was sheer for two-thirds of its height, offering only a few widely-spaced fissures and inconsiderable holds; yet more than a score of La'bo men, including Palimbong and others older than he, did the climb by way of a crazy succession of ladders, so-called, while younger men carried the coffin and *tao-tao* up. It took them more than an hour, and I watched them through my field-glasses in tense fascination.

The " ladders " were simply single bamboo poles in which notches had been roughly cut, loosely bound together where the top of one met the foot of another by a scrap of twisted bark and held in place at wide intervals by wooden wedges driven into small fissures in the rock face. The whole flimsy thread of scaffolding sagged and swung and strained, and more than once came apart, as one tiny figure after another swarmed up it and four sweating slaves edged the flashing red cylinder up the cliff.

A rock tomb, cut in a low cliff or a high precipice, is the last resting-place for most people in La'bo and the surrounding valleys, for only a minority are placed in the wayside death-houses for good. Some precipices have been wrought by daring, patient stone workers armed with primitive tools into little villages of the dead. A single family vault may take more than a year to carve out of the solid rock, complete with a railed gallery at the entrance, in which the *tao-taos* stand crowded together in travelling dress, their hands outstretched and their eyes fixed upon distances. Poorer folk's tombs have no galleries, just wooden doors, with perhaps the protective mask of the bull carved on them and their hats tied to a peg.

In Lai' Sappa's tomb several of her kinsfolk and her little son who had died in infancy already lay. Through my glasses I could see their effigies crowding the balcony outside. They were in sad condition: some had lost their hats and even their hair; their sarongs were faded, dishevelled rags from which the cockatoos had torn shreds for their nests; but the air of vivid expectancy was still about them.

A climax of colour to my season in the Torajalands was contributed by the great death-feast for the mother of the Puang of Sangalla. For seven days and nights I was one of the four thousand guests of the Puang, who is the leading Toraja prince, on the high feast-field of the Sangalla royal family, with its truly majestic prospect of valleys and mountain ranges to the north.

The main features of the feast were the same as those at Menkendek and Pintu, though on a more lavish scale. There was the same convulsive excitement, mounting like a thermometer plunged into boiling water, as the vivid procession of the dead person started down a steep hill at a gunfire signal, and with the velocity of disaster plunged into the deep-flooded rice-field at its foot, with a herd of a hundred doomed bulls stampeding after it, their horns glorified with plumes and fringes of gold leaf. There were the same night-long, tranced circles of dancers, chanting in the starlight the massive cycle of elegiac hymns appointed for the obsequies of those of *puang* rank. (I was a wallflower, of course, sitting out most of the dances on the flank of one of the complacent bulls that drowsed beneath the megaliths. The children introduced me to those seats, which are agreeably warm in the chill upland night.)

Seventy fine bulls were sacrificed. Large and splendid delegations of mourners arrived hourly, some of them from places fifty miles away. Three famous troupes of dancers and the renowned Bunt'ao choir toured the seventy-three guest lodges, like carol singers, honouring and entertaining the guests, as well as performing several times a day before the dead princess in her high tower. One day there was darkness at noon and a violent hailstorm, an omen of profound significance on account of its extreme rarity in those parts. (Salu, who had listened with sympathy to my regrets over ice-less Scotch, collected a mug of hailstones and I shared with him the welcome drink thus improvised.)

An hour before the third dawn of the feast I attended one of the rarest of all Toraja ceremonies—a *ma'aparando*. I am one of the two, or it may be three, white men ever to have witnessed it.

The *rante* was a thrilling place, with the moon pale behind wandering clouds and little glowing fires in a wide ring, and smoke drifting in fragrant plumes towards the east. Torches were lighted, huge torches of bunched bamboo canes ten feet high. Soon it was as light as day round the death-tower, and the drowsy, shivering children who had been sitting in rows on the reclining bulls came to life in the heat radiated by the torches. Two grave-eyed girls, a little past the age of ripeness and richly dressed, were brought forward by old women in mourning veils, and a big slave carried out a little boy of three or four, who exhibited all the boredom of minor royalty at an untimely function under a satin turban with feathers and gold brooches. These three were the dead person's great-grandchildren.

That is why the ceremony is so rare. It can take place only at the death-feasts of those of *puang* rank (and there are only three *puang* families), and only such of them as are survived by great-grandchildren.

A gong was struck and in a fierce blaze of torches the *to'ma'aparandan*, the dead lady's daughter who had been in intimate attendance on the corpse for every hour of the past three years, was seen coming down the ramp from the chamber in the top of the death-tower. She had thrown off her deep-fringed mourning headdress and cast a crimson and rust sarong about her head and shoulders. At the bottom of the ramp a magnificent slave waited and she climbed astride his shoulders amid a wild chorus of cries. In procession with a score of torch-bearers she was carried at striding speed three times round the base of the tower.

Meanwhile the old Puang, his stout form wrapped in a white robe, had appeared at the door of his pavilion and a slave handed him a torch. Despite all the uproar, the little prince had fallen asleep in all his finery on the slave's shoulder and had to be roused by gentle pats on his plump cheeks. The two girls, lovely in their Gothic, steeple-pointed headdresses and barbaric gold jewellery, mounted the shoulders of slaves and, with the Puang leading, the whole company made three circuits of the death-tower from right to left, the ritual expressing their gratitude for the long life and fertility of the dead princess.

It was a picture of unforgettable brilliance. The Puang manifested a noble presence as he strode under the forest of torches, his head uplifted, plainly moved and elated by the ceremony. The torches kindled vivid sparks of light in eyes and on teeth and jewels. The cliffs echoed back the triumphant cries from the surrounding darkness. Slowly roused to animation by the scene, the elder great-granddaughter raised her head and rode with parted lips, the three parallel gold swords rising and falling swiftly on her young bosom.

At the end of the third circuit the Puang led them all up the steep ramp into the presence of the dead, where they surrounded the coffin and wept ceremoniously. The echoes of the Puang's gusty sobs followed me as I stumbled away down the avenue of longstones, my eyes blinded and my face scorched by the torch flames.

Deeply impressed, I was also mortified at the thought of a unique opportunity missed. They had said there would be many torches, but I had never imagined that, in fact, there would be light enough for photographs, much less the noontide blaze that was just dying down; so I had left my cameras in the village. The spectacular *ma'aparando*, possibly never to be enacted again, has still never been photographed. . . .

The last ceremony of all at Sangalla I did not see, for only near relatives could attend it. That was the *enter bombo* or *ma'rondan bota*; as we might say, seeing the soul off to Paradise.

At the house of the princess, at midnight a few days after her entombment, the little company of her kin feasted on a black boar. For the last time meat was offered to her, and as the hour of dawn drew near it was time for her soul to make its journey to Puya, the Homeland of Souls. So the door was opened, and as her spirit left its earthly home the Puang and the others called their last farewells.

" Carefully! Carefully! " they cried. " Go carefully! "

" Don't fall! "

" Oh, watch for thorns! "

" Lose not your way! "

And then the old, primitive fear came over them. Like friends seeing off a traveller on a liner who fear it may

sail before they can get ashore again, the nobles feared lest,
having accompanied the soul so far along its road, they
should get drawn all the way to Puya and die. So they
changed their cries.

" Close that gate behind you! "

" Ah, break down that bridge! "

" Bar the fence! Bar the way when you have passed! "

And so her soul travelled on to Puya, along the dark
road, alone.

IV

SOME FRIENDS & NEIGHBOURS

MY best Toraja friend was Salu.

On Christmas Day, two days after my arrival in the Toraja country, I came out of the little mission church in Makale (where in the course of an extraordinary service I had listened to two sermons and contributed to three collections) to find a youthful, wiry Toraja with quick brown eyes and a responsible expression waiting for me in the road beside the lake. He advanced, bowed and handed me a note.

The note was from the Controleur, and said, " This is Salu, whom Mevrouw van Dijk recommends as a servant for you. He was formerly a servant of Dr. van der Veen. You should pay him thirty guilders a month and give him his rice daily."

I beckoned this newcomer into my life to walk beside me along the bank of the lake that reflected the dancing line of Makale's encircling crags; but this he was firmly disinclined to do. In the Torajalands only equals walk abreast; humbler folk walk just behind the great ones in friendly but not equal company. When I slowed down he came to a standstill; when I moved on he waited until I had gone two steps before he made a start.

In this preposterous manner we climbed the hundred steps up to the rest-house. In my room he accepted a cigarette and thawed to a small extent.

To a small extent only. I was not to be at ease with Salu for at least a week. Grateful as I was to the Controleur and the van Dijks for finding me a servant who had some acquaintance with European ways, I was disappointed at the

90

thought of sharing my house with such a sobersides. (Later he confessed that the summons to appear urgently before the head of the law and the government had unnerved him in spite of a clear conscience.)

" Would Salu like to look after me in La'bo? "

" Thirty guilders each moon, and food every day. Is that good? "

" How many assistants will Salu want? "

" Afterwards will Salu go with me to Pangala? "

" We will try for one moon. Then if Salu not like or I not like I seek another servant. Is that good? "

To all these questions Salu returned the same answer.

" *Tuan sahaja.*" In other words, Tuan knows best.

This was not encouraging. I dislike meekness. Would not this type of servant get cheated in the markets and let down by his assistants? Would he not expect almost hourly supervision? The strain of being confronted by so much submissiveness depressed me, and I soon rose to conclude the interview.

" I ask Salu to return here to-morrow evening," I said with the decisive, officer-like intonation his meekness invited; only I made one of my frequent mistakes in the Malay tongue. I meant to say to-morrow, but I actually said yesterday.

And Salu laughed. That is one of the things that make the Torajas so refreshing after some of the Javanese, for instance, who will hardly laugh if you slip up on a banana skin. In fact, a little of the unnatural atmosphere surrounding royalty closes round you in Java. But the Torajas do little to control their honest sense of humour. As soon as he laughed at my mistake I liked Salu. He laughed merrily, with me as well as at me, quite charitably. I sat down again and we had a less inhibited chat.

The chief trouble in those early days of our association was the figure, or the spectre, of Dr. van der Veen, which came hourly between us. The doctor, a missionary and philologist who has spent half a lifetime in the Toraja country, is the leading authority on South Toraja culture, the author of a Dutch-Toraja dictionary and grammar, and the translator of the Christian Gospels into the Toraja language. He is held in high esteem, not only by the small Christian community of the Toraja territories but universally among the unconverted. At that time he was in Holland recuperating after his ordeals in Japanese prison camps.

Needless to say I felt extremely unworthy at the idea of succeeding so august a personage in Salu's life, and uneasy at the thought of the daily and hourly comparisons that would be forced upon him. These, it seemed, he was frank enough at first to acknowledge. Whenever I gave him cigarettes he would mention how many a day Dr. van der Veen had been in the habit of giving him; when I told him I should be eating only two meals a day, like the Torajas, he did not fail to let me know the superior number of repasts served in Dr. van der Veen's house; when I firmly pointed out that I disliked the second course to grow cold on the table while I drank my soup I forestalled him by adding that possibly Dr. van der Veen, like most Dutchmen, did not mind lukewarm food, but Englishmen liked it either hot or cold.

I need not have worried, though. Salu was not really comparing me with the eminent doctor. He had merely taken it for granted that I could not fail to be interested in every scrap of information about his hero. Nobody in this world, I soon realised, could compare with Dr. van der Veen in Salu's mind. Me he accepted as a creature of normal good will and ignorance, exalted above himself certainly, but one of whom no perfections were to be expected. When he came to me with the excited news of his old master's return to Angin-Angin and the buffalo and pigs killed in his honour, I said that I looked forward to meeting him and wondered whether he knew English.

"He knows everything, Tuan," Salu said simply.

Salu believed himself more than forty years of age, but he looked younger. He was the father of seven children, the eldest of whom, the fifteen-year-old high-school pupil Isak, later came to live with us at La'bo.

Though there were times when, true to his Christian conversion, he scoffed at the faith and arts of his fathers, he was quick to understand my affectionate interest in his people's traditions, and I believe that in helping me to discover and comprehend some of them he may have rediscovered a pride in his blood that he had long lost. More and more as time went by I appreciated his common sense, his humour, his simple friendliness and his integrity, and when at last, after staying twice as long in his country as the three months I had intended, I said good-bye to him, I did so with keen regret.

Every two or three months now I begin a day with the pleasant surprise of a letter from him. It is thanks to Salu that I still know how the rice crop there is faring, what prices are falling in Rantepao market, who is in Rantepao hospital, how the bulls fight at certain big feasts, which children are moving up to high school and such-like welcome gossip.

From the first hour of my arrival in La'bo I had a good friend in my next-door neighbour, Palinggi. I shall never know the extent of my indebtedness to him, for he was one who did goodness by stealth. Among my retainers it soon became a habit to run to Palinggi or his slaves for anything I lacked. I would throw out some careless question and find later that Palinggi had spent hours digging out the answer.

"That was a good fish," I would say to Salu. "I ask you to buy more from the same man."

"Tuan Palinggi sent it," Salu would tell me. "Many times he gives me fish for Tuan." Gifts from Palinggi were handed into the cookhouse when I was not about.

" I come to help Tuan," he had said that first evening when he introduced himself to me, and he was abundantly a man of his word. It was seldom that I could do anything in return, for he was well off and understood that I preferred to reserve my few gifts for my poorer friends. I was able to give distinction to his Sunday school syllabuses and reports on his year's evangelical work by typing them out for him, but beyond such trifling services I could do nothing to repay his generous and understanding help.

I must have seemed to him boorishly unceremonious in the first weeks when I was feeling my way into village life, and my early abuse of the Malay language must have been excruciating to him. He loves eloquence, as all Torajas do, and it was delightful to watch him conversing with friends, gently balancing and relishing each word, with vivid eyes and easy tongue building phrases and sentences out of the supple, sensitive language which he knew as well as his own.

There was some talk among the village chiefs that owing to Tandilolock's age, his seeming minor interest in our end of La'bo and the complex's large population it might be split in two, with Palinggi as *kepala bua* of Karatuan, Menke'pe, Tambunan, Tandam Batu, Marante and Tandung. I hope it may happen.

Of the local village chiefs I liked Palimbong best.

One day I said to him that if I had enough money to pay for the air and sea passages between England and Celebes, I would build a house in La'bo and live in it for three or four months every year. (I would, too.) At once he offered me ground to build on—for white men may not own land in the Netherlands Indies—and all the help I needed in setting up an establishment. Often later he referred to the project as though I had only to show a little determination to accomplish it.

I followed his mother to the tomb and made several expeditions with him later into the mountain outposts of his village. He was a pleasant walking and climbing companion and, unlike most Torajas, not backward in giving an opinion.

" How much should I pay the porters ? "

" Ought I to give the night watchmen a meal ? "

" Is it all right for me to stay all night at the death feasts ? "

To such questions, which were in reality appeals for help, the normal and unhelpful Toraja answer was, " *Tuan sahaja*." " Tuan knows best," or, " It's up to you." But Palimbong would always give a straight answer. Often he would take Salu aside with suggestions for my entertainment and welfare, and to the end he took a liberal and fatherly interest in all aspects of my comfort.

" Tuan is truly our brother now," he said more than once in the last weeks of my stay. " Why return to your country where it is cold and the taxes are heavy ? "

I wish I could have listened to him.

Next to Palimbong I liked old Pong' Masa'aga, whose dignified good humour and hideous face was everything one expected of a retired head-hunter. But he could not speak Malay, so our acquaintance never went very deep despite my regard for him. Deppa was a little stand-offish always, and I used to wonder whether I had offended him until closer observation discovered in him a character curiously reserved for a Toraja.

Poi' Bunga, headman of Tambunan, was a complete contrast to Pong' Masa'aga, one of the new sort of chiefs; a former schoolmaster, good looking, young and neat, with the slightest touch of priggery to mar his normal good nature, intelligent. I got on very well with him, but not with the glum Chief of Tandung, who struck me as the dullest of dull dogs. His blank, unwinking stare I found almost desperately unnerving.

Kalasuso, the young Ampulembang of Bunt'ao, the district south-west of Kesu, was the only Toraja with whom I could chat in English. He had studied the language at school in Makassar, and during the occupation a Japanese officer who spoke English but not Malay used to visit him frequently, putting across the familiar totalitarian technique of large-scale spoliation combined with attempts at social ingratiation. The young prince's accent was good and his fluency moderate. No week went by without a call from him, and twice I was his guest in Bunt'ao.

Kalasuso had a primitive profile and a sensitive, handsome and sophisticated full face. His voice was low and melancholy. His sense of responsibility was strong, almost crushing at times, it seemed to me.

" We have trouble, sir. The bad worm is stealing the rice seed in Bunt'ao. Yes, sir, the roots are eaten and the leaves become brown. Last year also many fields in Bunt'ao were robbed by the worm. And the Controleur is angry because some of my people cut down trees in the forest, sir. They do not understand that cutting down the forest on the slopes makes the land slide after the rains. What is that word in English, sir? Erosion? Will you write it for me, sir? They do not understand. It is difficult for me."

It was often difficult for poor Kalasuso. But even when things went well the soft voice would never throw off its melancholy.

" The Puang of Sangalla has asked our singers to sing for four days at his mother's death-feast. He will give them a buffalo, sir. The Bunt'ao singers are the best, sir. Other singers get usually only a swine, but our singers always a buffalo. When you visit me, sir, I shall order Indoh Rero to sing for you." He studied his Dutch-English dictionary for a moment, and added, " No singer of the Torajas surpasses or excels her."

A week later, in his office beside the school at Bunt'ao, I heard this famous singer, the unrivalled *prima donna* of

The Hamlet of Ke'te

Lendu

all the South Torajas. When she sings at a death-feast her personal fee is a bull, and male mourners are seen to weep during her anthems of lament. She is a composer of note, evolving new songs at quite frequent intervals. At her command performance (I gave her a testimonial instead of a bull) she tried to sing a new one, a farewell to Rantepao, but she broke down in it, and despite the prompting of her accompanists, two brilliant flautists, could not finish it.

She is a young woman and has as yet no children, notwithstanding her famous name. *Indoh* means " mother," and in conferring that revered title upon her the Torajas manifest the depth of their affection and homage. (And do they, perhaps, manifest at the same time a healthier scale of values than we, who would scorn the suggestion of such a title as " Mother " for our divas?)

It was a pity that my tribute to the diva of Bunt'ao had to be largely insincere. For me the whole foundations of song yawned and retched as trills like death-rattles succeeded nose-dives of raucous and giddy *fioritura*. The melodies were exciting and the virtuosity remarkable, but I could do nothing about reconciling my ear to her voice.

When I was Kalasuso's guest I stayed at his office, not in his ancestral house. That was because of his father, who is a source of incessant anxiety and embarrassment to the young prince and all his family.

The old prince is mad. And not at all respectably mad, either. On such occasions as he has been allowed, or seized, his freedom in the past few years, he had painted Bunt'ao red with appalling gusto. So now he is kept under restraint, like Kent, in the stocks.

There are times when he is docile, resigned to his confinement or unaware of it; but there are others when he kicks madly with his locked feet and yells all manner of deplorable imprecations and obscenities.

In Makassar there is a well-run lunatic asylum, which the doctor in Rantepao has more than once recommended to

Kalasuso; but the family will not hear of sending the old man away. The death of a Toraja of high rank away from his home is fraught with deadly danger to his soul and entails a long succession of elaborate and expensive rituals. So the scandalous old prince will live his last years, and finally die, a prisoner in his own house.

Barra, our first night watchman and my friend throughout my stay in La'bo, was a good, simple young man of the *kaunan* or lowest class. In general he was laconic and unobtrusive, watching my various doings and the comings and goings at the basket bungalow with a bright, observant eye. In a crowd he seldom spoke, but sometimes he would come silently into my smaller room and squat by my table as I wrote. If I began talking then we would usually have a long conversation.

He was slender, alert-faced and very vain. He was about twenty-four years old and he had been married four times. When on one occasion he absented himself for several days I was not surprised to hear he had married again. The afternoon he walked in unconcernedly at last and squatted by my table I asked him why he hadn't told me he was going to be married.

" I am not married, Tuan," he said, smiling.

" All in the village say that you are," I pointed out, but he lit a cigarette and shook his head.

" Then where have you been since last market? " I asked.

" Oh, just back to my first wife, Tuan," he explained. " Four nights, that's all."

I couldn't decide whether Barra was for marriage or against it. One day I asked him whether he thought he would never be able to pick a good wife and live the rest of his life with her. We had not been talking very seriously, but at that his eyes met mine with earnestness.

" I want a son, Tuan," he said.

The slave Lendu always reminded me of a cock bird in spring: so vividly alive, so utterly content, so happily at home in the world. He would come down with a great load of firewood from Buntu Assa, singing as he strode through the gate, smiling broadly as he met my eye.

The Angel Gabriel must look like Lendu, I think. The same crystal glance of utter candour and good will, the same free movement of one who walks through a life rich with blessing. Yes, Lendu was for me the Noble Savage, the bright, unsullied being I had longed to believe in when the impatient idealism of youth demanded a pattern of human goodness far different from what I had been offered, far different from the grim stoic-puritan veteran of long campaigns with sin, pale and lifeless from the blood lost through many wounds.

While he set down the wood, squatted astride a log and attacked it with Palinggi's axe, I would watch Lendu through the window, asking myself whether I wasn't making a sentimental habit of idealising him. Wasn't he perhaps bored or ill-tempered now and then? Didn't he sometimes deceive others, or himself, despite the purity of his eyes? Was his self never an enemy? Didn't he ever envy the fortunes or the temperaments of others?

But those doubts seldom survived the first glance he shot me over the riven log. I believe that I knew in Lendu a good man and a happy man. Not good because a merciless will had flogged protesting body and nature into subjection; not happy from a conviction of happiness earned through the bitter defeat of self. But really good, really happy.

If, in fact, he was not, then he must have been so near as not to make any odds to one so far from being either as myself.

A small group of La'bo's playboys spent a good deal of time in my company. Tinggi, a son of Pong' Rantebambam, was one of them, and they frequently slept at his house and lounged round the basket bungalow through the following day in lazy gossip with me. There were five of them: Tinggi, Manga, Masak, Tira and Tambai, all about nineteen years old, all unmarried and inseparable companions.

Such groups of friends are fairly usual in La'bo; as usual, I think, as pairs of friends. These had all been school mates and they had circumcised each other around the age of twelve, an experience that often confirms childhood friendships and results in close intimacy during adolescence. They toiled not, neither did they spin, these young gentlemen, for by local standards their families were well off; but there is no organised entertainment available for leisured folk in the Torajalands, so they mostly rested with the graceful indolence that in the East is as attractive as good manners or any other of the everyday works of art of cultured people.

They stayed frequently in each other's houses and were much in evidence at death-feasts, singing and dancing and retiring at certain hours of the night to play with the best-looking local girls in the darkened guest-houses. They were vain and incessantly borrowed my mirror. They also begged paper and pencil now and then to write love-letters, amid a chorus of mutual teasing, to a few local girls of the modern, educated type—an immodest Western innovation in La'bo, practised only by this slightly disreputable quintet.

No doubt they had more charm than the playboys of the Western world, but they were not by any means free of the dullness characteristic of playboys everywhere.

From the first my most frequent visitors and to the last my most faithful friends were the children.

There were several reasons for this. I usually like children, anyway, and the children of La'bo would win the heart of a Herod. Children are less put off by considerations of awe for high rank. Children have rather more time than their elders for gossiping. The majority of the La'bo children, but only a minority of adults, understood Malay. I felt more at home, too, with the everyday Malay of the children than with the polished periods of the accomplished grown-ups.

I was good fun, as well, for the children; an oddity whose next move was always agreeably incalculable. I taught them games and sometimes gave them cigarettes, sweets and even dinners. And I was the only grown-up in the village who bothered very much about them.

Lindung, I suppose, was the first of my smaller Toraja friends. He is the ugliest child in South-East Asia, and when his head has been newly shaven, which is often, and scarred by the slips of his father's knife, the sight of him is enough to bring on a miscarriage. His face is small, yellow and mean. His arms and legs are spindly, his belly pot. The only nice things about him are his voice and his nature.

A bad conscience was the foundation of my friendship with Lindung. Not many of the smaller children (he was six or seven) knew much Malay and in talking to them I had to use my fifty words of Toraja. I got a good laugh when I pointed to Lindung's pot belly and said, " *Buda bawbaw*," much rice. I did it several times, and while the other children laughed Lindung hung his head and clasped his small hands.

A day or two later I found him snatching out of the rubbish-pit a chicken bone that I had left on my supper plate. I told Salu, and he said, " Yes, Tuan, some people here are very poor."

" But they have rice," I said, gazing round the rich terraced valley.

" Their crops will not feed them for a year, Tuan," Salu told me. " Lindung and many children here will have no rice now for six moons, until the harvest. Only vegetables."

Buda bawbaw. . . . . Lindung shared my meals from that day onwards and every six days I gave a dinner party for seven or eight children. My money would not run to more.

Lindung's home was on the lower slopes of Buntu Assa, but he used to spend most of his time round our bungalow. His sarong was a pitiful rag of coarse pineapple fibre cloth, but when I gave him a new sarong of marigold-coloured linen and a small scrap of white calico from which his mother made a pair of shorts, he at once became the best-dressed individual in the village. The day his buffalo calf threw him and he stumbled, wounded, in through the gate, I dressed him elaborately with sulfa powder, bandages and sticking-plaster to the envy of all his companions.

He was a grateful little creature. He would go off climbing for hours to find me a flower I hadn't seen before, often one I never saw again, either. He attended me on shorter expeditions, carrying my mackintosh. Reproved one day by Salu for entering my room unceremoniously, he took to studying his manners and in the end almost awed me with their polish.

Often nowadays, when I am weary of the limitations of post-war diet in England, I reprove myself with the thought of Lindung and wish sincerely that I could still put aside a part of my rations for him.

Duna was my first slave.

Properly speaking, he was no slave. Properly speaking there are no slaves in the Toraja country, because the Dutch abolished slavery when they took over the Torajalands in 1907. But household servants among the Torajas, who are ex-slaves or the children of slaves, are usually referred to as slaves still and refer to themselves so. Some of them, indeed, consider themselves still bound to their masters by the old obligations, but legally they are free to leave them, just as Duna was, of course, free to leave me and did, later on, to work with his father on a bridge being built over the River Sadang.

Duna was neither a beauty nor one of the world's thinkers. He was fourteen years old, had no nose to speak of in profile and took some time to reply to the simplest question. It was very like having a pleasant domesticated animal about the house.

Indeed, often he would remind me irresistibly of a good-natured mongrel of limited intelligence who longed to please, but distrusted his ability to do the right thing. Duna would rush off to perform some service he was almost certain was what I had ordered, but the doubt remained and he would fix a bright glance of devotion on me, ready to desist cheerfully in a moment if I frowned. His heavy-handedness with crockery was incurable.

When I decided to regularise his voluntary assistance to Salu and asked him if he would like to continue the job at a salary of a new sarong and shorts, two meals a day and a cake of tobacco at each market, he was overjoyed. He presented me that evening with one of his own cockerels, as good a bird as Deppa had given me on my arrival. Throughout the district he was envied a situation so generously paid.

Sipa was fat and sniffed. He used to sit on the floor watching me and keeping up a running commentary on everything I did, which was sometimes amusing, but often a little distracting. It seemed, too, that I was more demonstrative and theatrical in my manner than I had supposed.

"Ah! His pen will not write. He curses. He is angry. The pen is thirsty. It is drinking from the bottle. He has three such bottles. Now he can write again. He is not angry any more. He drinks *ooiskeh* that Salu brings him. He loves it very much. It makes him contented. Us it would poison. It has the price of thirty *rupias* a bottle!

He goes to his room. He will fetch us *golla-golla* (candy). No, it is not *golla-golla*. Another book only. He has a hundred books. He writes fast now because he has drunk the *ooiskeh*. *Wah*, so fast! Faster than the schoolmaster...."

Though Sipa was distantly related to the Puang of Sangalla and had a drop of divine blood in his veins, his parents were poor, and so he had gone to live with his rich kinsman, Pong' Rantebambam. Toraja children, even eight-year-olds like Sipa, have considerable freedom in choosing where they will live. Quite a number of them leave their parents to join the household, temporarily or permanently, of some better-off or better-loved relative, or even to take up residence with a close friend. Sipa did not like Pong' Rantebambam much, but food was plentiful in the old man's house and he liked his cousin Sulo, Pong' Rantebambam's youngest son.

It was Sipa who first modelled clay bulls for me. His heroic portraits were the foundation of my large herd.

Duna's friend Sesa, who often recalled how he had been the first child in La'bo bold enough to address me, was a member of the nicest family I knew there. They lived in the tiny hamlet of Parrara on a little hill opposite our back door, and Sesa and his small sister Mina were my daily visitors.

Their mother, one of the sweetest human creatures I have ever known, came seldom to the bungalow, but we often met at the bathing-booth, where she did her laundry, and by their poor little house in Parrara. She was the eternal mother; warm hearted, patient, selfless, with a twinkle of indomitable gaiety about her. She had married at about thirteen years old a boy a few years older, and they were still happily married. The father of Sesa (I never knew his own name, for a man of La'bo is customarily addressed as the father of his eldest son) was what I would call a typical Toraja; artless and faithful, modest but having a notable dignity. We borrowed things from his poor, generous home when I grew ashamed of our incessant demands on Palinggi.

Poor Sesa suffered a good deal on account of his hair, which was the only example in La'bo beside Pong' Masa'-aga's of the tightly curled Papuan type. He was as much ashamed of it as he was proud of his little sister's " white " skin. To my eye, Mina was much the same colour as other little girls in the village, but Torajas have a very keen eye for subtle variations in flesh tints, delighting in the lighter ones and mocking the darker. It was Sesa's small flock of brown ducks that supplied my breakfast eggs, and his patient schooling that helped as much as anything to improve my tongue-tied Malay. He will be just such another man as his father, I think, in spite of his high-school education in Rantepao and his unusual intelligence, both of which can be of doubtful moral value to a young Toraja of to-day.

Timbo the clown, and Massang the visionary, who succeeded Duna as household slaves, will be introduced in later pages. So will Isak, the son of Salu, and Lelang, the outlaw of Karatuan village, as well as Tu'ugun and Sulo and others of the press of eager children who used the bungalow as a club.

But what, you may ask, about the girls?

The answer to that question is that the word " friend " in La'bo implies a favoured comrade of the same sex. Between unwed male and female there can be love and passion, and a certain amount of un-intimate and impersonal *camaraderie* in the few jobs that are shared between the sexes; but not friendship.

You do not, in La'bo, talk about your girl friends, because they are your friends for certain intimate exploits only, every approach to which must be hidden from the eye of day. Talk about sex in general is utterly free, even to debate on the most intimate nuances of technique; but to identify your partner in any of your experiences of the night is considered the worst of bad manners.

I approve.

Any woman who paid visits to me in daylight would have deeply shocked public opinion in La'bo. Not even Palinggi's wife would have done so. The few women who came to me for medicine or treatment were always chaperoned, at least by a baby, and I soon learned never to attempt to develop the occasion into anything in the least social. When Loedia came by day so that I could take her photograph, she was so painfully shy that I had to use a fast shutter speed to arrest her nervous trembling. The only feminine acquaintances bold enough to enter my rooms regularly by daylight were Likku and Mina.

It was extraordinary that ugly old Pong Masa'aga should have had such handsome sons and such a lovely grand-daughter as Likku. She was eleven years old, one of the very few children in the village whose age was accurately known, and very much a leader among her shy companions. While they clustered bashfully in the background she would come gracefully up the steps on to the veranda and lean on the table, smiling into my eyes. Already she inflamed the imagination of several of the village boys; what it will be like in a year or two when she is the beauty queen of La'bo I can scarcely imagine. . . .

" Why do not Likku's friends come and see me, too ? "

" They are shy, Tuan."

" But Likku is not shy."

" No, Tuan. Because Tuan likes me."

" Yes, Likku, but I like your friends, too."

" Some of them are very ignorant."

" Often I do not like clever people. The Bugis are clever and I do not like them."

" Yes, Tuan. Will Tuan take my *portret* again? "

" Yes, if Likku will smile and not make strange shapes with her mouth."

" I will smile, Tuan, and wear my new dress."

" If it is a dress as the Dutch children wear I do not like it."

" Why, Tuan? "

" Because people look silly in other people's clothes. A man looks silly in women's clothes. I would look silly in a Toraja loincloth and fillet. A Toraja looks silly in Dutch clothes."

" The prince wears trousers and shoes like Tuan."

" He does not look good in them. In Toraja clothes the Toraja girls are very beautiful."

Likku was delightfully honest. She was not interested in me apart from my interest in her, but she did not, like so many of her irritating elders in Europe, put up a transparent pretence of interest in me for myself and in the things apart from herself that interested me. I liked her especially for that.

Mina was five or six years old and the sister of Sesa. She was quite tiny, only a little higher than my knee, and she wore one of the largest hats I have ever seen: a huge flattened cone of dull-gold straw. Her hair was not yet long enough to twist into the smallest bun, so it hung in the dankest of rat's tails about her small, vivid-eyed face. The tinniness of her voice was almost, and the width of her smile quite, indescribable.

I was her hero, and though we held daily conversations we understood each other through sympathy and affection rather than any interplay of intellect, for Mina always spoke in Toraja and I in English. A dozen times a day she would stagger back from my bathing-booth under a long bamboo pipe of water to her home in the groves of Parrara. Sometimes she would prop the pipe against the booth before filling it and dart across the lane for a chat with me.

" My dear Mina, what a delightful *décolletage!* "

The smile. Mina looks like a baby alligator in a hat.

" I saved you this silver paper, Mina. And here's a raspberry sucker."

A flood of tinny Toraja and a grab at the sweet.

" It ought to be a box of chocolates, Mina. You can't get them in Rantepao market, though."

The water supply is urgent. With a parting smile bisecting her face she races off. Her tiny foot-and-toe prints in the mud are charming, and somehow pathetic.

V

NEIGHBOURS I NEVER MET

I WAS never aware of meeting a *batitong*, though there were known to be one or two in the village, and I must surely have come face to face with them in the course of my daily wanderings and the occasional gatherings at the bungalow. Unlike Pong' Sakuru, however, I had not the gift of detecting a *batitong* under his mask of a blameless villager, and I knew better than to ask either him or old Sapondama to share their secrets with me.

By day a *batitong* is a normal man, living with his family, working in the paddy-fields, going to market for his *sireh* and tobacco. Usually at night, too, he is an ordinary parishioner, eating his rice or spiced vegetables and gossiping with kinsmen and friends in the smoky shelter of his cabin.

But there are moonless nights when a cannibal hunger comes upon him, and he is obliged to go into the darkness and strike himself thrice with his fist on his brow. At once he becomes invisible to human eyes and a light springs up in his forelocks, like a miner's lamp; by its invisible beam he finds his prey. A lone woman running down to the water-pipe, a young boy looking for love, perhaps an old man late on the road home from market. They know nothing amiss as the *batitong* attacks them, tearing out the heart and gobbling it greedily in the darkness; but soon they sicken and suspect the truth.

They will die, of course, unless Sapondama can help them. It is no use their going to the hospital in Rantepao, for such cases are beyond the white doctor's competence. A wizard, though, can sometimes recover a heart from a *batitong* who has not yet eaten it and restore it to the victim. Many a time has Sapondama successfully treated in this way patients who had appeared to be dying.

Unlike the healers of Harley Street, Sapondama expects payment only for satisfactory results. Only patients restored to full health are required to pay him with baskets of rice and eggs.

" Are there many *batitongs* in Tuan's country? " asked Massang one day.

" We have many wicked people," I told him; " but none of them are *batitongs*." Then I asked, " Do you know who is a *batitong* in La'bo? "

He folded his hands tight between his thighs and looked down at his feet.

" How can we know, Tuan? "

I never saw a *bombo*, either.

A *bombo* is a ghost or soul which has an existence semi-independent of the body. During sleep, for instance, the *bombos* of La'bo folk sometimes left their bodies, perhaps to visit Puya, the Homeland of Souls, where they met and spoke with the souls of kinsmen who had died; or they might visit the sleeping-mats of certain girls and enjoy them; or perhaps they just went inconsequently to market or a feast. In the morning a villager often remembered his soul's night travels.

Even during the day a *bombo* sometimes left the body and wandered. Once in a *sisemba* contest Lendu was kicked in the crutch and he fell, and his *bombo* went away down into a dark place where there were crocodiles and a tremendous heat. Until his *bombo* returned to his body he lay on the ground as if he were asleep and could not hear his friends talking to him.

Psychic persons like Pong' Sakuru can see *bombos* in certain circumstances of crisis. If they see the *bombo* of a living person with its face distorted as if in pain or tears that is a sure sign of that person's imminent death. But if they should tell the doomed person or anybody else what they have seen they would themselves die. The *deata* would kill them.

This does not mean, though, that a clairvoyant will keep his discovery entirely to himself. He may disclose part of it in a number of oblique ways.

For instance, one night Pong' Sakuru interrupted a lull in the conversation of a group of villagers who had enjoyed a rare supper of fish following a day of *ma'bale* in Palimbong's biggest rice-field to announce in a dreaming voice that he had seen a *bombo* that morning at dawn.

And fear descended. The older men and women, who had been leaning against the pillars of the two rice-barns with quids of tobacco poised between their lips, straightened their spines and their old eyes blinked. Nobody asked a question.

I never knew whose weeping ghost it was that Pong' Sakuru had seen, but certain details of its identity could be deduced from his subsequent words.

" A baby's *bombo*," he said, after a painful pause.

Oberammergau, at my side, relaxed his tension at this. That was because he knew it was an old person who was going to die. Forbidden under pain of death to disclose their visions, Toraja seers often adopt the course of announcing the opposite of what they see. Their audience, familiar with this convention, may then gain some idea of the truth. When Pong' Sakuru spoke of a baby's ghost the older people grew more anxious, and Oberammergau, a twenty-year-old, stopped worrying.

" A little boy's *bombo*," the clairvoyant declared at last, and the poor old women closed their eyes. It was an old woman's ghost he had seen. They never doubted Pong' Sakuru; so often he had been right. Many times he had announced, by contrary inference, the approaching end of a girl baby or an old man, and when, soon afterwards, a certain baby girl or old man died he was able to reveal that it was their *bombo* he had seen. The next time an old woman of the village died they would remember their seer's words on the evening after the *ma'bale*. . . .

When a psychic person sees a *bombo* with its face normal and not distorted it means that the person concerned is in a condition of danger. There again the seer may not warn the threatened one, but he may, for instance, try to tempt his appetite or reinforce his reserves of strength with a gift of meat or eggs.

"Once a *bombo* struck Pong' Sakuru," Oberammergau told me afterwards. "From midday till near sunset he could not speak or move his body. His wife thought he was dead."

Cats, too, can see ghosts. When they dash crazily about for no apparent reason it is known that they have seen a *bombo*.

How many souls has a Toraja?

I could never find out for certain.

Massang said three. One was immortal and went to Puya, the Homeland of Souls, soon after the final death-feast; the second stayed near the body's earthly dwelling-place for a time after death and eventually died; the third lived for many years close to the body in the tomb.

Kalasuso said only one.

Dr. van der Veen, requested to give a ruling, was uncertain. After that I made no very serious attempt to clear up the point, hardly supposing that I could succeed in a few months where he had failed in a quarter of a century.

It was a pity that I never saw the Cat with the Iron

Collar. This large wild cat wears a metal collar that is luminous at night, and anyone lucky enough to see it is suffered to approach and unfasten it from the beast's neck.

Its possession confers much strength; that word implying, of course, magical power and soul-strength. Sapondama had such a collar.

The cat is held in high honour by the people of La'bo. That is to say, the Toraja breed of domesticated cat is. The wild cat and the common breed of knot-tailed domesticated cat that has come up from Palopo on the coast have no higher status than dogs. But the small Toraja tabby is known as *serreh datu*, a cat prince.

These cat princes are never in any circumstances allowed to touch the earth at any time between birth and death, nor indeed after death. Normally, they never set paw outside the house in which they are born.

"We don't have to keep our *serreh datu* in," Sulo told me. "She never wants to go out, except when she needs a man cat and then we fetch her one. It would be very bad for a *serreh datu* to touch the earth, Tuan. When one dies we weave a special mat for it and wrap it inside with a small knife, and a boy climbs a *po'pong* tree with it and fixes the body safe in a branch."

I never discovered the reason for this ban on contact with the soil. That cats who protect the clothes and fabrics of their masters from the incredibly voracious Celebesian rats should enjoy a favoured position as guardians of household wealth is natural enough, but the ritual elevation of their lives and deaths I cannot explain. I was also told that in some districts, though not in La'bo, a cat had to be apprised in formal words of its master's death, and then be carried to another house until the corpse was finally removed to the *rante*.

Prince cats are sharply distinguished from the ordinary coastal cats, which are called *serreh la'o*, cats that walk

about. Certainly they are prettier than the rather disreputable prowlers from Palopo.

I shall now have to say something about the *deata*, none
of whom I met during my stay, though their everyday
presence in the village was vividly manifest to my neighbours.

The following brief outline of Toraja myth may hold good
in the barest essentials for all the million Torajas inhabiting
the middle of Celebes; but most of the details are true for
only the small area between Rantepao and Sangalla, where
they were collected. In preliterate societies the place of
written documents is taken by human memory, and though
in such societies memory is normally far keener than with
us, the absence of any central authority and the former lack
of contact between the various Toraja tribes has resulted in
wide variations in beliefs that had a common source.

Life began, they say, when the sky descended to the
earth and gathered her in an embrace of love. Of that
union three sons were born. The Lord Gauntikembong
ascended to the region of the sky and remains there; the
Lord Pong' Bangairante remained and remains on earth;
and the Lord Pong' Tulakpadang descended under the
earth to Tokengkok, where he rules the gods of the underworld and also holds up the surface of the earth.

Simultaneously other divinities must have come into
being, for when the boy-gods were ripe there were goddesses for them to marry. Pong' Bangairante married one
by the name of Talloh Mangkakalena and they had a
family of eight, who are the chief *deata*.

The first was Pong' Lalondong, who eventually went to
Puya, where he established, and still presides over, the
Homeland of Souls. His sisters, Indoh Pare Pare and Indoh
Samadenna, went to the sun and moon respectively and still
dwell there. The Corners of the World are guarded by
another son, Puang Radeng, and the Edge of the World is

the kingdom of Saripi Bula'an. The sixth child became Timbalo Kila, the Father of Lightning, which he sends out from the rocks which are everywhere his home. Of the last two sons, Tandiminanga became Rajah of the Sea, and Pong' Tulangdenna is Rajah of Rivers.

All but the first three punish humans for offences in their sphere of majesty, and all can be appealed to for help and protection.

The nearest the Torajas come to a conception of an Almighty is Puang Matua, literally " the old lord." He was a grandson of Gauntikembong and it was he who created mankind, forging the first man from gold with his divine bellows. Christian missionaries in the Torajalands have taken his name for the Supreme Being of their faith, and many prayers in their churches begin *"Puang Matua . . ."*

The first human was named Datu Loku by Puang Matua, who married him to a goddess, Bonga Lang'ina; but it was not until the sixth generation of man that human feet first walked the earth. There was soon trouble. The first human to be born in the world, Pong' Mulatao, lived happily with his wife in the region of Makale, but of their two sons, though Londongdilangi was an Abel, the other, Londongdirura, was a Cain.

When Londongdirura gave his son to his daughter in marriage, Puang Matua in a fury flooded the earth, drowning the incestuous innocents and their parents. As the waters rose the good Londongdilangi and his wife were able to escape to heaven by the staircase of rock which in those times stretched between heaven and a spot a few miles west of Makale. The pair returned to the world when the waters subsided and peopled the earth with their progeny, their children apparently multiplying themselves without guilt of incest in the manner of the children of Adam and Eve. At Rura, a little place south of Makale and formerly Londong-dirura's domain, a small lake can now be seen which is all that remains of the flood.

Toraja legend has its share of the familiar myths of Asia, as even these few paragraphs have shown. The origin of life in the bridal of earth and sky is an ancient Chinese belief; the good and bad brothers and the flood are found, of course, among the Jewish myths of the Old Testament. A detailed account would reveal other parallels.

It is only about twenty generations since the first puang descended from heaven. He was not a man but a *deata* by the name of Tamborolangi and he married a mortal called Sandabilik. They had three sons, or perhaps it was four, the three becoming the first Puangs of Sangalla, Makale and Menkendek respectively. It is in Kesu that they say there were four; the fourth, they claim, was called Puang Tuman Bulibuntu and was the ancestor of the present Ampulembang of Kesu.

Twice Tamborolangi descended to earth, first of all by way of the rock staircase to visit a kinswoman of his who lived in Sangalla. To his horror he came upon her as she was being ravished by a human whose name is given variously as Pong' Bulukuseh and Kate'ebak. In a rage the god consumed the ravisher with fire and returned to heaven up the staircase, revolted by the ways of man. Some say it was he who on that occasion threw down the staircase, for ever cutting off earth from heaven; others say that it was Puang Matua who wrecked the rock ladder in his disgust at the crime of Londongdirura, leaving only its bottom step standing, which we can now see as the noble Buntu Kandora, and strewing the wreckage across the district of Kesu, a long pile now known as the mountain range Sarira, where the baboons live.

Those who favour the latter tradition say that Tamborolangi descended from heaven in a house. Both accounts agree that he travelled by house on his second descent, and you may still see the spot where his house grounded at Ulin, near Rembon, when he arrived to found the dynasty of the puangs who rule to-day in Sangalla, Makale and Menkendek.

Ordinary villagers know only the main points of this story, but the wizards and chiefs are familiar with a vast amount of further detail and believe it implicitly. The Puang of Sangalla is perfectly persuaded of the truth of this account of the origin of his family. King Charles the First's view of his position and prerogatives was modest by comparison with that of the Puang.

Under white influence some undermining of belief in the ancestral Toraja divinities has, however, taken place. There are some young people in Rantepao and Makale who, though not Christians, are not good heathens either. Even so, these school-taught moderns would not go so far as to swear against the gods.

The three proto-divinities, the Lords of Heaven, Earth and the Underworld, are no longer in the forefront of Toraja belief; but if you swear against the *deata* it is still they who administer condign punishment. The Lord of Heaven pulls you up by the hair, the Lord of the Underworld pulls you down by the feet, and the Lord of the Earth cuts you in half.

The root, though, of all Toraja belief is animism.

There is something, they believe, that is neither matter nor force. Let us call it soul. It is this soul that makes all living things tick—men and women, birds, beasts and fishes, flowers and trees. It exists in differing quantities or concentrations in different living things. There is not much soul, for instance, in a frog or a kapok tree, but much soul in a man's head (which is why the heads of enemies were sought and taken in the Torajalands up to forty years ago). The crimson-leaved *tabang* plant is strong because of its much soul; so is the rice; so is a bull.

This soul-material or soul-energy is the basis of both physical and spiritual strength. Naturally a man safeguards his own reservoir of soul and reinforces it as far as he can. He plants *tabangs* close to his house, he eats rice and receives the rice-soul into his body, and when he eats bull meat at a death-feast he enjoys an accession of magical strength. Particularly when he is sick he is greedy for soul-matter to fortify his threatened reserves.

The reason why Pong' Rantebambam, a rich man, wore an old and much-stained sarong and tattered basket hat was that they, through long contact with his body and absorption of sweat, perhaps a little blood and other body emanations, held minute quantities of his soul-matter in their fabric. As a gravely sick man, unable to stem the draining of his essential reserves, he could not risk the loss of such particles of his vital treasure by discarding his garments, or even by having them washed. If, however, he had decided to discard them he would have been careful to burn them and scatter the ashes, for fear a sorcerer should get hold of them and with such traces of his Self be enabled to work bad magic against him. Pong' Rantebambam believed that a sorcerer was responsible for his disease; a powerful sorcerer, too, since Sapondama's strongest magic availed so little to help him.

Even some inanimate objects possessed soul, my La'bo friends told me. A panel of dead wood enshrined only the most negligible amount, but that panel after Munu had carved the mask of the bull on it was "very strong;" strong enough to serve as the door of a tomb, beyond the power of any evil spirit to pass.

One consequence of their animistic faith is that the Torajas are in no danger, so long as they retain it, of the spiritual ill-health that is sometimes attributed to our own divorce from Nature. Moreover, by reason of that faith their conception of their place in Nature is not that of dictators or super-beings. They are not, as we tend more and more to become, uneasy strangers in the world of Nature, at war with her and obsessed by a passion to subdue her wholly. They are at home in the world, with no vaunting notions of themselves as Lords of Creation. It seems to me that they are the happier for that.

VI

MARKET DAY

THE rough division of a moon into four weeks of seven days is known to the Torajas and they have the same name for "week" as the Malays, *minggu*. It is an alien concept, of course, derived from the Portugese who, four centuries ago, taught their first Malay converts the unique importance of Sunday, the Day of the Lord, or *Domingo*. Sunday is called *hari minggu* by the Indonesians, and a week is *minggu*, but it is seldom that the word passes the lips of anybody in La'bo. They have a month, or moon, of five markets instead.

The great market of Rantepao, the chief focus of Toraja commerce, takes place every six days, and over a wide surrounding area local markets are all held at a corresponding interval. On the morning preceding each Rantepao market day Salu would hand me my mug of sunrise coffee with the reminder, "Tuan must bathe quickly. It is the Little Market."

The Little Market was the humble affair held round my bathing pavilion, at which the locals bought their chewing tobacco, lime and *sireh*, their hot peppers and a few vegetables. It assembled early, and unless I took my bath within half an hour of sunrise I would find myself cut off by the earlier market women and their first customers. For about three hours it lasted, with the women perched in tiers up the little hillside with their baskets before them and buyers wandering between them, all to the tune of the gentle, contented murmur of chatter that rises from any Toraja gathering. There would never be more than fifty people there at one time and by mid-morning attendance would already be falling off.

By the time the last market woman shouldered her basket, fixed the carrying-strap across her head and moved away, the first traders for next day's market at Rantepao had passed the bungalow. These came from Palopo, the little town down on the Gulf of Boni, having climbed more than forty miles of alpine paths with loads of salt and coconut oil. They were not coastal Malays from Palopo, but Torajas living near Rantepao who made the journey to the coast every six days. Often they freshened their feet in my bathing-booth and rested a while under the bungalow eaves. Salu was thus able to buy our supplies of coconut oil, in which all my food was fried, at his cookhouse door.

I went to Rantepao market most weeks. It was a festival in its way, with all the wholesome animation of a country fair. Next to a big death-feast it is the most vivid scene of Toraja life that I know.

This is how I remember a typical market day. . . . .

Almost unbroken files of wayfarers passing the gate from daybreak. An early breakfast. Salu a little abstracted, his best shirt and sarong laid out on his bed. Duna in close attendance on me even before breakfast. A small knot of acquaintances gathering on the veranda to give me their company along the four miles to Rantepao. Salu coming in with a list that has taken him ten minutes to write. It says, in Malay, " Rice, 4 chickens, 1 carp or goldfish, salt, potatoes (if have), beans, tomatoes, onions, bananas, sugar, charcoal, 1 big pot, lamp oil from Dr. Goslinga, smoking tobacco, chewing tobacco, *sireh*. 25 guilders."

" Is there anything else Tuan wants? " he asks. " It will not cost twenty-five *rupias*, but perhaps I see something else or perhaps I am able to buy many potatoes. We need a new pot because Duna has broken another. His hands are truly not clever."

Duna hangs his head. I hand over twenty-five guilders,

ten in notes and fifteen in the tiny silver coins which the Torajas greatly prefer after their experience of the valueless paper money with which the Japanese cheated them. Those on the veranda gaze upon this outpouring of wealth like a crowd watching the unloading of bullion.

A few minutes later, shining in his varnished brown hat of Javanese straw, his white shorts and cream and chocolate patterned sarong, Salu looks in to take his leave. He departs, attended by Lendu with a shoulder-pole and deep baskets which we have on permanent loan from Sesa's father.

I leave a little later, and Barra, under orders from Salu, bolts the doors almost before I am through them and instals himself on the veranda as a quite superfluous guard. Duna and Lindung are in attendance upon me, wearing my livery of marigold-coloured sarongs. Lindung is there to carry my mackintosh, Duna to carry one camera and any purchases or gifts I may acquire.

Poi' Bunga, the young Chief of Tambunan, joins my party at the gate, as do Palimbong's writer and the eldest son of Pong' Masa'aga. The brilliance of the morning is not to be described: it is as though light were growing and burning out of the earth, irradiating every water surface, every grove and glade, even the files of bright, hurrying folk along the path.

" *Umbara miola ?* " Where are you going? Again and again the people on the road ask me that. It is quite obvious where I am going, but that is the customary Toraja greeting on the road.

" *Lalokan tama Rantepao,*" I reply. I go to Rantepao.

" *Manda'akomi,*" they say. A good journey.

Now and again Duna or another of the lesser ones in my party is asked for details of my identity, title and business in those parts. The marigold sarongs are much admired. We can see the fretted peaks of Sarira over on our left, sometimes reflected in huge flooded fields. Then there is the charming hamlet of Ke'te, where old Tandilolock lives, the clustered roofs of houses and barns like granny's bonnets in the sun beneath the green woods and the great black precipice. The *rante* of Ke'te is directly alongside the hamlet, but from the disrepair of the guest-houses it is plain that there has been no death-feast there for the past year or two.

The artist who is Salu's friend sits outside his hut a little farther on, preparing the lumps of earth from which he makes his black, white, ochre and scarlet paints. The waters of one of the Ampulembang of Kesu's finest fields reflect him and his small hut and the mountain beyond. The country is open before us now, and we can glimpse the huge blue mass of Mount Sesian overhanging the rice-plain of Tikala. The sun is hot, but whenever the path passes through a cutting the *taruk*-scented shade is deliciously cool.

One immense megalith, perhaps forty feet high, towers above the slope to our left, its foot railed off from the sweet-potato plots surrounding it. To our right the Ampulembang's deep fields shine, with the infant rice vivid and sturdy and the water sparkling through the green blades. Some women in a wayside hut have woven a tiny *baka*, or shoulder-basket, for a little naked tot of two years. She staggers up and down with its strap in position across her brow and a few wisps of rice for a load, while the women encourage her with admiring words.

The Ampulembang is such a miser that I take pleasure in calling at his house, where they are obliged to offer me coffee and cake every time. He is not at home, but his senior wife, a handsome woman with gold earrings and teeth, receives me. Two large plates of cake and biscuits are brought, which I share with Lindung and Duna.

I am surprised by this unusually lavish hospitality until I reflect that Mr. Sukawati, president of the new dominion of East Indonesia, has been expected in the Toraja country for more than a week. A beautiful triumphal arch of woven palm fronds and bamboo spans the steep lane to the house. Doubtless new refreshments are baked daily against the president's call, and we are merely helping them to eat up some of the stale accumulation.

Though the exterior scene of three houses and a fine row of rice-barns is most handsome, the reception-room is deplorable. The table supporting my coffee tray and cake dishes is covered with a cloth of nameless crochet and bead-work. On the wall above my head there is a pair of antlers, a Victorian lithograph of a Gospel scene I am unable to identify and a hideous framed motto in Dutch, " Oost, West—Thus Best." Suspended from the ceiling is a lamp-shade with what look like hundreds of furry caterpillars the colour of milk chocolate hanging from it.

Down to the road again. It really looks like a road here, for a gang of men performing their annual service to the government are weeding and raking it and filling in the larger ruts. This is not appreciated by the wayfarers, for all the tiny smooth tracks that normally run like veins along the path have been obliterated by the operation. The sole of a Toraja foot, that carelessly stubs out a burning cigarette end and is no more ticklish than the shell of a tortoise, is not entirely insensitive all the same, and as if by instinct Toraja travellers will pick out the tiny, thread-like tracks, worn satin-smooth by thousands of naked soles and heels, that wind between the stones and flints of the road.

Past the Ampulembang's fish-ponds and now we join the wide main road that begins at Tondon in Pangala, twenty-five miles to the north-west, and ends on the sea-front in Makassar, 210 miles to the south. Here it runs parallel with the Sadang River through a narrow valley of smiling beauty. To the stream of wayfarers from Sangalla, Rante Bua and Bunt'ao who have passed our gates at Pintu, is now added the larger flow of travellers from the area of Makale, coming up the main road.

More than half of them carry loads.

Men carry their loads on shoulder-poles; women carry theirs in beautifully woven baskets on their backs, supported by bands passing across the top of the forehead. Rice, for instance, is carried either way, according to the sex of the carrier. Young boys and girls carry similar but smaller burdens, for Toraja children always share the work and play their elders.

The procession is now lavishly picturesque, like a slightly overdone travel poster. Against a background of magnificent crags, olive and black under a gentian sky, the merchandise travels to Rantepao on patient shoulders of bronze and broad bare feet. There are chicken in airy globular baskets, and special cocks with their heads emerging from what look like wicker bottles or carried lovingly in the arms like babies. There are dazzling clusters of giant goldfish dangling from shoulder-poles, dipped from time to time in the waters of a paddy-field to revive them. Pigs ride to market slung beneath a pole resting on the shoulders of two men; small ones hang in harnesses of green bamboo bark, but big ones recline comfortably on platforms beneath canopies of leaves. A weaver of the big primrose-coloured straw hats wears a dozen balanced on top of each other. A naked boy, who has only nine or ten cobs of maize to sell, has tied them together and balanced them like a spiky halo round his head—women would pay twenty guineas for a lightweight replica of it in a Bond Street hat shop. Vegetables are carried by the women, but fruit burdens are shared. So graceful is the walk of either sex that great bunches of bananas are often balanced securely on the almost flat hats.

Most spectacular are the pot-sellers. The large, fragile rice-pots are very light and men balance shoulder-poles twelve feet long with chestnut-coloured pots tied to them all along their length. Women pile half a dozen, one on top of the other, on their shoulder-baskets, the top one towering more than a yard above their heads, usually surmounted by their hats, since the broad-brimmed hats must be discarded when loads protrude more than a little way from the baskets. There are two men with shoulder-poles balancing twin open-work baskets four feet deep with foaming white loads of kapok, which grows in pods on trees in these parts.

A poor man from the mountains leads a quartet of white dogs. They are young table dogs, relished by the poor mountaineers but despised as food by the valley dwellers. Mention the Torajas anywhere in South Celebes and the Bugis will spit, and say, " They eat pig and dog!" The Torajas are very sensitive over this, and when I asked friends in La'bo whether they cared for dog meat their eyes widened in gentle reproach that I should have thought them capable of such indelicate appetites.

The lead of each smooth-haired Toraja terrier passes through a pipe of bamboo a yard long. This is because they are inclined to be vicious, and a dog led in this way cannot get near enough to the ankles of his purchaser to bite him.

Now we are entering Rantepao, the London and New York of the South Torajas. Up a bank to the left is the office of the Ampulembang of Kesu, a little square one-story hut of stucco, with a front veranda set with chairs for the meetings of chiefs. Each chair has the name of a village or village-complex on its back, and is reserved for the chief in question.

On the right are the barracks built by the Japanese during the occupation, more handsome than most barracks I have known. Along the road a detachment of some of the first Toraja soldiers are drilling under a Menadonese sergeant and a Dutch lieutenant. They are doing English Army drill but wear American Army uniforms. They do a creditably smart " Eyes—right " as I pass, a courtesy to which I am no longer entitled, for my release leave has now expired and I am a civilian again; and in any case, I have no right to be wearing British Army uniform here, even with my badges of rank removed.

On the left now the missionary's pleasant house and the little white-walled church that with its mountain background has a bright, Swiss air about it. On the right a little farther on is the hospital, with a crowd of out-patients and kinsmen of patients squatting round the entrance. The wards are always full of sick, except for the small private ward in which the Rajah of Boni enjoys the best of health. He is serving a sentence of banishment for his enthuasiastic collaboration with the Japanese and his part in terrorist outbreaks after the capitulation. He travelled from Makassar into exile in the same convoy with me, enthroned in a large easy-chair mounted in the back of a military truck.

The doctor's white house is next door to the hospital, but the boundary line between the districts of Kesu and Tikala runs between the two buildings.

A forbiddingly alien note is struck by the pounded-out hymn sung by a class of high-school children. Rantepao has several schools, even a small Chinese one. Altogether there is a metropolitan air about the large village, with a lorry parked outside a Chinese dealer's store and a number of clerk-like young Torajas in shoes and well-creased trousers, even one or two *horizontales* with European dresses and artificially waved hair. At the wooden cottage that calls itself the Tjong Hoa Hotel, I stop for a word with my rich friend Sampe, who owns the lorry and has once or twice done a little business for me in Makassar. Then it is Serang, the postmaster, I must greet.

I have to be on my best behaviour with Serang, and even then I cannot hope to match either his gracious cordiality or the air of consequence with which he surrounds himself. Seeing me approach, he waves away from his window several of the clerk-like individuals who are before me, much to my embarrassment, and with flashing smiles extends a cordial hand before I am within ten yards of him.

" Greeting, Tuan! I have been expecting Tuan. Yes, I have letters. I regret that the mail from Makassar was not yet sorted when the child who calls for Tuan's letters came yesterday. There, Tuan, I tied them together for safety. Three from Groot-Brittannie, one from Amerika, one from Java, one from Singapura, one from British India and one from Makassar. Eight altogether. I am happy that Tuan called, for there is a paper Tuan will want to see. My new directive on air-mails. It came yesterday only. The charge on letters to Groot-Brittannie remains the same, but there are alterations for some other countries. . . ."

Serang is happy. While I am there he has a man of affairs to talk with, one whose interests, like his own, are world-wide, one who has been known to receive twenty letters in one post, all dispatched by fabulously expensive air-mail from important capitals in four continents. It would be brutal not to linger, not to ask him to be good enough to look up the air-mail rate to Egypt or Denmark, not to buy a few of his large, expensive stamps for next week's letters.

Good-bye to Serang, and a few steps more bring us to the first of the market gates where a policeman, also in American uniform, collects the small tax on all the merchandise taken in for sale. The crowd is dense at the gate, thinning only around the dog-seller as one of his curs begins to snarl.

It is only when I am in a crowd like this that I realise momentarily what a small-statured race the Torajas are. I am scarcely more than six feet tall, but even the tall Pangala men come only an inch or two above my shoulder. Just for a moment they all look like children.

Hats.

Hats are the master-motif of the market scene. If you were to take a photograph of the market from above, slightly out of focus, it would look like a close-up of a great bed of marigolds. The huge yellow hats, flatly conical, are

worn by all the women and some of the men. I suppose
there are six or seven thousand Toraja hats here, those worn
by the long rows of squatting sellers a fixed pattern and those
on the heads of buyers weaving in slow flourishes among
them.

Eight long sheds shelter a large proportion of the sellers,
but hundreds squat in rows in the great open spaces between
the sheds, so thickly that it is difficult to move about. The
size of the market is astonishing in relation to the size of
the village, even when you realise the enormous area it
serves. No wonder the Toraja divides a moon not into four
weeks so much as five markets.

The sun is hot. I am fatigued. I want to read one or
two of my letters. I need a haircut. The barber's chair is
obviously the place for me.

My favourite barber is free, so I pick my way through
the dense ranks of the women vegetable-sellers and mount
the step up to the first enormous shed. The near end is
occupied by seven or eight barbers, with stout Lee Tong
conspicuous among them. His chair, too, is vacant for the
moment and I feel guilty as I pass him with a greeting and
sink into Kaladin's chair. The Chinese is much the best
barber there and the only good haircut I've had in the
Toraja country was in his chair; but I prefer to patronise
Kaladin because he is a Toraja, so far as I can gather.

I haven't gathered much about Kaladin, for I have never
yet understood anything he said to me. Either he suffers
from a vocal impediment or else he speaks a dialect I have
not encountered elsewhere. Kaladin is probably a mere
approximation to his name, but that is what it sounded like
when he told me. His smile is broad, however, and it is a
habit with me now to spend my first ten minutes at market
in his chair.

If I were fussed by a little dirt I should not patronise him.
But then, if a little dirt fussed me I should not have stayed
in Asia, I should never set foot outside the Anglo-Saxon or

North-West European countries, and even at that I should be scared to eat in some of their most famous restaurants. But I find it more fun to get an indifferent haircut in Rantepao market than to yield my head to an expert in the scented stuffiness of any west-end saloon.

Kaladin's establishment is modest. His mirror, which returns an alarmingly poxed reflection, hangs from a nail driven into a pillar of the lofty shed. Beneath it stands a rickety table with a similarly poxed complexion, for most of the varnish has long blistered away. On the table stand two hand-clippers, two combs, a razor, an old sardine tin half full of dirty water, a shaving-brush with not many bristles left, a minute lump of soap and a pair of scissors. All these, particularly the clippers and the sparsely-toothed pink and green combs, are liberally coated or choked with coconut oil and snippets of black hair. An old leather strop hanging from the pillar, a couple of yards of soiled pink calico to swathe customers in and the chair in which I sit, complete the equipment of Kaladin's business. Drifts of coarse black hair, clotted with coconut oil, litter the pavement round the chair and a spittoon would be an improvement.

Kaladin has merry brown eyes, two rows of flawless teeth, a shock of gleaming hair, an old khaki shirt, a lilac sarong, a horn bracelet and a brass ring with a glass ruby in it. He smokes a cigarette as he works on my hair. A few of the milling thousands pause to enjoy the spectacle, for it is customary for a *tuang kapua* to summon a barber to his house and not disclose the secrets of his toilet to the gaze of the multitude. Lee Tong, however, turns his plump back and close-cropped grey poll on me to the end. . . .

After the cool shade of the shed the climbing sun is like a flame on the shoulders. The fruit and vegetable market is colourful with its scores of piles, set before each seller, of green and red tomatoes, small pineapples, strings of pink *katambi* fruit, brilliant white bamboo shoots, pawpaws picked unripe to be eaten as a vegetable, huge green Bali oranges cut open to show the rosy flesh, bananas of many kinds, strange limp greens, a few little onions, fat cucumbers, green beans, the huge, murky crimson flower of the banana which can be steamed and served as a vegetable, a fruit that looks like a Victoria plum but disappoints the palate, honey-coloured *langsas* and small, green tangerines. The sellers squat with open knees tightly stretching their sarongs, their faces invisible under their great hats unless one bends low to speak to them. I have my camera open, but the moment I get it focused on the profile of a smiling hill girl her friends warn her, the smile fades and she turns her back on me so that I am made to feel a prying, ill-bred outsider.

I am, however, sure of a smile from my favourite salt-seller, a buxom *vendeuse* who reclines on a pile of baskets under an awning devised from a woven sleeping-mat propped on crazy wooden pillars. I pause before her heap of coarse grey salt and mop my brow.

" Hot, Tuan, hot! " she sighs, delicately fanning herself with a sheet of banana leaf.

" But the lady has a good shelter from the sun," I say. " It must be cool in there."

" Indeed, no, Tuan. Dreadfully hot. No breeze."

Like the postmaster, she enjoys our momentary intimacy, two sensitive creatures that we are, adrift amid the coarse crowds and the excesses of the sun. . . .

The next shed is chiefly occupied by Buginese women who sell cotton cloth at exorbitant prices, and, again at exorbitant prices, swiftly run it up into sarongs, tunics or shorts for the purchasers on their old-fashioned sewing machines. With their hair dressed in high coils and their vivid blouses of violet, petunia, rice-green and gold, these women are conscious of their superiority. They and their husbands remind me of city cheap-jacks at a Wessex country fair, and I esteem the simple Torajas as far above them as Wessex rustics above city cheap-jacks.

We halt at the row of tobacco-sellers, not the humble purveyors of chewing tobacco who crouch in rows in the open, but the dealers in Buginese cigarette tobacco who have opened shop along the edge of the third shed. The tobacco is packed in dark-brown tubes of giant bamboo (locally grown) and each week Duna receives a shilling cake of it, from which he will manufacture scores of small cigarettes with the aid of the thin pages of my air-mail edition *Spectator*, or even sheets of toilet paper. The tobacco-sellers offer little books of cigarette papers, but Duna will not let me buy them because they are too expensive.

After staring for some time at several different brands he demands a sample of one of them. This he twists briskly into a thin tube with the scrap of paper the vendor hands him and lights at the smouldering end of rope coiled from a pillar nearby. His bright eyes close and he frowns a little as he inhales slowly. Then he shakes his head and a little to my embarrassment moves on to another seller and demands a further sample.

He is satisfied at last, the cake of compressed *tembaco* is wrapped in a square of banana leaf and fastened with a long thorn, I pay the fifty cents and we move along to the smelly corner where durians are sold.

My dictionary defines a durian as an oval fruit with a fetid smell and a pleasant taste. They are oval all right, as big as coconuts and handsomely armed with spikes something in the manner of a pineapple. These spikes are more formidable, however, and a number of people passing or lingering beneath durian trees have been killed by falling fruit. The creamy interior is rather strongly aphrodisiac. Its pleasant taste is a matter of opinion, though the fetid smell is not.

South-East Asiatics esteem the durian above all other fruits, a view that is shared by only a small proportion of white people. Word descriptions of flavours are seldom strongly evocative, and the usual characterisation of the cream of durians as combining the flavours of chocolate, clotted cream and garlic fails to take into account the whiff of carrion that hangs about the smooth delicacy. I was greatly disappointed at my failure to appreciate it, for exotic foods are one of the minor adventures of travel.

The durians look rather like green-gold Mills bombs arranged in pyramids and secured by slings of green bark. They are far too expensive for most of the poor Torajas passing by the squatting boys, who seem indifferent as to whether they sell or no.

The sellers of coconut oil are busier. They are a cheery crowd and their arms and hands gleam with the lustre of the oil. The bottom sections of the biggest giant bamboo stems are used as containers for the oil that is distilled down on the coast at Palopo and they are a glowing brown from their long pickling in it. The corner beyond is the market for the ingredients of *sireh*-chewing and is full of women crouching and gossiping over supplies of *sireh* leaf and fruit, of areca nut, of gambier, of chalk and the little balls of tobacco which are popped into the mouth after two or three minutes of *sireh*-chewing. Buyers take no pigs in pokes here; every purchase is well turned over and sniffed over before a deal is closed.

Duna suddenly attracts my attention to an old gentleman I do not know, a very dignified old gentleman with a staff.

" He is that one of whom Salu told Tuan some nights ago," says Duna. " He who murdered the white man."

About thirty years ago Mr. van der Loosdrecht, a Dutch missionary, spent the night at the schoolmaster's house at Bori, a few miles north of Rantepao. In that district a number of men had resented more violently than most the Controleur's new ban on gambling and other interferences with tribal *adat* and a small group of them had decided to do away with him. When the missionary arrived at Bori the mistaken word went round that the Controleur had come and the plotters resolved to wait no longer.

After nightfall, as Mr. van der Loosdrecht sat writing by lamplight at the open window, he was hailed from the darkness outside. He answered, and the next moment the gentleman who now chatted genially with a wine-seller at my side threw a spear and killed him.

Murder is not a capital crime in the Netherlands Indies. The murderer was given the maximum sentence of twenty years' banishment, several years of which were later remitted, and he returned to his old village, where he was warmly welcomed and where he has lived ever since.

That is one of the difficulties of bringing white man's law and morals into other civilisations. You can impose them, but you cannot necessarily mobilise respect for them or social disapproval of the law-breakers. By no means all the prisoners in Makale jail lose face. The chief's clerk who has helped himself to a cut of the tax money before sending it in is jailed, but on his subsequent return to his village he may not find that he has even temporarily forfeited the respect of his neighbours.

The missionaries grieve, too, over the pretty Pangala girls who now and then migrate to Makassar, ostensibly to work as domestic servants but often actually to earn the wages of shame in *maisons de plaisir*, where their skill and beauty are much appreciated. When they retire and go back to Pangala no stones are thrown at them, perhaps because none of their neighbours pride themselves on being sinless. Instead, they are welcomed back with open arms, and sometimes with proposals of marriage.

I met one of these retired charmers in Pangala. I thought she was nice.

I am thirsty and would like nothing better than to buy one of the bamboos of *tuak* which sellers from Tikala and Nanggala offer to let me taste. I would, too, if I had found the way to drink from a long tube without pouring so much of it down my neck. As it is, I sit down at a table under one of the sheds and order a glass of coffee and a plate of fried bananas.

While I am sipping the good coffee and chatting with a soft-voiced Javanese soldier and a strange old man from Palopo who looks rather like John L. Lewis in a turban, Salu appears. He brings an invitation to lunch with Dr. Goslinga and his family. The soldier has a watch and tells me it is past noon. Time for one more look round.

The hundreds of green pipes full of *tuak* are ranged like organ pipes against rails with tempting froth bubbling from their mouths. Behind them are the sellers of rattan, offering great coils of the immensely strong creeper they gather from the forest. Beyond them four dog-sellers. The old man who walked into Rantepao with us has sold all but one of his dogs. Sesa's father has sold two ducks for eight guilders, a good price. The pot-sellers take up a great deal of space, squatting among their fragile pans and bowls, the glazed ones ablaze in the fierce sunshine.

The dusty black pigs, lying trussed on their sides in the shade, watch passers-by with little slanting eyes and scream hysterically if you tread too near them. A boy offers a cluster of thin eels, drawing them out of their travelling tank of a water-filled bamboo cane; I shake my head and they are tucked back in again.

Nobody presses you to buy. Nobody shouts. The hum of gentle chatter is almost musical. I am reminded of the poor Estonians and their strange, remote language that in any assembly sounded like the twittering of birds. They used to claim quaintly, in those days when they were enjoying their short spell of freedom from Russia between the wars, that they possessed the second most beautiful language in Europe.

Yes, it is a pleasant sound, the hum of Toraja conversation. Sane and good humoured. There is nobody with " nerves " here, nobody twisted and ugly from arid battles

with his self. Nor is there any of the stink of bad men here
that chokes you with moral suffocation in the big cities of
the West. The evil here is simple, more like the naughtiness
of children.

Everybody meets friends in Rantepao market, and I am
no exception. Elisa, eldest son of the Ambonese missionary
at Sangalla, is there, and a Toraja boy I last saw on duty as a
guard in the seventeenth-century fort in Makassar, and the
wizard Sapondama and one of Kalasuso's clerks and Indoh
Rero herself, the Toraja Nightingale, paying an enormous
sum for a few yards of cheap lemon cloth.

The rice, in weeping sheaves and husked in baskets, is
tragically expensive; fifteen pence a pound husked. Everything is dear, from 1,500 to 5,000 per cent above pre-war
prices. I pause to buy a pineapple and three Bali oranges.
Though I bend low to ask the price, the girl is so shy that
even then I see only her lips and chin below the wide hat-
brim as she replies.

" Tuan, in the street there is a crocodile," Duna tells me
after a word with an excited friend. " A Chinese man is
buying it. He will kill it and sell the skin in Makassar."

I do not care for crocodiles. Giving Duna and Lindung
permission to go off and see it, I pass through avenues of
vegetables and fruit, push my way past the knot of barbers
and greet several La'bo friends with fresh haircuts, step
carefully to avoid the little nests of eggs and the garlands of
eggs tied in long palm leaves like huge bead necklaces,
shudder slightly as I turn from the bluey-white masses of
sago and the baskets of violent red peppers, pause to admire
the weaving of the thin, pliant bedmats, snapshot a group
of hill-men with wild locks and swift, bird eyes who are
buying knives, return the parting smile of my favourite
salt-seller and then I am out on the main road again.

It is a relief to relax the perpetual caution against treading
on naked toes which is an obsession for a white man in any
Toraja crowd. The road is hard after the sticky mud of the

market-place, with its litter of discarded banana-leaf wrappings, bits of durian skin and orange peel, and the hæmorrhage of *sireh* spittle over all.

Buffaloes are sold outside the market-place. At the end of the village a large bull, on his way to the market, is causing concern by his nervous inability to cross the bridge. The sight of the torrent twenty-five feet below is too much for him and he has come to a standstill. Nobody dreams of beating him. I join the group which rather apologetically heaves at his flanks, but the wide-set hooves will not budge. Finally, the young man in charge of him strips off his rose-pink sarong and drapes it over the noble horns.

It works. Ponderously the blindfold beast advances and everybody is pleased.

Dr. Goslinga is a heavily-built, calm man of middle age with close-cropped flaxen hair. He is a medical missionary and runs the hospitals and the health services of the province with the assistance of a Dutch sister and a staff of orderlies and nurses whom they have largely trained between them. He is a devout man who moves as the centre of an aura of peace and confidence. Every day of his captivity in Japanese prison camps he read his Bible and also Shakespeare in the English and Homer in the Greek.

Both he and his hospitable wife speak English well. Three boys who are almost small-scale replicas of the doctor sit round the luncheon table. Their elder brother and sister are on their way to Europe and there is a baby in the nursery. Before we eat, one of the little boys is asked to say grace for us.

I forget how long the doctor and his wife have been out here, but it is a long time. There are not many questions about Toraja life which one or the other of them cannot answer. Mevrouw Goslinga has educated all the children, and now the little boys, who began their education in

Japanese prison camps, are beginning to learn English. They find certain English words screamingly funny; two of them almost choke over " horseback " when I use it in discussing with their father the possibility of an expedition into the mountains of the west. When we have finished lunch the doctor reads a chapter from the Bible, I following the reading from an English Bible which is set beside my plate.

The rain-clouds are gathering when we join the returning stream of wayfarers along the road to La'bo. In little roadside booths and under trees a number of women have kindled fires and fry bananas in a thin, golden batter over them. We have our favourite cook among them and wait while my rather large order is fried; large because Lindung and Duna have been joined by Siu and Sesa, out of school, and Duna's new friend Riri.

" The crocodile was not large," Duna tells me. " A male."

" His mouth was tied up but he knocked down a child with his tail," Lindung adds.

Along the stretch of track weeded and levelled by the roadmenders new little paths have already been traced between the sharper stones. The children instinctively follow them.

Just as we come in sight of Ke'te young Siu says in a slightly awed voice, " Tuan *parenge*! "

It is the Ampulembang, returning from a village tax meeting. Four handsome attendants accompany him two paces to the rear. No doubt he finds my train unimpressive. At any rate, I have finished eating my fried bananas and thrown away their leaf wrapping. To hell with him, anyway.

" I visited Tuan's house and he was not there," says the squeaky voice when we have shaken hands. I am disgusted at myself for wishing momentarily that I had been mounted and in my best uniform.

" I also, Tuan. I visited Tuan's house this morning and Tuan was not there."

A polite titter and a pause.

" Tuan has been making *portrets?* " (An eye on my cameras.)

" Yes, Tuan, at the market."

" Tuan's Kodaks were surely expensive."

I am small enough to lie.

" On the contrary, Tuan. This one only fifteen hundred *rupias* and the other two thousand." (Together they are not actually worth more than one hundred pounds.)

" But that is *very* expensive," exclaims the prince, and, impressed, he passes on these false values to his suite. I make no reply, but glance up at the sky and hold out my hand.

" We must both be home before the rain, Tuan."

" Truly, Tuan."

A concentration of more than twenty tribesmen has been waiting for leave to pass the *tuang-tuang kapua.* I wave them on and we start on the last sunless mile to the bungalow.

" The *parenge* has chocolate shoes," says Riri; " but he has no great boots like Tuan."

" He has no Kodaks, also," says Siu.

The big field-boots sound clumsy and noisy among the scores of silent bare feet. Near Marante two little girls are trying to round up half a dozen ducks that have strayed too far from home. I tell my companions about the discipline of the ducks of Bali, which never wander more than a hundred yards or so from the feather-tufted staff the duck shepherd drives into a bank when he takes them out in the morning. As the first shadows of night fall they assemble close round the staff and wait for the shepherd to come and lead them home.

Sesa, himself the owner of a small flock of ducks, is particularly interested. How, he asks, are they trained. I don't know the answer to that one, unless the old birds train their young like the swans on the moat of Wells Cathedral, who educate their cygnets to pull the rope that rings a bell asking for food. I tell the children about them, too, and so we reach journey's end, with me, as so often, telling them of the wonders of the world they will never see.

VII

MY DAY

THE heart, said Sterne, is for saving what it can.

One night when I was no longer a newcomer to La'bo I fed a clean sheet of paper into my typewriter in readiness and went to bed with the resolution that I would set down some record of the next day, minute by minute, from reveille to lights out. Because I knew that the time would come when I should look in vain in the mud by my gate for Toraja footprints and open my window on to a garden for ever empty of Toraja smiles. I was afraid that when that time came I should be homesick in my own homeland . . . and so I am . . . and I thought it might be pleasant for me sometimes to read over a record of that February the twenty-sixth in La'bo . . . and so it is.

This chapter is a shortened version of the running commentary I set down at short intervals next day.

I was wakened as usual by Duna's black cock crowing under my bed. He isn't Duna's really, but a kinsman's. He roosts up at his home in the cliffs of Buntu Assa and struts down here every morning before sunrise to wake me and flirt for hours with the poor doomed little hens that are bought every market day and served up one by one for my supper. A handsome but over-indulged bird.

He was under the floor as well as under my bed, of course, pecking about in the dust beneath the bungalow piles. There was a little light in the room, shining up between the floor-boards and through a thousand chinks in the basket walls. Sometimes I wait in bed for the moment when all these points of light suddenly turn gold as the sun bounces up over the ridge of Buntu Sanik; but I'm always sorry when I do that. This morning I threw back my two blankets before the cock had stopped crowing and went out in time to see the day begin.

It's never twice the same. The eastern sky is seldom quite clear; there are usually a few little clouds of amethyst or cream or lavender, puffed or smeared or frilled round the peak of Buntu Sanik. This morning there were baby puffs like forty-millimetre shell-bursts, a dozen or so, faintly rosy. One of the big, fragile white herons was flying very slowly across Palimbong's big field, drawing a primrose reflection across the water surface. That girl who sings as she bathes was down at the pool under Parrara with the sun glinting on her arms and thighs, but not singing this morning. No wind at all. A few women pounding rice in Marante and somebody playing a flute up the cliff side.

Is it fanciful to speculate on how many of our Western ills of mind, spirit and even body, might be eased if we could all start each day with a few moments of silence, watching the dayspring?

I wonder.

Found Duna, Timbo, Isak, Massang and Sesa perched like sleepy birds round the edge of the fire-bench in the cookhouse, their toes buried in the warm ashes from last night's fires. Rather glum replies to my "*Ma'siang melo.*" The poor little bastards are cold, of course. I should hate to sleep here in nothing but a cotton sarong.

Temperature: 67 degrees Fahrenheit.

I am the village sluggard. Nobody else gets up as late as sunrise. The old men began singing the Kambori

Song at the first wink of light more than an hour ago. I wonder if that old man will come to-day to tell me the words of it. . . . Salu says most people get up an hour before sunrise.

The children are all bathing now. That will wake them up. Timbo is back already, jigging about and hooting and yodelling. I think I like those cries as much as anything here. They catch your breath and seem to draw you back to the very morning of man in the world. Hearing them is like seeing Stonehenge for the first time.

I never really liked coffee till I came here. This is delicious stuff. Nice name, *Arabica*. The *Robusta* we drink in Europe is bound to be inferior with a name like that.

This is really the only hour of the day when I know what time it is. It must be twenty minutes past six now. Of course, if we could see the sun set, we should know when it is six o'clock p.m., but it sets behind mountain and cloud every day, so there's no telling. But who cares?

Just been to the lavatory. When I write my book I must remember to describe my lavatory, because the prisoners of the twentieth century set great store by bathrooms and privies. And there you have a picture of the tame captive of our civilisation: the man who takes a deep interest in the settings for his lowly private moments and has a nose and palate so debased that he eats stale food daily without a murmur and sensibilities so weak that he is seldom aware of the tyranny of manufactured ugliness under which he lives.

One day, of course, a coconut will fall on to the roof of my lavatory and that means *through* the roof, for it's little more than an untidy, though rainproof, wig of black hair from the trunk of an *induk* palm. It would be hard luck if I were inside just then, though. It is quite a pleasant place, airy on account of its basket walls and often with a little bronze lizard for company. I've noticed that all the ants and spiders that live in there are the same auburn colour as the plaited walls.

As for hygiene, I'm sure any M.O. would pass it with honourable mention. The flooring is of the largest kind of bamboo, set on a gentle backward slope. A large slot has been cut in the central hollow log and there are two bamboo pipes of water for flushing. Replenishing these is one of Duna's lowlier duties.

Callers. They begin at about six-thirty daily. School children first, invariably saluting me formally in Malay, though I always answer in Toraja.

" *Berdiri betul! Satu, dua, tiga. . . .*"

" *Tabe, Tuan!* "

" *Tabe, pia-pia,*" I answer, and they break ranks and get in my way until the school opens. Bongga, who was in the first lot, has learned to wink, a grimace I seem to have introduced into the village; his is a dreadful distortion of his whole face. Black Bombai brought me a *taruk* taller than himself, a huge cluster of fragrant cream blooms and rows of stiff leaves like arms thrown up for joy. They can't understand why I have them in the house. When I sniff them and say, " *Wangi bagus!* " rhapsodically, for they are sweeter than lilac, they frown and spit as Eastern people do whenever a stink is encountered or thought of.

" The girls are in your place of bathing, Tuan," young Sampekanan said.

" Good," I said to him, and they all laughed. They think I show consideration to the girls merely to amuse them. " You should have let them wash first before you went in," I added, and then they knew I must be joking.

By the time I went across to bathe six of the little girls were drawn up at the gate with clean, sparkling feet. They greeted me with a tiny, mousey " *Tabe, Tuan!* " only vaguely in unison. The boys, perched at ease on the veranda railings, laughed aloud, so to my good morning I added,

144

" I ask you to use my place of bathing whenever you wish."

They stood with downcast eyes, too confused to reply. To underline my point I made a great show of brusquely ordering out Barira, whom I found splashing under the spout. As he came scuttling out, naked and glistening, I slapped him over the head with his little shorts. The girl with dimples who is Lepeh's cousin or sister giggled at this, but I wonder whether I'm not being merely mischievous in trying to disturb the age-old conventions of the village with my alien prejudices. It isn't as if women had a bad time here; they must be among the most emancipated in all the East.

One of the village ladies has been washing fish again in the booth. As long as Salu doesn't get the scales on my uniform when he does the laundry. . . .

How pleasant mud looks with plenty of naked footprints in it! Round the gate there is a good crop this morning after the one storm yesterday afternoon and no night rain. Large, medium and small prints, wide and staunch, with far-set toeprints—many villagers could tell me who had visited the bungalow in the past twelve hours by studying those prints; the spidery stamp of Duna's cock; the marks of Deppa's horse and Salu's bicycle; the trail of Pong' Rantebambam's staff and the paw-marks of his dreadful dog; and my enormous nailed bootprints, of course.

No trace, I'm glad to see, of the wild cat that stole the hen four nights ago. Let's hope it stays away a few nights longer, for the little black hen sitting at the foot of the coconut palm will surely hatch her brood very soon.

Small dinner for the kids to-night. Invited: Mina, Sesa, Timbo, Siu, Kalo'udun, Tu'ugun and Koton. There's a calf's tongue that was sent from the death-feast yesterday; they can have that and some of Kalasuso's goldfish.

It can't be more than seven-fifteen, but the sun is high. The shadow of the tallest palm has come racing down the fence and across the grass towards the foot of the trunk.

About a hundred children have been in with greetings. I suppose every single one of them has been to the waste-paper basket. Everything it ever contains is a treasure—old envelopes, tooth-paste cartons, exhausted flashlight batteries, film spools, odd scraps of paper or tinfoil and empty match-boxes—all trophies to be solemnly asked for and hooted over exultantly when granted.

I left my soap out again and that rat has eaten a big corner off it.

Likku is up at the window. She watched me shave from start to finish. She says Pong' Masa'aga is going into Rantepao Hospital. Her two plain little friends won't venture nearer than the fence and hang their heads in silence when I include them in the conversation. Likku is every inch a chief's granddaughter and quite lovely. I wish she wouldn't screw up her mouth like Salu being prim whenever I point a camera at her.

Now it must be nearly half-past seven, for here's the *guru*, in his scarlet shirt and large European boots, coming down the lane to open the school. (Later.) He sent me a bunch of zinnias from the school garden yesterday, so I made a point of going out to wish him good morning. I must have him to supper one night.

The thrill of the day!

Just as the *guru* passed my gate, Saleko, Pong' Rante-bambam's superb black and white bull, came down the path

146

behind my bathing-pavilion and turned into the lane with Lameh up wearing a hat four feet in diameter. While he made his way southwards, *maestoso*, the fat black bull Kandilli, with Timbo up, advanced from the opposite direction. At their meeting Kandilli went so far as to snort defiance at Saleko and the great beasts squared up to each other. In a second Timbo and Lameh were off their backs, urging the monsters on with insane cries.

" *Hoi! Hoi! Hoi! Gooo-ra-rah! Hoi! Hoi!* "

Children came racing onto the scene from every direction, whooping and shrilling and yelling like demons. They nearly knocked the *guru* off the narrow school path into the paddy-field. The clash of horns echoed like a thunderclap and the children yelled with ecstasy. I don't blame them for that; the two best bulls in the village had never fought before, I believe, and they looked splendid with their horns locked and their foreheads laid along the ground, breathing fire and fury back between their legs.

It lasted no more than forty seconds. Just as men came bolting out of the groves of Pintu and Parrara, roaring and yodelling, one of Kandilli's back hooves gave an inch or two. He had chosen his position badly, for the momentary giving way meant that his hoof slid over the edge of the bank and with a resounding splash the black monster fell five feet into Kappa's field.

Saleko, with Lameh mounted again, has now moved out of sight like a Derby winner in the paddock, the centre of a demonstration of affection. Timbo has rescued Kandilli from the water and brought him in for a consolatory browse on our lawn. He's still puffing and blowing prodigiously and Timbo is swearing in Japanese over the prolonged bath he will have to give him now.

Duna has just been in, carrying the enormous bunch of bananas from the wall of Salu's room. I tried not to laugh as he gravely turned it to reveal the one fruit with its end gnawed off by a rat.

" I ask leave to eat this banana, Tuan," he said in a low voice, his bright eye fixing mine.

" You may, Duna," I replied, and he left the room rather more quickly than he had entered. Night after night the little rat comes and attacks a banana; morning after morning this formality is gone through. I have told Duna he may take a damaged banana at any time, and in any case help himself whenever he is hungry; but he likes to do things right.

Now another daily ritual. Here is Lindung, who is acquiring the most polished manners. He furls his marigold sarong down to his waist and bows with a flashing smile. His head has been shaved again and he is revoltingly ugly.

" Good morning, Lindung," I say, and reach down the tin marked FOR R.A.F. OPERATIONAL CREWS ONLY. From it I take three malted milk tablets and hand them over.

" *Kurre sumanga, Tuan,*" says Lindung smoothly, and puts one carefully into his mouth. He is a firm believer in their strong magical power and in my assurance that they will make him fat. The astonishing thing is that the occasional meal and daily scraps I give him, plus the malted milk tablets, are unmistakably putting flesh on his spindly limbs.

Salu is washing my yesterday's shirt, trousers and undershorts in the bathing-pavilion. Sesa's nice mother is there to borrow a rub of the soap. Nobody in La'bo has soap. I've told Salu to leave the tablet with her.

The clothes-line stretches between the taller coconut palm and one of the roof pillars. It is a highway for certain large blonde ants and the children were more amused than I the morning one of them was found to have escaped

148

Salu's massive charcoal flat-iron when he pressed my trousers.

Salu doesn't wring out the clothes, merely throws them dripping over the line: my army shirt, trousers and undershorts, a shirt of his own and Isak's second-best sarong. They will all be dry in less than an hour.

Now I've had breakfast.

There were two boiled duck eggs, a bowl of fried rice with chopped onion and tiny scraps of last night's chicken in it. Bananas. Cold water.

I read some pages of Norman Douglas's *Alone* as I ate. He doesn't like ants, either. " These insufferable communists," he calls them. But out here, of course, they are useful scavengers. Whenever I swat a fly I have no need to remove the corpse. A small working party of ants will quickly roll up and clear it away. I suppose if I dropped dead and nobody noticed they'd clear me away, too, and pick my skeleton clean.

Salu has just taught me the Toraja word for " whisper."
Sibisibisi.
I call that perfect.

I cannot look out of the window without seeing something beautiful. Over by Parrara one of the frail white herons has just alighted on a tall bamboo spray, which dipped slowly and delicately as the feathery weight met it. The bird kept her wings outspread to soften the impact of her feet. The harmony of movement between bird and plant . . . could I even begin to describe it!

How beautiful a plant the bamboo is altogether! We have many varieties in La'bo, from the huge *patung* as thick as my thigh to the tiny, wispy *ao*, all miracles of grace and delicacy and all serving the needs of my neighbours in a hundred ways.

A bamboo branch starts life at the base of its parent clump as a cone of tightly packed leaves of a crisp white substance a little like chicory. At that stage you can steal its green and dancing future and eat it as a delicate vegetable. If spared it becomes a fat, straight stem tapering to a point and throwing out what look like pointed leaves of chocolate colour. Quickly this rather gross, fungoid pole is transformed into the mature branch, drooping at its end in a weeping drift of fresh green leaves the shape of a Chinese girl's eyes.

When cut down it is strong and surprisingly durable. Its hollow interior is exquisitely smooth and clean, and if the joints are pierced it becomes a strong, lightweight water-pipe. Many fitted together can swiftly be arranged to form an aqueduct a hundred yards long. Sections are used as containers for water, wine and oil. Unpierced, the larger branches are used for the building of bridges, houses and sheds. Split in halves, they form the high, elaborate roofing of houses and rice-barns. They are wrought into several varieties of decorative fencing.

Scaffolding can rapidly be thrown up of bamboo poles secured by thongs of split and twisted young bamboo. Ropes strong enough to sustain the weight of a great megalith and the pull of a hundred men can be devised in a few moments from split half-grown branches. It takes no more than an hour for half a dozen men to make a house wall or partition by splitting and flattening and then plaiting the medium-sized branches. Exquisite hats, baskets and mats can be woven from the " bark." A short section cut at a joint can be carved in an hour into a fine cup or bowl.

If I stayed here five years I don't suppose I should learn the full list of the uses of this blessed plant, for there seems to be no end to its employment. There is flooring, for instance, and cooking containers, scarecrows, ladders and musical instruments, shoulder-poles and bellows, forked spears for eel-fishing and protection from the bites of led dogs. . . . I could go on like this for another page.

Is it possible that the fall of a bamboo leaf inspired the early Toraja musicians? It is so beautiful that it draws a seeing eye like a flame in darkness. The leaf, torn off by an afternoon breeze, dives steeply like an arrow and then suddenly falters in its flight to spin in the sunshine like a slender fish under a waterfall, spinning rapidly but descending slowly and diagonally until once again it poises itself on its axis and sighs into a swift, steep dive to the earth. Similarly the music of the Men of Before alternates long, smooth notes with flickering brilliances of trills and shakes.

> *Mara'ana donga delamba,*
> sings Lindung;
> > *Beke di'sabiangan,*
> > *Di'paurani di'padingin-dingini* . . .

It is his favourite song. His voice is sweet. He leans over the veranda rail, poetically twirling a great cream, purple-throated convolvulus in his fingers, the ugliest child in all Celebes.

> " I am a little deer, homeless and forsaken;
> I am a kid, lonely and forgotten;
> Wet and so cold. . . ."

There is a whole history of short rations behind the unfailing interest here in anybody who is eating. There are seven boys from Menke'pe here now and the twins have brought hard-roasted corn-cobs for their elevenses. The moment they began to chew them every eye turned on them and conversation lapsed. With the touching unselfishness of Toraja children, they are now sharing out all but their first mouthfuls and our work on the extension of my Toraja

vocabularly will have to wait, no doubt, until the last grain
has been noisily crunched and swallowed.

The average Anglo-Saxon in his ignorance thinks of
Hunger as torment and tragedy, a hideous spectre of raging
evil. To half the folks of La'bo it is just the common lot,
not worth sighing over, as familiar since early childhood as
the chill of dawn and the heat of noon. For that matter, more
than half the human race are in the same situation. In the
years before the war only a third of the world's population
had enough to eat and fewer than ten per cent had the daily
3,000 calories considered necessary for health by authorities
on dietetics.

Yet with populations rising and millions of acres of
productive land reverting annually to desert and waste,
there were insular fools in England who could twitter of an
Age of Plenty. . . .

A big, handsome red and black wasp is building a nest
under the wide eaves outside the window. She works all
day. Now it's the size of a golf ball and apparently almost
ready. There is an elaborate tunnel entry. The one who
sealed up the lock of my bookcase with mud doesn't come
any more.

Just now a swift, urgent butterfly went through the
window like a bird. A swallow-tail. Warm, velvety black
and thin, polar green-blue, the coldest colour in the world.

Resting on the veranda rail is one of those queer, semi-
detached dragonflies. In flight, with its black body and
black disks at the end of completely transparent wings, it
looks like five creatures flying in perfect formation—a big
bomber with an escort of four fighters.

When I went across to wash out the developing tank I
found Barra bathing in the booth. His fillet crowned a
corner post, and beside his sarong hung a small, beautifully

woven frail basket holding four sprays of one of the smaller
sorts of bamboo, which he told me is called *biang*. While he
finished his bath he explained.

"So' Kampu's seed-plot is sick, Tuan. The rice seed
loses its colour in one corner. We made some fault when
we prepared the field or sowed it. Now we ask the *deata* to
forgive us and save the seed. I take those four *biang* sprays,
Tuan. I shall erect them in the bank of the plot and weave
a platform between them with the leaves. Then the old
man will kill a cock (not a black one, Tuan, for truly a black
cock is the same as a dead man and would kill the rice), and
we will look at its spleen. If it is big and clear and green,
with a white tip, the *deata* may help us. Then we will cook
the cock with rice in a bamboo and offer it to the *deata* on
my platform. Afterwards we will offer *sireh* to the *deata*
and we will eat the cock and the rice."

"I hope it will be good," I said.

"I bathed at sunrise, Tuan, but now I bathe again for
the *ma'biang*," he explained.

This is the way he bathes. A foot and leg under the
spout, vigorously massaged with the hands. Then the other.
Then he crouches under the spout, letting the water flow
over head and shoulders and the whole body, with a great
deal of brisk massage. After that he rinses his mouth and
massages his teeth with a forefinger, and next a great deal
of combing through oily hair with the fingers. Finally, a
brisk rub down with both hands and the clothes are put on
the wet body. Nobody in La'bo uses a towel.

Barra has a comb, so all the time I was washing the tank
he was titivating his hair and deciding the set of his long
tresses and the angle of his fillet. Now he has gone off
up the path looking as clean as the inside of a bamboo stem.

"I ask to take Tuan's letter to the Puang of Sangalla,"
Salu has just appeared and said.

"There is no need," I told him. "Duna can go."

"I ask to take it on my bicycle," he said. "I want to clear out my sweat, Tuan. I will ride fast. It is not good to stay in the house always and keep my sweat."

So he has rattled off down the track on the solid rubber tyres of the bicycle that stamps him a man of some substance.

The school orchestra is practising. The flute melodies come only faintly now and then up the pathway, but the boom of the *pompangs* fills the valley, sounding almost like tubas. The boys of the class not under instruction have rushed down to Pong' Rantebambam's big field, throwing off their clothes as they went, and now they are swimming and aping about in the warm water. Very noisy. Some of the girls are headed this way.

(Later.) It seemed a good moment to open the *golla-golla* tin. I have to be careful now about choosing a moment, for stocks are running low already and my efforts to get more from two continents seem unlikely to succeed. The first big tin holds no more than about two pounds of sweets now and two ounces of ants. The girls never get their fair share of sweets, but they did better this morning; about thirty girls to half a dozen boys got a ration.

There was a painful scene when Nimpa inadvertently swallowed his orange-drop a moment after he had put it in his mouth. A misadventure, of course, because an orange drop should last at least ten minutes, even all day if you only take a suck now and then. I thought he would rupture himself in his efforts to recover it. He clung to a pillar, stamped his feet and broke into a passionate sweat, with powerful eructations shaking him from head to foot. Gave him another.

Gave them all some writing-paper. Much grateful cooing. Dressed several cut feet. Thank God tetanus is unknown here!

Several of these children are really thin, and that is not

154

the characteristic Toraja shape. If only I could have come here before the war, when there appears to have been almost as much malnutrition as now, I could have fed a hundred children a day. Prices then were between a twentieth and a fiftieth of what they are to-day: a grown pig for the equivalent of half a crown instead of four or five guineas; a good chicken fourpence instead of six shillings; eggs threepence a dozen instead of fivepence each, and rice, now more than a shilling a pound, less than a halfpenny a pound.

It was lucky that Kalasuso and the old man who was to sing me the Kambori Song came at the same time, for with Salu out and Palinggi evangelising somewhere and only Duna in attendance, I should have been hard put to make any sense of the words. Duna's Malay is punctuated by the word *anu*, three or four times in every sentence. (*Anu*— what-is-it, so-and-so, let-me-see.)

Only a chance remark of Timbo's revealed the existence of the song to me. Neither the Controleur nor Dr. Goslinga had heard of it. Soon it will be forgotten, but now a few of the old men still sing it in the ancestral way, crooning it in a whisper as they lie on their mats when the very first pallor of dawn appears, singing so softly that the children seldom wake.

It is a song of the old time, formerly sung in every house before every dawn; but when I asked Lendu whether he sang it, he laughed like an Oxford undergraduate who'd been asked whether he wore bed-socks.

The poor old man who was here half an hour ago still sings it. I can't remember his name, but he is Kalo'undun's *neneh*, which may mean either his grandfather or his great-uncle. The unfamiliar setting of daylight and a listening stranger distressed him and again and again his memory failed. In the end I let him go, with thanks and some chewing tobacco, though he had never got past the first stanza.

It is all in the form of couplets, the second line repeating the sense of the first in other words. Is there a name for this construction? I don't know. Much of the Old Testament is in the same parallelist idiom. The song begins as a reveille, waking the sleeping family, warning them of the danger of slave-raiders and head-hunters; then it becomes a prayer for blessing on the young people of the house, on the growing crops and the beasts.

Well, with Kalasuso's kind assistance, I've set down a rough and ready translation of the opening:

> " *The Light will come again;*
> *The Light comes already.*
> *The Light calls you from sleep;*
> *The Light calls you for the day.*
> *The Light will clothe you*
> *The new Light will fold itself about you.*
> *Be silent!*
> *No sound!*
> *Be watchful!*
> *Be wary!*
> *Be roused and use your eyes!*
> *For the slave-raiders prey on the sleepy heads;*
> *The sluggards fall into the hands of the head-hunters.*
> *Wake!*
> *Wake!* "

Now I've got a baby. His mother has come to have a burst boil on her leg attended to, but it is mud-splashed and I've sent her to wash it first in the bathing-booth. The baby had begun a conversation with me, so she just dumped him on my knee and went out.

He's an agreeable baby, a bit more than a year old, I think. Naked except for a heavy old English silver crown-piece on a string round his neck, portly, warm and very smooth to the touch. His face is jovial and saucy and when he smiles you see some nice teeth. I'm typing this with one hand and keeping him more or less still with the other. I suppose he's too young for a *golla-golla*.

(Later.) They've gone now. The baby's name is Bangri. I pointed to George III.'s bust on the coin round his neck and told his mother that he had once been *maharajah besar* of the Torajas as well as the English. Even with Duna's unskilled help she could not understand what I was driving at. It is a fact, though, that the Torajalands were for four years, after the British conquest of Java during the Napoleonic Wars, part of the British Empire.

From 1811 to 1815 George III. was Emperor of the Torajas, though we may be sure the mad old king never heard of the Torajas any more than they ever heard of him.

I'm being watched now as I type this by a horrifying apparition which has come earnestly asking for medicine. It is a small boy whose whole face is monstrously bloated and swollen so that his eyes are narrow slits and all the inflamed and tightly stretched skin of his face is shiny like a huge boil ready to burst. He keeps shaking his head like a horse when flies attack its eyes.

Not until I had heard the whole story did I recognise the unfortunate as young So' Lipan. That isn't the way to put it, though, because I still don't recognise him; I only recognise his little striped shorts.

" I was playing with my kinsmen, Tuan, and they chased me into the forest. I fell and my face went into some *kabosien* leaves. Much pain, Tuan. I could not sleep in the night because my brain is hot."

Duna tells me that the *kabosien* plant is poisonous, and most people, if they touch it, suffer from severe skin inflammation for a day and a night. I've asked him to fetch me some of the leaves. Fortunately he told me that if victims bathe while the inflammation is on them it is increased to a point where it drives them almost insane. Unwilling to admit that I had nothing to help him, I had been preparing to bathe So' Lipan's face with Dettol and water. I've given him an aspirin instead.

If I were ever to be crippled or paralysed I could wish for no better viewpoint to watch the moving world from than this veranda. The track past my gate is a pageant that is never held up for more than a minute of the day. I can see two hundred yards of it, rising to the north to pass under a screen of weeping bamboo and vanish against a narrow vista of blue Mount Sesian, falling to the south past the school and passing into the bamboo grove beside Chief Deppa's half-built *tongkonan*.

At no time in the past hour has the road been empty. Only during heavy rain is a minute likely to go by without a single passer-by. As I type this line there are six humans, a horse and a buffalo in sight, though now I have reached this next line two of the humans have gone out of sight and another horse and Duna's aunt rise up against the dreamy blue of Buntu Sesian.

The old man nursing a gamecock takes him into my bathing-pavilion and refreshes him at the spout, speaking tenderly to him and caressing the chestnut feathers. He looks more like a hen than a cock, for the combs of fighting birds here are amputated so as not to give a hold to their opponents. Two young men with long hair wait their turn under the spout, abstracted after nights of dancing and love-making at a death-feast; one of them carries his last share of buffalo meat. The fat stallion, led by a slave, is ridden by a woman carrying a baby. She wears one of the huge rain hats, four feet in diameter, and round it she has draped a sarong so that the baby rides in a sort of heliotrope-curtained pavilion. Duna, returning from Buntu Assa with a spray of the venomous *kabosien* leaves, exchanges a word with the slave, who tells him that the baby is feared to be dying. They are rushing it to the hospital in Rantepao.

The big grey bull from Marante, whose name I forget, lumbers by with his small groom sitting cross-legged on his heaving back. Duna's aunt smiles to me as she sidles into the bathing-booth to wash some clothes.

The horseman is a paragon of Toraja elegance. He bestrides a spirited white stallion, with a rose-pink cushion in place of a saddle. His graceful torso and fine legs are bare, for he has furled his indigo and gold sarong into a noble turban that falls in streamers down his back. He wears several horn and ivory bracelets and there is a sword in a finely-carved scabbard at his hip. Approaching my gate, he dismounts with the grace of a Diaghilev star, and, as he passes, bows to me, leaping astride the rosy cushion as soon as the stallion has trotted past the garden corner. We are not acquainted.

The slave with a letter carried in a cleft stick turns to stare at him as he passes; then he stares through the gate at me.

Five little children in soft and grave conversation approach the gate and hover out of sight behind the fence, too shy to come in because they are comparative strangers. When I call them they come trotting in, the eldest (about four years old) carrying the youngest (not one yet) astride his hip. Lindung, still singing, is the only other child in sight, so the *golla-golla* tin can be opened.

I know the two girls walking away now to their home in Bunt'ao. They were guests at the death-feast for Palinggi's father. This, of course, is an entirely different occasion, and village gossip would have burst into flame if they had come into the house in daylight to greet me; so I went to the gate to greet them. Now their slim figures, stepping delicately under the shadow of their wide, golden hats, are receding into the groves of Parrara.

Neither Lai' Melambi nor her sister is a beauty, I suppose, but there is beauty about them, about their presence. What is it, this wholly delightful and subtly rousing quality about Toraja feminity? I think it is best described as sweetness, though one is shy of using that word nowadays on account of its misuse by the insipid to describe the merely vapid and pretty. Yes, that is the word—sweetness. A stranger to our brave new world, but delightfully at home in the everyday life and human intercourse of La'bo. As far as it concerns the charm of Toraja women, I suppose it is compounded of the racial guilelessness, good nature, inner serenity, modesty and an unmaimed sex life.

A smart aleck from Rantepao in European clothes has just greeted me through the gate. The sweetness is fast dying out of him as he goes along despising the yokels who have not, like him, played traitor to their blood and the faith of their forefathers. He smiles at me confidently, the poor unconscious quisling, sure of my approval. Don't we both wear boots and trousers? Don't we share the one and only *Herrenvolk* religion? Aren't we the masters of the poor ignorant heathen?

I hope it is not presumptuous in me to feel compassion for him.

Lendu has arrived with the axe we are constantly borrowing from Palinggi. He comes and watches anxiously as I take the *kabosien* twig from Duna, break it and rub the milky sap and the leaves along my forearm.

" Tuan will find no sleep to-night," he warns me.

" Perhaps white people are strong against *kabosien*," Duna says. " Lelang can rub it on his tongue and it does not swell."

Some schoolboys have borrowed my scissors and are

cutting each other's hair on the veranda steps. The washing on the clothes-line is bone dry and stiff as with frost as Duna gathers it in, shaking out the ants. A few small clouds, dazzling white, are advancing from the west. The little white hens in the big globular basket gaze dreamily out at Duna's cock strutting round them; he has made a track in the dust round the basket. When they are given a small handful of rice he heaves against the basket and sometimes manages to overturn it and steal their ration.

On her nest near the foot of the bigger coconut palm the little black Leghorn-like hen pants with open beak. The cock never goes near her, though Duna says he is the father of the eggs.

Two men carrying rice freshen their feet in the bathing-booth and come across to rest under the bungalow eaves. They are father and son, and they tell me they have been down into the Duri country to buy the rice, which is cheaper there. A two-day journey each way. They are glad of a cup of *tuak*.

It seems that they live in the rocks of Sarira, so they should be home before the afternoon rains. They squat on their hunkers at the foot of the steps, talking about me in low voices. The four great weeping sheaves of rice, dark golden and bridal flowing, hang from the ends of their thick bamboo shoulder-poles. When I picked one up just now I was astonished at its weight. I should be sorry to have to carry it a mile.

The large callouses on the shoulders of porters are easily accounted for. The older man is disfigured, though not unpleasantly, by abnormal convexities on his shoulder-line at the points where the smooth pole has ridden. The boy's are so far slight, but the one on his right shoulder is inflamed. When I soothed the dry heat of it with a little vaseline he winced as though I had touched his eyeball.

Other rice-carriers are passing in the opposite direction. The progress of these toilers is beautiful. They advance with a light, dancing step upon timid, fastidious feet as though the earth scorched them. The whole golden, sweating body glides up and down, the black forelock and the golden bridal sheaves of rice rising, floating and falling together. One hand grasps the polished bamboo *pikul*, the other wavers in rhythm before the breast, preserving a delicate balance. They cover the ground at trotting speed, their motion a consummate system of balance and economy of energy. To change shoulders the step falters and the elbows perform a swift opposite movement, one jerking up and the other falling, and the pace renews itself.

Lendu has chopped a heap of firewood and now he is singing one of the rather rare Toraja love songs.

> " *Karimani to'nambela,*
> *Sola to'landolalan;*
> *Mase'idika ma'simbo simbo'angin. . . .*"

> (" Do not refuse me food, girl,
> And let me sleep in love with you;
> For I have come from far.
> Do not shut me out alone in the cold.")

That is the nearest I can get to a translation. The melody is poignant and Lendu sings it well, one arm wound round a pillar, one knee bent, his cheek pressed to the pillar. I don't suppose, all the same, that many girls can have shut him out alone in the cold.

I wish I were like Lendu. He is almost everything I admire. Profoundly simple, good natured, utterly at home in the world, hard working, transparently honest, with good manners and considerable sensibility. He has lots of fun, too.

I am going out now to try to photograph the *puarangs*.

These monitors or river lizards inhabiting the swift stream along the Bunt'ao path have been shy whenever I looked for them, but now young Koton has run in to say that a pair are frolicking under the little thatched bridge. Lindung is already carrying one camera and Koton the other. Koton has to take the Super-Ikonta, which is on a short strap; if he puts the Rolleicord round his neck it hangs down to his ankles.

What next, I wonder.

Returning from the bridge, where no *puarangs* were to be seen (" They are sleeping under the water," said Koton), I found a lovely girl from Menke'pe lying nude on my back veranda. One of Sesa's elder kinswomen was massaging her abdomen and Lendu was conversing with her while delicately turning his back.

For a perplexed moment I deduced abortion and wondered whether it was up to me to react at all.

" Are you sick, *Nona*? " I asked the girl.

She smiled faintly and said something I did not catch.

" She has conceived, Tuan," explained Duna. His back was turned too.

I found her brow hot and she confessed to a headache, so I fetched her an aspirin and a mug of water. When I came back she was sitting up and the old dame was replacing her sarong. It seemed that she had been taken queer by our gate and Duna had fetched the old party, who is our local midwife. He had also summoned the girl's mother.

Now they are leaving, the girl hand in hand with her mother, stepping with delicate care across the grass.

" It will be her first child? " I ask Duna.

" Her first, Tuan," he tells me.

It must be near noon.

The trunk of our big coconut palm rises from the very centre of the small rosette of shadow round its foot. The few clouds increase the brilliance of the meridional sunshine, reflecting the strong rays as they glide through the heights of blue. Even the hush of the multitudinous little waterfalls from terrace to terrace below the garden sounds lazy in the noon heat.

The temperature is 80.5 degrees Fahrenheit.

I like Palimbong. His men are working in his big field down on the valley floor and he has been in for a chat.

He has no presence. His hair is always very untidy and the gap in his upper teeth gives him a slightly disreputable look. The print tunic which confines his torso in scores of pink rosebuds and blue true lover's knots is a mistake too. But he is a good friend to me, thinking out little journeys of exploration or giving me introductions that help. From the first he has concerned himself with my intimate comforts and his conversation is usually very acceptable.

This morning I spoke of the extreme timidity of Toraja women, and even men, in places away from the main paths when I approached them or their houses. What was the reason?

" *Biasa*, Tuan," he said; but with Palimbong that familiar reply is seldom the last word, which is what it usually is in La'bo. No, he said, it was not on account of Japanese harshness, nor had the Dutch ever ill-treated the local people. " Those village people cannot like strangers, Tuan. When they know you they are friendly—Tuan has hundreds of friends here already. But their blood fears a stranger."

" It is nearly forty years since there were head-hunters or slave-raiders in La'bo," I said. " The old people remember those times when a stranger might kill or capture. But the

young people are as timid as the old. Why should they think
I will harm them?"

"They do not think Tuan will harm them. They do not
think anything. They are simple people, Tuan." He put
his hand to his forehead. "It is dark for them here."

When I told him about my idea of a month in Pangala
he said, "No, Tuan, stay here with us. My sons say you
are like their kinsman. Those people in Pangala are strange
people. Why go there, where you have no friends?"

Now he is down by his big field again, where a dozen
men are drawing two *ma'salaga*, implements like gigantic
coarse combs, through the water. The great teeth tear at
the mud underneath the water and admit moisture into the
soil that baked so long during the dry season. The men
laugh and yell at their work and flocks of white *koroks*
follow them like gulls behind a Wessex ploughman.

Shall have to slow down on whisky. This double has
meant breaking into the last case.

Some pages from a famous American magazine had been
used as padding for the bottles. Glancing through the
crumpled sheets, I find the world they reflect more incom-
prehensible than ever.

An example. The principal of some high school had
allowed negro students to use the school swimming-bath
once a week. The white students had gone on strike in
protest. Even that is less fantastic than the sequel, which
is the assumption that a crooner's plea for tolerance is worth
reporting and photographing!

And am I expected to respond to this advertisement for
a perfume "originated by men for men, that makes for that
cool, clean, tingling aliveness that's grooming plus!" (Must
ask Salu to bring some of that back from Rantepao Market.)
Or some of those underpants that "give you that smo-o-oth
tailored look." Brave New World!

Perhaps the sports article is healthier. It begins: " Above all other sports professional hockey is a game in which rough and dirty playing is a high and necessary art."

There are advertisement photographs of automobiles with overdressed dwarf models occupying or entering them. In the drawings the human figures are even more stunted, so that the cheapest and smallest sedan looks like the sort of thing Hitler used to ride about in.

Everything gives the overpowering impression of swindling and sharp practice. All the women in the photographs look like *horizontales*, many of them frowning with the strain of holding in their breath so as to push forward their busts. They remind you of those cheap-jacks who spread out all their shoddy stock on the pavement and draw your attention to it with hoarse, crude patter.

Under a lyrical landscape in pastels I read, " The Bells of Pleasant Valley. The story is about the bells that ring in a little village in the foothills of the Alleghennies. In the year of Our Lord, 1865. . . ." It is an advertisement for an armaments concern.

And so on. La'bo looks even sweeter and healthier as I screw up the pages and throw them into the waste-paper basket. I expect my face betrays something of the puritan primness I sometimes see on Salu's as I fish them out of the basket again and set a match to them. I can't face a spate of children's questions on the meaning of those pictures and their captions.

I turn and there is fat Sipa in the doorway, dancing the *pa'gellu*. As usual, his nose needs wiping, and to-day there is a crimson moustache above his lips from eating a bunch of *sadipeh* berries. But his grace is exquisite as he floats round on one spot, his fingers fluttering. When he sees me looking he stops and grins, and Lindung stops banging the tempestuous rhythm on the side of my leather trunk.

It is no hardship to be confined here to the radius
accessible to a healthy pair of legs. The more we of the
West conquer space, the more time enslaves us. The
Torajas have neither sought nor won victory over space,
but then time is no enemy to them and I think that is better.

Sesa's father and mother, yoked together, are drawing
one of the heavy comb-shaped cultivators through the deep
mud of their tiny, shelf-like field. His grandfather guides
it. In the next field Kappa is repairing a breach in the
terrace wall made by Kandilli when he fell from the road in
his fight with Saleko. He heaves up mud in armfuls from
under the warm water and moulds it against the two ends
of the breach until they meet and begin at once to dry in
the hot sun.

Why don't I go and take Sesa's mother's place in the
yoke? I'm a friend of the family. I'd be glad to help. I'm
uncomfortable at the sight of her straining to drag the heavy
ma'salaga through the thick mud. Why don't I go out
and lend a hand?

It would shock Salu. So what? It would shock the village
and shock the tiny white community of Makale and
Rantepao if word went round. Does that matter? I suppose
it does; it is no good bewildering and embarrassing a lot of
well-intentioned people just to ease your own conscience.
And Sesa's mother would be the most distressed of all.

I hope that is honest.

Back from a walk. A short one to-day. Accompanied
by Sipa and Duna, and a small rabble of Marante urchins.
First of all to the valley floor, where I chatted with Palimbong
and his men for a while; then up the little forest path to the
forge, where I tried to photograph the boy on his high seat
operating the pistons in the big bamboo cylinders that fan

the charcoal fire beneath. After that, along a path I'd never seen before that moves up and down among the little hills of Marante.

One tiny steep valley no bigger than a rugger ground was like a little zoo. The slopes were alive with lizards and there was a monitor. A flock of white *koroks* shared the air above the one rice-field with thousands of gold and ruby dragonflies. One of those emaciated herons that look like a grey skeleton of a bird's ghost was there, eating a lizard. Several kingfishers. Some pretty flowers the same colour as the sky lay on the warm waters. Sipa saw a snake. A herd of swine trotted off as we approached.

The brute creation can show few uglier profiles than that of the Indonesian pig. When first you see one you conclude that it is probably a freak that should not have been allowed to grow up. The snout reminds you of a tapir, the convex backbone is razor-peaked and fabulously dipped, so that the sows' bellies sweep the ground even when they are not gravid. Like Toraja hens, they spend a great part of their lives in being shooed away.

I rested in a fine compound on a steep hill-top. Half a dozen pairs of female ankles vanished up ladders and round corners as I came in sight, but a stately old man resting under the best of the three *alangs* made me welcome. A calm little girl, too, went on searching her mother's or aunt's hair for intruders, and a large golden baby, half hidden by the curtain of black hair, went on feeding from the woman's breast. Sheaves of rice lay drying in the sun; there were fighting cocks in large, beautiful bell-shaped baskets, one of them standing with a swollen, injured foot in a saucer of medicine; a long hand-loom, deserted as I made my sudden appearance, was set beneath the pillars of an old, shabby house with a section of coarse pineapple leaf fibre cloth half completed on it; a few single french beans climbed tall poles; the strongly magical *tabang* plants with their crimson leaves were planted in a protecting circle round the compound; two dogs of lowly breed barked naggingly for a few moments and then fell back exhausted in the heat; later a small *serreh datu* gazed down from a glassless arcaded window at the ground its feet would never touch in life or death; an assortment of beautifully woven basket-containers was tied to the walls of the big house, beside twenty pairs of sacrificed bulls' horns, mounted on a panel from roof to pile-head; best of all, an orange tree in bloom wept cataracts of ravishing fragrance about us.

An extraordinary and alarming sound began soon after I had taken my place on the rice-barn platform, a human sound that wasn't human, a wail with a vehement pulsation that was almost unendurable. When I inquired I couldn't understand the reply and suspected all sorts of horrors; but a young fellow took me by the arm to the smaller bamboo house and showed me lying inside it a boy in a fit of raging fever. His whole body was in violent, machine-like motion, and as he kept up a high, unhappy moan the ague shook it into the disquieting noise that had so much perplexed me.

" I will send some medicine," I promised, and the young man accompanied me when I left. Now he's just gone off with sixty atebrine tablets, having learned the dosage by heart. Strange that I should have waited two years in the East to see my first malaria case with the fever in action. . . .

Clouds began to veil the sun momentarily before I left the hill-top. A rising wind ruffled the huge, glossy rococo leaves of a *kamassi* tree.

" Our soil is thirsty, Tuan," said my host gravely. " Every day too little rain."

He spoke only of the past week. Before that we had a heavy daily rainfall. I am so happily at home here already that every day I look anxiously for heavy rain—an unfamiliar preoccupation for an Englishman. Already, too, I think of a field instinctively as a pond, which is what fields are here.

On the way back I became aware of a strangeness in the

atmosphere. What it was I didn't discover until I took a dizzy little eight-inch path between two paddy-fields. I saw then that I advanced with a dull rainbow circle enclosing me, like a ring of oil film three yards in diameter, one half reflected in the waters of one field and the other in the other. Looking up, I saw how the sun was surrounded by a vivid corona, a wide, glittering circlet poised like a miracle in the sky.

" A *ma'panku*, Tuan! " the urchins exclaimed.

" It will make the pigs grow," said Sipa.

I was reminded of the sick green afterglow that followed a recent sunset, causing many of my visitors to shake their heads in concern. It is not so good for mortals when the gods are suffering from an attack of dysentery.

Salu is back with a letter from the Puang of Sangalla, written by the prince's son in Malay and signed by himself in the strange Buginese script. All it amounts to is the news that the date of the big death-feast for the princess his mother is still not fixed.

It had shocked Salu to find the house unguarded on his return. Children had been playing Snakes and Ladders on the veranda floor, but no member of my staff had been present.

" Why does Salu worry? " I asked. " People here do not steal."

" Truly they do not, Tuan," he agreed. " But sometimes bad people from Palopo come along the road. They might steal the Lamp! "

Now he is making coffee and *sanggara*, tiny bananas fried in a toffee-like film of paste, and stoking up his big iron.

I never contracted the siesta habit, even in the heavy noon heat of Batavia, and should never dream of missing a

minute of my few days here. Now the clouds are massing
and it looks as though the rain will catch the children on
their four miles from high school back to Karatuan.

Here is Salu with the mug of coffee and a plate of fried
bananas. I began here by having only two meals a day, but
I think Salu found that too un-European. He has in-
sinuated the coffee and *sanggara* into the daily time-table,
and they are too good to cancel.

The first appalling thunderclap, seemingly only a few
yards above the roof, took me straight back to Cagny that
morning in July, '44. For a split second there was the
same wry feeling of " I suppose this is it," the same
resentfulness at human dignity so assaulted and the same
feeling of disgust with the sordidness of man-made horrors.
I am tempted to say that I smelt again the spouts of cider
which drenched me from the huge, shrapnel-riddled casks
before they collapsed, and that I choked again at the
memory of the clouds of dust rising from the barn roof as
it fell about me; but that would be going too far. Actually,
that wasn't one of the moments of fuss I remember most
vividly from the weeks in Normandy.

Salu won't stop teasing me over my claim that a hen can
lay eggs without the help of a cock. I don't remember how
the subject arose a few days ago, but my statement burst a
bombshell upon the company. Up to then they had believed
I knew almost everything, and they were bewildered to find
me maintaining such a preposterous theory. Since the *vita
sexualis* of Toraja poultry is as free as human sex-life here
and local hens are never kept under restraint, the truth of
my assertion will never be discovered by observation.

Salu has now reported this gap in my omniscience to half
the village and I am twitted with it hourly. The short

lecture on the nature of the ovum which I delivered to a
small group last night was plainly considered ingenious
rather than convincing.

I must go and prepare my dark-room.

Needless to say, no apartment of the bungalow, with its
basket walls, spaced floor-boards and open gables, can be
rendered dark. For the minute or two it takes to feed an
exposed film into my developing tank I have to retire into
total darkness, so I'm reduced to making a tiny light-tight
chamber or hutch by throwing all my blankets and sheets, as
well as spare shirts and towels and Salu's second-best sarong,
over the table and blacking out the floor beneath it with
Salu's and Isak's sleeping-mats. Into this black hole I creep,
with Salu hovering near to tuck in folds and block light-leaks
with kitchen cloths, socks and handkerchiefs, or even a
sarong snatched off the back of one of the Snakes and
Ladders players on the veranda floor.

Once inside this hutch, I am gambling with time. If the
film doesn't jam and runs easily into the spiral grooves of
the tank-spool all is well. But the tank, like almost every
other product of our gadget civilisation that I've brought
here, is defective. Often the film jams.

When that happens all depends on whether I can delay
the onset of perspiration long enough. The slightest trace of
moisture on film or groove makes it impossible to feed the
film into the tank. But 170 pounds of human flesh will not
stay for long sealed in about forty square feet of warm air
without sweating. I have spoilt several films in that way.
It is best not to think about such things or I may start to
sweat before I get into the hutch.

(Later.) No hitch. Duna is now turning the knob of the
tank, his eyes glued on my watch. The developer must stay
nine minutes in the tank, and I know that practically nothing
short of death could vary the set time by so much as five

seconds with Duna in charge. Nine matches are laid beside the tank and his bright eye follows the second hand round. Every time the hand reaches the top of its circle he replaces one match in the box.

The watch says seven o'clock. It is only brought out for these occasions. But the gadgets of the twentieth century will not last long out of reach of a repair shop. " Tuan! *Jam suda mati!* " The watch is dead, cries Duna, and I have to shake it to start it again. This necessitates leaving the developer in the tank for some seconds after Duna has returned the ninth match to the box, an adjustment that causes him deep anxiety. Then I take over for the decanting of the developer, the rinsing and the addition of the fixer. A dozen children watch, while Sipa keeps up his usual running commentary.

" Tuan turns the small handle all the time. He will not let us turn the handle. The *portrets* are in the little box, being washed in strong water to make them good. The watch tells Tuan when the *portrets* are clean. Without the watch Tuan cannot make *portrets*. Now he pours out the strong water. Now he pours in water and salt. It is not salt, but it is like salt. If we drank it we should die. Ah, he wastes it! He is angry. We must not touch. . . . Now he pours away the poison in the gutter. The black box makes water like a man. Now he puts the box under the spout in the place of bathing. It must stay there for long. If we move it Tuan will shoot his *pistole*. . . ."

It seems that I am immune to the poison of *kabosien*. There is no sign of swelling or inflammation on my forearm.

" Tuan has much strength," says Lindung.

Down comes the rain. Racing the last hundred yards to

the gate, Siu almost beats the downpour. The letters inside his shirt are hardly wet.

Most of my letters have come more than ten thousand miles, but the preoccupations of my correspondents suggest life on another planet. It is good to hear from distant friends, but the hard greyness of their lives in post-war England troubles me with a sense of unworthiness. It is disturbing to feel too lucky.

A correspondent who has been slightly sickened by reading my first rhapsodical letter from here in a temperature below zero with a bad cold in the head asks, " When next you write, dispense a little comfort. Tell us what you *miss* in your sugar-plum paradise. Wouldn't you sometimes give all your sunshine and noble savages and Indonesian houris for a Mozart symphony or a pint at the local? "

Well, what do I miss here?

Easier, perhaps, to list what I don't miss. I don't for a single moment of the day miss the society of white people. I never miss newspapers or radio. I don't even miss Mozart symphonies. I never sigh for a play, an opera or a movie. Least of all do I miss the tame, grey world of parties and ballrooms, of restaurants and the rich brothel hotels of the West, all the feeble dreariness of a " good time."

But there are one or two little things I miss. A glass of pure water, for instance. Boiled water, flat and usually flavoured with smoke or some nameless, sick taint, is one of the curses of the tropics. And I'd like an arm-chair, I think. Now and then I day-dream a little about good food—but so they do at home. I'm better fed here than they are in England.

And I think that's all.

This is good rain, falling in rich, steady volume. It looks like falling till past midnight. The one shattering thunderclap has not been repeated.

Salu is ironing my uniform. The firm in China which made his iron seem almost to have designed it for use here, for the prow of the great boat-like utensil is surmounted, like a rice-barn gable, by a cock. Its capacious interior is filled with glowing charcoal, upon which he sometimes blows through a small bamboo pipe.

I wonder if he is really colour-blind. He keeps calling my jungle towel red. Like all equipment designed originally for troops in Burma, even underclothes and toilet paper, it is khaki-green to render it invisible from enemy aircraft, though some fading has made it more khaki than green. Now Timbo has come in after putting Kandilli to bed, and I've asked him what colour it is.

" It is no colour, Tuan," he says.

Only the primary colours have names in Toraja, and that is almost true of Malay. A range of colours from purple to nut-brown is called red in La'bo.

> " *Da mutunai kandope*
> *Da'o tapai-tapai. . . .*"

It is my singing lesson. Timbo is teaching me *Pa' Kandope*, which I selected as one of the simpler Toraja songs.

A mistake, it seems. I can make little progress beyond the first easy phrase and Timbo is surprised at my failure. One difficulty is that he cannot recapitulate an isolated phrase, but is obliged to begin again from the beginning every time, often in a different key.

Salu suggests that I should learn something easier and he mischievously proposes one of the village women's nonsense ditties. He sings one that must be less than thirty years old, younger than the first road in the Toraja-lands, a rhyme about the chauffeur, the cornet (the former chauffeur's mate who cranked the starting-handle) and the horseman.

" If the chauffeur has no money
    And the cornet has money,
    Or the horseman,
        I like him best! "

Enter Palinggi, sighing.

" What can I do with my child, Tuan? They have sent him away from school and will not take him back."

Palinggi's child is a vain youth of seventeen. I don't care a great deal for Peter Palinggi (as I think of him, though the patronymic is, of course, wrong) and am not surprised that he is an anxiety to his father. His most recent escapade, however, does not reflect any real discredit on him.

The tribes of Kesu and Sangalla have not gone to war or hunted each other's heads for forty years, but the former enmity remains, and in the high school at Rantepao the youths of the two districts occasionally fight it out. Now Peter Palinggi has slapped down the youngest son of the Puang of Sangalla and rubbed his face in the mud. The headmaster, provoked to decisive action, has expelled them both.

" What can I do, Tuan? " sighs poor Palinggi. " The Puang is a rich man. He can send his son to school in Makassar. It would be hard for me to afford that."

Unversed as I am in the management of headstrong youths given to rubbing the faces of scions of reigning princes in the mud, I'm unable to do much more than look sympathetic and pour my friend a glass of Portuguese brandy. The father of the new hero of Kesu drinks it, shaking his head. He is so worried he looks almost thirty years old.

" When the Puang's son has gone to Makassar perhaps the headmaster will take Peter back," I suggest. (Note: this was what eventually happened.)

" I shall ask him," Palinggi says. "*Adohi*, Tuan, one son only and so much trouble! "

176

Rice Planting in La'bo

Kadang ready for Ma'Bale

A daddy-long-legs was blown across the veranda just now. When I saw Timbo and Salu and even Palinggi back away from it I wondered what evil power it was supposed to yield.

" A malaria fly, Tuan," Salu said.

I put him right, but I doubt whether any of them is entirely convinced by my arraignment of the small anopheles.

" Those little *kassisi* bite us all every night, but most of us have no fever," Timbo objected.

With a very serious face and twinkling feet Koton, the younger brother of Duna and the oldest boy in the village to go naked, comes dashing through the rain down the track for his supper. As an umbrella he holds a banana leaf five feet high over him, making a fine picture of attractive savagery, but the wind twists and tears the great leaf, and he is streaming with water as he climbs the veranda steps. Coughing, too. I hope that doesn't mean anything serious.

" He has eaten four spiders, Tuan," Duna tells me, " and still he coughs."

The large, meaty spiders that live in the *atap* thatch are a favourite Toraja cough remedy. Unfortunately, my box of medicines does not include an alternative.

The other supper guests take squares out of the giant leaf and fold themselves large, neat scoops from which they will eat their food. The ironing is finished and Salu, assisted by Isak, is now cooking our meal.

I've been asking Palinggi which virtues Torajas most admire. He says faithfulness, honesty and good temper. He said nothing about courage, which did not surprise me, for I've noticed how Torajas show no shame in admitting fear.

Kalasuso told me the other day, " When the Japanese arrested my people, sir, and gave them to me to imprison until the soldiers took them to Rantepao, I sometimes unbound them in the night and let them escape. But I had to stop, sir, because I was afraid of the Japanese. They made me very afraid."

Torajas, in fact, rather scorn the Japanese traditions of bravery, in much the same tolerant way in which Englishmen smile over the ready emotionalism of Latins and Americans.

Have hung the film to dry by my bed, so must remember not to take a light in there for an hour or two or a thousand and one insects will fly in and get stuck to it.

One or two passable pictures. A rare sunset view from the track near Parrara and Lendu sitting on the front door-step looking fastidious. The forge one is a dud and there's yet another of Likku with her mouth screwed up—I shall have to build a hide like a bird photographer and steal a picture of her unselfconscious beauty.

The sun is setting and Salu calls us to supper—or rather, he calls me, for the guests have been in position round the floor of the back veranda for some little time.

The *menu*:

Fried Eggs
Fried Chicken
Fried Goldfish
Braised Calf's Tongue
Green Beans
Green Tomatoes
Boiled Papaya
Steamed Rice
Red and Green Peppers

*

Cold Water

*

Acid-Drops

178

The party went well, I think. I sat with them on the floor of the back veranda. Timbo, Sesa and Siu on my right; Mina on my left; Tu'ugun, Kalo'udun and Koton facing me.

The comparative silence might have given a white stranger the idea that the party was freezing over. By " comparative " I mean that conversation ran quite dry, but that we did not eat in silence all the same. A Toraja child is a hearty eater when he gets the chance, and he so seldom gets the chance to eat like this that he would be a fool to distract himself with talk. He does not compliment his host on any dish, but a host as sentimental as myself is liable to find tears in his eyes at the sight and sound of so much vehement enjoyment.

Every six days I give a little party like this, inviting my closer small friends in rotation, with one or two less intimate guests each time. This week is the first time for Koton and Kalo'udun; they are lucky, because the gifts of goldfish and calf's tongue happened to be handed in last night. Issuing invitations is a sad and difficult business; everyone of the thousand children in La'bo would like to come, and two or three hundred of them need the food. . . .

Even when I went round with third helpings there was only one refusal, and that was from Kalo'udun, who shook his head at the vegetables.

" We eat only vegetables all the time at our house, Tuan," he said, twirling together a lump of rice and fish and tossing it deftly into his mouth. His is a very poor home and he has balanced on the edge of subsistence all the ten or eleven years of his life. I took care to eat slowly, for Sesa and Siu, at any rate, would have been embarrassed by the sight of their host's plate empty while they were still eating.

Tu'ugun, as thin as a reed after his malaria, had constructed a second banana-leaf scoop which he kept in the shadows behind him. In it he stowed a handful of rice, a fried egg and a lump of fish for his little sister, who was waiting out by the gate, too shy to come in. I wasn't supposed to see that.

If only I had a little money! If I had even four hundred pounds a year I could feed a little group like this every day. It's horrible to have to go into details of how much it will cost to invite one more child and wonder whether, after the year or so, my army savings will see me through, there will be any money at all coming in. . . .

Every dish was cleared. Not a rice grain or a leaf of vegetable or shred of meat left. Even the fish's backbone was scrunched up with relish by Tu'ugun. There were sighs of content and everybody leaned back to ease the downward journey of the viands. Then Duna appeared with the big earthenware coffee-pot. Starting with Mina, he refreshed the company in turn with a draught of water. Each diner, squatting open-thighed in the candlelight, held up his face with his mouth open while Duna poured in a steady stream of water which was swallowed noisily without closing the lips.

Before the guests rose to throw their leaf scoops into the rubbish-pit and wash their hands and faces, I opened the *golla-golla* tin and dealt out two acid-drops each. The silence was at last broken and they hooted and yelled as they ran to the bathing-booth in the gently-raining darkness.

Nobody said thank you, but a form of words would have been redundant after the sighs of content and repletion, and the gentle stroking of each other's swollen stomachs. I suppose Mina may have said thank you, for she was the least untalkative guest. We had one of our English-Toraja conversations after I shut the *golla-golla* tin, having favoured her with raspberry suckers instead of acid-drops.

" It is raspberry suckers you like, darling, isn't it? " I began. " And did I tell you how much I like that necklace? "

An *oiellade* and a torrent of coy Toraja from Mina.

"A pity it couldn't be just the two of us, without all these others. But then the village would talk, I suppose."

Mina laid an earnest, greasy hand on my arm and popped a raspberry sucker into her mouth. There was an interval of inward concentration as she began briskly sucking.

"You're the only girl in the village I ask to dine, you know. The rest don't mean a thing to me, Mina."

Mina's feet, which are the size of match-boxes, curled up rather at this and she smiled. Hers is an all-out smile and reminds you of crocodiles and the girls in advertisement photographs. You can see all her back teeth and a close-up of her uvula. She rattled off a non-stop spate of eager tinniness, pausing only to draw a gasping, croupy breath while Sesa washed her tiny hands in a bowl of rain water.

"I'm going to miss you, Mina, when I go home again. Ten thousand miles, Mina. A long way. It won't be many moons before you forget your English sweetheart."

Like a pipe-smoker taking two meditative puffs before answering, Mina slid the raspberry sucker briskly round her palate for a moment. There was a note of gay reassurance in her reply, which was reinforced by another smile, another alligator gape with the pink fruit-drop as a centrepiece.

I'm very fond of Mina.

A slave has been in with a message from Palinggi. He is entertaining some aristocratic friends of Peter's—sons, no doubt, of the Puang of Sangalla's hereditary enemies—and he would like some brandy to regale them on. A piece of paper the lad showed me was inscribed with the single word "BERENDI," in case I should fail to understand the message.

I've poured out doubles for myself, Salu, Barra and Lendu, and sent my neighbour the half bottle that remained

To hell with Pong' Rantebambam!

The intolerable old man is always asking Salu for things; for paper, soap, matches, cigarette tins, even for *golla-golla*. Salu invariably replies in a grave voice, as I have instructed him, that Tuan has only a few things to give away and they are all for poor people. Pong' Rantebambam just goes on asking.

An hour ago, as we sat playing cards, he came in, sank with a groan into his corner and then brought out a Player's cigarette tin and began taking *sireh* leaf from it. Astonished at what appeared to be Salu's disobedience, I asked the meaning of it. Isak interposed the information that it was the tin I had given Sipa. Pong' Rantebambam had taken it away from the child.

I was furious, because Sipa had been overjoyed with his tin, which had long been promised him, and I got up to take it away from the old bastard. I didn't, though, reflecting that Sipa, a poor relation feeding on Pong' Rantebambam's charity, would not be helped by that sort of row.

My ill temper demanded some outlet, all the same. Frowning round, I saw Pong' Rantebambam's unspeakable dog lying in the corner where Duna sleeps, an obscene, evil-dispositioned collection of sores.

" Take that bloody thing out of here! " I shouted in English at the old man and I strode into my room and took down my revolver. As the children drove the snarling brute out into the darkness, I went out and fired two rounds into the air. I felt slightly better for that, but it had no effect whatever on Pong' Rantebambam. I think he would be quite pleased if I did shoot the dog.

The firing delighted the children, though. They started yelling and banging on their Adam's apples as they do when bulls fight, and other children began to answer back from the houses up the slopes of Buntu Assa.

Pong' Rantebambam is still sitting in his corner in his stained geranium robe, fingering his ill-gotten tin and blinking mildly across at me, at a loss to understand why a high-born white man should take more pleasure in the company of slaves and children than in that of his rich next-door neighbour. I'm a fool and worse to lose my temper with him. Maybe when I am old and dying I, too, shall be surrounded by strange, uncaring people who do not understand me. . . .

Bed-time.

The temperature is 72 degrees Fahrenheit.

Barra has won six cigarettes with the best rummy score. He liked the brandy, but Lendu only pretended to like it. Salu sipped his with a worldly air and told me grandly that he was *biasa* brandy, whisky, genever, porto and beer.

Barra, Duna, a *ronda* whose name I forget, Podoh, Timbo and Massang are sleeping in the next room. Actually they are singing a ribald song for the moment, while they settle themselves for sleep.

Just before we parted for the night there was a terrific outcry in the garden. I was the last to realise what was up. Lendu was the first, and more or less jumped over me to get to the door and outside, shouting and hissing like a maniac. The others followed him, and Duna suddenly came to my side and slipped my revolver into my hand.

The confounded wild cat had molested the little black hen. When I shone my torch on the nest we saw that four of the seven eggs were broken. The hen was up on the bungalow roof, clucking distractedly. Of the wild cat there was, of course, not a glimpse. The hen is still on the roof; I don't suppose she'll risk returning to the nest now.

I've issued a categorical order that nobody will ever touch my revolver. I had left the safety-catch off and there were three rounds in it when Duna snatched it from the wall by my bed. There might have been a wretched accident.

Thank God for this good rain. The frogs are filling the cool air with their preposterous chorus. There are pale ochre lightning flashes behind the rainclouds.

One more day of my life fallen away. One of the better ones. I've made a poor job of recording it because I haven't the resource and the skill to communicate the abiding, quiet joy of my life here. What way is there of describing in unsentimental language the emotion that moves me to blessing, time after time, every hour of the day?

Sterne knew what it was like, perhaps. See him riding through the Bourbonnois in the heyday of the vintage, " *with my affections flying out and kindling at every group before me.*" It is something like that.

It must be nine o'clock, or half-past. I'm the village sluggard and also among the later retirers for the night. The hills and valleys are sleeping. The man and his son who brought the rice from Kalosi are sharing their wives' sleeping-mats after their hard trek. The sick baby and its mother—has Dr. Goslinga been able to help them? The boy with fever—how soon will the atebrine help him? The young girl who has conceived—is she afraid as well as happy to-night? Is poor So' Lipan's swollen head still sleepless on his mat or is the poison dying in him? Will health return to the sick young rice, now that the feathers of the sacrificed cock flutter from Barra's little woven platform close by?

There is not a single light to be seen in the valley. All my friends and visitors are asleep or playing love in the dark houses. Those pampered monsters, Saleko and Kandilli, are at rest in their bamboo pavilions. And my small dinner guests will be sleeping contentedly with full bellies for once, if not indeed kept awake by the unfamiliar

184

strain of digestion. In only seven hours Kalo'udun's *neneh* will be crooning the Kambori Song in the dying darkness, remembering all the words he forgot while the white stranger listened this morning.

It is good to hear the rain that will bring to my good neighbours a little of the plenty they deserve.

Good night to them, and God bless them all!

VIII

THE KIN OF MAN

"I WILL tell you, Tuan," said old So' Toding. "*Puang Matua* in heaven made the first man and the first rice and the first buffalo on the same day. The first man was called Datu Loku, the first rice was called Takebuku and the first buffalo was called La'elo. They were brothers. Their seed was strong. They were our ancestors, Tuan, and the living generations of men and rice and buffaloes are still kin. Truly, we could not live without each other. . . ."

The Torajas are a poor people, but what wealth they have comes from their rice. The standard of life round the terraced valleys of La'bo, for instance, is much higher than on the cruel neighbouring slopes of Sarira, where the shy mountain folk depend on pitiful little crops of maize and vegetables raised in cherished pockets of soil.

It is sad that the climate of Central Celebes does not allow of the two rice crops a year common in Java and Bali; but even the single annual crop supports a large population in the districts of Kesu and Tikala. In good rainy seasons the yield is bountiful, but quite often the rainfall of those months from December to June is poor. Then the rice in the small, poor men's fields suffers first, for it is highest up the hillsides; but in a really dry year even the deep rich men's fields on the valley floors are sad with thirsty rice.

From sowing to harvest-time the rice lives in water. One morning I watched a man sow rice in the little plot he and his son had prepared the day before. He had waited till the sun was well up and the quarter-inch of water above the level, weeded mud was warm. He took the seed in his hand and spoke softly to it and then broadcast it, speaking again (but this time to the gods) as it flashed in the sunshine and fell like a little hailstorm into its bed. For a while he gazed down upon it, then he shouldered his narrow, curved spade and walked off with his black cur.

In a few days there was a flush of green, flame-vivid, on the water. By the end of my first moon in La'bo the valley was dotted with dozens of those gleaming plots of seed rice.

A paddy-field need never lie fallow. Every year the wooden plough, sometimes drawn by buffaloes, more often by men, cleaves the sun-baked soil after the first rains of the season have lain a few weeks upon it. The heavy, toothed *ma'salaga* later assists the deeper penetration of the water and the *ma'bale* has the same purpose.

On my third day in the village Palinggi took me to see a *ma'bale* in his largest field. The word really means "fishing," and that is the secondary or incidental purpose of the occasion. Nearly a hundred men, women and children had assembled on the slope above the field, equipped with a variety of finely-woven baskets. At a signal they went down into the almost knee-deep water with large, bottle-shaped baskets in each hand. These contrivances, which went by the name of *da'dak*, had open necks and open bottoms, surrounded by rings of strong spikes, which were the *raison d'être* of the whole affair. Advancing in no particular formation through the warm water, the villagers plunged their *da'daks* deep at every step, so that the rings of spikes penetrated the soil beneath to admit the enriching moisture.

The sun flashed strongly in every water-drop. Under the dark olive shadow of the bamboos it was miraculously cool. The humble little Toraja doves cooed more passionately than their English kinsmen and the workers were attended by flocks of white *koroks* and white, grey and tawny rice-birds. I saw grey wagtails, too, and a solemn pair of cranes in the next field. A small crowd of babies and toddlers played quietly on a bank while their mothers earned their dinners in the water.

The rice was, of course, not present, so no special decorum was necessary and the company cheered themselves frequently with the wild cries they love, drowning the echoing plunges of the *da'daks*. Now and then a tribesman would stop and thrust his arm down the neck of one of his *da'daks*. He had felt the wriggling of a fish imprisoned by the basket walls. With a yell of excitement if it was a good-sized one he drew it out, flashing in the sunshine, and popped it into the square basket fastened to his belt. The paddy-fields are the homes of many small fish and the villagers may keep any fish they catch on such occasions.

Two moons later I went with Palinggi to watch the same field planted. When we arrived, a crowd of women were uprooting the vivid seedling rice from a plot near-by and men were carrying sheaves of it on shoulder-poles to dumps on the banks of the field. An old man sacrificed a cock to the *deata* and a long line of women, perhaps fifty of them, stepped backwards into the water, the level of which had been lowered for the planting. With the precision of guardsmen and the grace of a *corps-de-ballet* they began to plant at great speed.

In her left hand each woman held a bunch of seedlings whose wet roots had been dipped in ashes and manure. She took one step back, and swiftly, like an act of benediction, pushed three bright seedlings into the mud, one right, one centre and one left, her upper body moving gracefully to right and from right to left. Then another step back, while her right hand plucked three seedlings from the bunch in her left, the gracious sweep of head, shoulders and arms to the right—and one, two, three, the plants were thrust home. It was beautiful.

And now that the rice was in the field there were no raised voices and everything was gentle, seemly, a little exalted. The lovely line of the women's great straw hats and golden arms moved back and back in the sunlight. They planted an acre in about three minutes. Little girls not yet ripe, wiry old dames who had served the rice for sixty seasons, golden girls in the first lustre of their blooming and their calm, plain mothers—all moving in perfect unison like priestesses in a water-temple.

It is only in La'bo and a small surrounding area that women in large numbers plant with this spectacular technique. In Sangalla, only five miles away, men quite often do the planting, and there is little or no attempt at precision or pattern in setting out the rows of seedlings.

At first the planted fields have no more than a stippled look; then as the blades grow the water surface becomes more and more hidden until finally the ducks are no longer able to spend their days plupping and guddling in the warm tides between the plants. Twice the growing leaves are cut and given as fodder to the buffaloes. After the second cutting the grain stalks appear.

Four moons come between planting and harvest. When I left the Torajalands the rice in La'bo was not yet ripe, but I had glimpsed the earlier harvests of Pangala and Tikala. I shared the hushed, smiling content of the harvest field when naked toddlers and wrinkled ancients joined the troops of reapers, each one armed with a tiny knife hardly bigger than a safety-razor blade. Each stem of standing rice was cut separately, the reaper approaching it with the knife concealed in his palm so that his brother rice should not see the blade coming and be afraid. At the day's end reapers were paid at the rate of one sheaf for every ten sheaves they had harvested. I noticed that the smallest children were usually paid at a more generous rate.

Next day I went to a *mangrakan* ceremony, held to enable the people to eat the first rice of the harvest.

That was a strange morning. The remote village stood on a ledge and through a screen of bamboo we could look down on one of the small, lost valleys of Pangala, in which two or three fields had been harvested on the previous day. In the shade of one of the chief's rice-barns a wizard recited a long incantation in the esoteric language of his order over a trussed black boar. His voice, rising to a little shout on what appeared to be the openings of sentences, droned on for twenty minutes or more, undeterred by the squealing of the propitiatory beast, the quiet conversation of the crowd or the crowing of game-cocks under their big, bell-shaped baskets. Then he touched the boar with a leaf of *sireh*, dedicating it to the *deata*, and an old man pierced its heart with a long knife.

The crowd took more notice then. The young man who had wrapped himself in his sarong and gone to sleep under a rice-barn was roused and all pressed forward to see the carcase split open. There was a murmur of satisfaction at the large size, lustre and blueness of the gall bladder. A fire of the white leaf-husks of bamboo singed the corpse and gave its skin an unpleasantly fungoid look. The chief's clerk had been collecting trifles of money from members of the crowd and these now took small cuts off the carcase and began to cook them over a number of fires.

Several old men had with extraordinary speed prepared a high branch of bamboo. The thin green bark or skin had been cut off in delicate patterns in certain places, and in others shredded off in long streamers which were plaited to form little lacy platforms and pockets for the reception of offerings. The raw head of the boar was set high on the pole and morsels of the cooked pork were laid on the web-like platform. Other hanging pockets and shelves had been swiftly woven and were now attached to the pole while women brought out a huge pot of cooked rice, the harvest firstfruits. This was placed in bowls and small horn-like packets, and soon the pole was hung and surrounded with scores of little offerings, while a great pile of rice and pork rose round its foot.

It was not, after all, so unlike our harvest festivals at home. As the more prominent villagers fussed forward to place their choicer offerings in commanding positions on the pole I seemed to hear a well-remembered voice. (" That large bunch of grapes, dear. The lectern or the front of the pulpit, would you say? ") When, however, the wizard had concluded his dedication, the crowd pressed forward to reclaim and eat their offerings with none of the embarrassment I always experienced when a pre-war Salvation Army landlady of mine served me at breakfast with boiled harvest festival eggs inscribed with such texts as " Lo, He cometh! "

My neighbours in La'bo urged me to stay for two more moons to join in the prolonged festivals that follow the reaping of the final field. " Much pleasure then, Tuan," Barra would say. " Many days of *sisemba* fights, and the Burakke dances round the fields with his tambourine and at night we dance the *ma'bugi*, and there is no work but very much love-making."

It is the climax of the year for them. Certainly I hope that I may one day see the *sisemba* combats, sometimes between teams of a hundred foot-boxers from rival villages, and the strange performance of the priest-priestess from Tokesan who leads the mysterious *ma'bugi* ritual, dancing and singing in his falsetto voice.

That ritual is one of the Toraja mysteries I am far from understanding. The *Bugi* is a powerful spirit to which entreaties may be addressed. Particularly is it petitioned for the relief of an epidemic among men or buffaloes, and after a harvest for the promise of a good crop in the next season. But its identity is obscure. Several times as I returned to my idle questioning on the subject the answers convinced me for the moment that the *Bugi* was identified with the victorious magical strength of the white man; and indeed that appears to be one facet of the enigmatic force called

Bugi. Like some other preliterate peoples, the Torajas do not hesitate to incorporate alien gods in their pantheons for extreme occasions; Jesus and Mahomet are sometimes entreated to add their mercy to the grace of the *deata*.

Sometimes I wondered whether the *Bugi* was a devil, or the devil, for it seems that preliterate people tend to identify the devil with the race they most fear, and it was the Bugis of South and Central Celebes who preyed on the Torajas for centuries. But when I asked whether the *Bugi* was wicked the answer was usually " No."

The beautiful chorus of invocation to the Spirit Bugi was frequently on the lips of my neighbours, so that I came almost to know it by heart.

> " *Iriko, iriko angin,*
> *Tsimbo ko'darinding;*
> *Mangiri rekekoh buntu. . . .*"

I did my best to translate the opening lines, but they are not particularly clear.

> " Oh, Wind, fly far,
>   Speed far on your unseen wings;
> Fly to the mountains,
>   Seek the high hills;
> Ask the mountain ' What is your name?'
>   Oh, strong crag, tell me your name!
> Oh, fair encircling foothills,
>   Like a necklace round the great mountain,
> Where is the Spirit Bugi?
>   Where can I find him?'
> Ah, help me to make my *ma'bugi* perfect,
>   Help me to lovely song and invocation.
> I am bold to ask this,
>   Not shy to beg this favour;
> Though this throng of people surrounds me
>   I am not shy. . . ."

One Field's
Harvest

Salu

The dance is a great circle, with the slowly moving dancers chanting for hours under the harvest moon. By midnight the impatient boys and girls drift away to resort in crowds to the " women's houses," houses whose menfolk and older women are away for the night, either by arrangement or happy accident. There groups of girls who are kin or friends receive their lovers and play till dawn.

" Sometimes forty of us in one house," Barra told me. " It is not bad, because we are all friends. And there is no light. It is like our play in the dark guest-houses at a death-feast. We never sleep, for it is a short time to dawn and we must leave before light."

This festival is termed " orgiastic " by the enemies of Toraja culture; but that is surely a slander, for there is never drunkenness nor any vestige of the public disclosure of preliminary approaches to sexual encounter which provide the familiar unsavoury spectacles on Western beaches, parks and even dance-floors. It is true that individual performances are vigorous to a degree that would rank as excess among whites, for the Torajas are not half-hearted lovers, and on those rather infrequent occasions their preferences are those of the Young Lady of Spain.[1] But I found it impossible to work up the puritan hatred of the body and its playtimes which could condemn such innocent delights.

Rice is of the East and Life; Death comes out of the West. The two *adats*, of the East and West, may never be associated, so rice is forbidden to a circle of the kin and household of a dead person until the final death-feast is held. This interval may be as long as three years in the case of a dead noble. The *pemali* on eating rice is therefore

---

[1] *Not now and again,*
But again and again,
And again and again and again.

a severe deprivation but it is never ignored, for a man wearing the beaded *poteh* and under the *pemali* who ate rice would be driven insane by it.

Rice is at all times treated with respect by Torajas. To honour a stranger they ask him to sit under their best rice-barn. A man's rice-barn is always as finely built as his own house, usually more so. I was told that so great was the respect shown by Pong' Maramba, the late Prince of Kesu and Tikala, that he always swallowed rice without chewing it, so that he should not damage the soul of the rice.

More charming than their respect is their affection.

I shall always remember the first time I heard a *poni-poni*. That is a sort of whistle or pipe which the boys make out of a rice-stalk as soon as it reaches a certain stage of growth. It sounds rather like an oboe—a remote and pastoral note.

I was chatting with Salu and a group of Pangala tribesmen when the antique piping of a *poni-poni*, the first to be heard that season, sounded from a cliff-top across the valley. At once smiles of affectionate delight broke over their faces and they paused to listen in silence for a few moments. Then the oldest man turned to me and said, " It is good, Tuan. Soon the rice will be ripe." And he looked round with simple amity upon the green, stripling rice that stood in crowds about us.

> " *The Bull that is the sign of life,*
> *Its sombre, phallic will.*"
>
> W. J. TURNER

I said that from their rice comes the chief wealth of the Torajas. But the token and unit of that wealth is the bull.

The high spiritual value they set upon rice is in harmony with its intrinsic indispensability. The high spiritual and commercial value they set upon bulls is, however, largely extrinsic. The pampered bulls of La'bo are symbols of wealth and prestige. Where rich Europeans and Americans accumulate a diversity of treasures—jewels, great paintings, yachts, libraries, racehorses, even postage stamps—a rich Toraja accumulates only bulls, while the poorer Toraja will deny himself and his family needed food and clothing to buy and maintain a bull or bulls to be sacrificed at his own or his parents' death.

Bulls very seldom work. It is only occasionally that they are yoked to a plough. There are no vehicles for them to draw, for the Torajas never invented the wheel and until the lifetime of their young men there were never enough level tracks to make wheeled vehicles practicable. Even to-day I doubt whether the smallest cart or automobile could reach the houses of more than one Toraja in five hundred.

Cows are very seldom milked. The job of a cow is to give birth to bulls and the job of a bull is to manifest his master's wealth in life and death.

But there are bulls and bulls. Pong' Rantebambam's big black and white Saleko would never be bartered for fewer than fifteen ordinary grey bulls; he is the type of piebald bull held in highest honour by the Sadang tribes. A large black castrated bull plays an important rôle in death-feasts and may be worth eight ordinary bulls. A *bonga*, a grey bull with a white face, has a high value; but an all-white bull is valueless and may not even be eaten by the people of Kesu.

Toraja buffaloes are a large breed of water-buffalo, but the partiality of their kind for hour-long wallowing up to the eyes and nostrils in mud-holes was not indulged in La'bo. As befitted beasts of such high origin and destiny they were kept spotlessly clean. Timbo frequently invited me to feel the purity of Kandilli's lustrous coat and inspect the freedom of his skin from ticks and fleas. He would make the invitation in the way one might offer another a rose to smell.

Though at all times submissive to the tiniest Asiatic boy, these beasts are often said to be hostile to white men. I can only say that I was never affronted by a Toraja bull or cow, and that I was on terms of friendship with several of them, notably Kandilli. Just once or twice I felt a momentary qualm as I moved at feasts between the bulls tethered to the close-standing megaliths, and friends would sometimes call me from the close vicinity of the more highly-strung candidates for sacrifice; but it seemed to me that Toraja buffaloes had not seen enough white men to develop an antipathy to them.

Each bull and each cow has a personal attendant, usually a small boy, whose day's work it is to exercise his beast, bathe it, groom it and feed it. The cows receive less attention than the bulls and are usually assigned smaller and less experienced grooms; moreover, they are not given personal names. The groom of a bull, a boy usually between the ages of six and twelve years, rides his charge out in the morning, often singing as he sits, either astride or side-saddle, or squatting on his hunkers or even kneeling on the broad, lurching back, directing his mount by a rein threaded through its nose-ring. He may drowse under his immense straw hat while the beast grazes on a grassy slope, or he may dismount and with his small billhook cut grass from ledges the bull cannot reach.

At least once a day the bull is thoroughly bathed. In our corner of La'bo there were no mud-holes or rivers with pools in which bulls could submerge, so Timbo, like the other Karatuan grooms, had to halt Kandilli at the edge of a deep paddy-field, jump into the water and for five minutes keep up a storm of splashing over the complacent creature. Then he got out, turned him round and jumped in again to drench the other side. After that the horns—seventy inches from tip to tip—had to be polished, the face prinked, the tail groomed, the hooves cleaned and the skin searched for ticks. Kandilli, though black, had not been castrated, so Timbo was expected to perform a soothing and intimate service probably familiar to concubines in attendance on elderly potentates.

Only twice did I see the diminutive grooms at odds with

their powerful charges. Once was at the buffalo inoculation described in another chapter. The other time was in Marante, when I was startled by a torrent of shrill abuse echoing along the path ahead of me. So peaceful are Toraja lives that I had not yet witnessed a single quarrel, so I hurried forward to watch and note what sort of insult and invective might be used. But it was only a little boy whose bull had absently trodden on its rein and so could not be jerked or guided into motion. It stood placidly while the infant kicked and pummelled it with tiny feet and fists, yelled abuse and finally ran up its shoulder and seized the great horns in an effort to jerk back the noble, stupid head.

" May you have the anthrax! " the shrill voice fumed. " To the sacrificial spear with you! Pleasure your mother! "

(That last, by the way, is the most extreme insult one Toraja can offer another. As with most of our own stronger oaths, however, it is almost never used in earnest, though frequently in friendly jest.)

At length the mild bull took a step forward and the boy recovered the rein, deeply mortified by the discovery that I had witnessed his loss of temper, a grave offence against the temperate seemliness of Toraja life.

The mask of the bull is the dominant motif of Toraja art. A modelled buffalo head, fitted with a pair of real horns, is the figurehead of their ship-like houses. Among the carved and painted panels that cover the walls, those representing the stylised bull mask are most important. The same mask is painted on the doors of the rock-hewn tombs. Real horns surmount the gigantic headdress worn by the *manganda* dancers; collections of the horns of sacrificed bulls cover the walls of old houses; and forty years ago the men who had captured enemy heads were entitled to wear a helmet surmounted by a pair of horns.

But it is in the manifold rituals of the death-feasts that

197

the bull plays his supreme rôle. If rice is the Guardian of Life, then the bull is Lord of Death.

Bulls are immortal beasts. Their high destiny is to be sacrificed at death-feasts to travel with their dead masters to *Puya*, the Homeland of Souls, and live in endless bliss in the pastures of Paradise. Before they die they fight among the megaliths, thrilling the Toraja crowds to the very soul with the clash of their mighty horns. And before the procession of a dead prince to the feast-field is carried the *belotedung*, the banner of the bull, radiant with the mightiest magic known to the Torajas.

The Dutch administration has imposed limits on the numbers of buffaloes that may be slaughtered at death-feasts, for the prodigal tribesmen and nobles used sometimes to ruin themselves completely, so great was the temptation to honour the dead and impress the living with extravagant sacrifices. But so important are these sacrifices that even to-day an inheritance is commonly divided between a man's sons in proportion to the number of bulls contributed by each of them to the father's death-feast.

Early during my stay in La'bo fat Sipa, anxious to make me a present in gratitude for some small favour, angled unsuccessfully for a whole morning in his grandfather's small field in efforts to get me a fish. When he gave up at last he stayed disconsolately at a distance from the bungalow for a while; then I saw him busy near the Parrara bathing-pool, bent in concentrated toil till the afternoon rains began.

Shyly he came then and offered me a bull modelled in clay. I was delighted with it, for there was an admirable vitality about it. I put it on my bookcase, where it fell forward onto its face because the horns had been conceived on too heroic a scale for the body.

As soon as it was seen that I took pleasure in such primitive sculpture, the other small children turned to modelling and soon I had been presented with a herd of clay bulls. Everyone was so proudly horned that at times the whole herd fell forward and appeared to be grazing with their sterns in the air. When I showed the children how a stone set inside the rear portions would balance the weight of the horns, they used the device to enable even lustier horns to be fitted.

Eventually I had a corral of about fifty selected mud bulls set at the end of my writing-table, each one conceived in a spirit of impassioned hero-worship. A few were portraits of the village's more famous bulls.

The day a wild rainstorm blew the bungalow roof off, my fine herd was reduced in thirty seconds to a low mound of mud and stones. But one or two horns still arched defiantly skyward.

IX

AN EVENING AT CARDS

A TRAVELLER into remote parts of the earth naturally likes to take with him a stock of trifles to distribute as gifts among the acquaintances and friends he expects to encounter; but the assembling of such a stock was hardly possible amid the chronic scarcities of post-war Batavia. From N.A.A.F.I. canteens and officers' shops I had managed to collect 4,000 cigarettes (which included my rations for six months), forty-eight yards of cotton and linen cloth, fifteen pounds of candy, a few mirrors, clasp-knives and pencils, a Snakes and Ladders board and two packs of playing-cards—and that was all.

Most of these small offerings went down very well, but the last two were the most deeply appreciated, though they were not given away until the night before my departure.

Actually, I gave the Snakes and Ladders board to Torri, the little son of Palimbong, one day during my first fortnight in La'bo and showed him and his companions how to play it. A few minutes later, however, Torri had been elbowed back into the outskirts of a crowd of elders, in the midst of which a quartet of the village intellectuals were dicing, ascending ladders and descending snakes with impassioned concentration.

It can be said that Snakes and Ladders took Karatuan village by storm, but in the case of the elders initial enthusiasm waned after a day or two. That was lucky for the children, who had been waiting their turn with impatience. It was lucky, too, that Torri did not understand that I had intended to give him the game outright, for it became one of the chief items of equipment that turned the bungalow into a sort of children's clubhouse during my stay.

The playing-cards attracted the higher age groups. Not, I should add, the village gamblers who met secretly now and then on the wild slopes of Sarira for games of chance that were forbidden by law. Rummy for a few cigarettes for the evening's highest score could not be expected to attract them. But the circle of youths and boys whom I taught formed a rummy school that lasted my time there, and, for all I know, may continue to this day, for I left the cards with them. The infinitely variable game may by now have developed a La'bo variant.

On most evenings I joined the rummy school, which provided a setting and characters for endless village gossip and all sorts of incidental sidelights on local manners. Now and then I tried to introduce a new game, but the only alternative to rummy that caught on at all was the innocent affair known as "Thirty-Ones" that I had learned in the ranks. Poker and *vingt-et-un* came to nothing, chiefly because every Toraja seems to be born a wildly irresponsible and foolhardy gambler, going the limit on every card regardless of value.

I thought I would try to give some idea of an evening at cards in the basket bungalow, an evening that followed a rainless market day during the planting of the rice about six markets after my arrival.

I have finished my usual evening meal—soup, chicken, green beans and potatoes, and Bali orange—and on the platform in the cookhouse Salu, Isak, Barra and Duna are eating theirs. Lindung, promoted lieutenant-colonel this afternoon and wearing my old gilt crowns and stars on his marigold sarong, is gnawing a leg of chicken that I left especially for him.

There are several groups of callers on the front veranda.

A rather crazy old man who is the brother, or at any rate a kinsman, of the woman Ampulembang of Rante Bua is the only one who expects formalities. Respect for his age and birth require a chair, two cigarettes and grave attention to the rigmarole I have heard half a dozen times and still understand imperfectly about his long association with the Dutch rule in the Torajalands and his series of promotions in the imperial service. (He had, I believe, something to do with the maintenance of roads.)

Ignoring him, Sipa, Torri and Tu'ugun play Snakes and Ladders on the floor in the twilight, watched by tiny Mina in her enormous hat, and young Koton. My playboy friends, Tinggi, Masak, Manga, Tambai and Tira, are waiting to play rummy, three of them lolling in a corner and Masak and Manga on a chair in one another's arms. The fuzzy-headed Sesa and Siu, a schoolmate of Isak, are perched on the veranda rail.

Grouped in each doorway are a number of strangers, travellers returning from market, resting and seeing what there is to be seen. This is not much until Salu, having bathed after supper and failed to make the abominable pressure lamp work, brings in two flickering candles. The west monsoon is stronger than usual, flattening the flames every few seconds, so I lead a move into the small front room, where a form and chairs are arranged round a bare bedstead of massive rough-hewn hardwood.

When the cards have been dealt and cigarettes handed round, the idle quintet of youths who have been hanging about the place all day, bathing lavishly, washing their clothes and drying them in the sun, singing, smoking and lolling, come to life and play a keen, fast game. Their conversation is, as usual, little more than an endless questionnaire.

" How much did Tuan's great boots cost? "

" Is Tuan as rich as the Controleur? "

" Has Tuan a house of stone in England? "

" Had Tuan an airplane in the war? "

" What are the girls like in Java? "

" In Bali? "

" In Singapura? "

" What did Tuan's typewriter—pen—shoes—cameras
—camp-bed—blankets cost? "

" May we see the *portret* of Tuan's wife? "

It is time to say a word about my wife.

I am a bachelor, a circumstance which on balance I
had seldom regretted before my second visit to Bali. There
I dropped a bombshell among the happy folk of Manokayana
village by informing them casually, shortly before my departure, that I wasn't yet married. It took them a day to
believe it, and they didn't begin to understand even after
putting me through a long cross-examination.

I had spent a happy week with them, losing money at
chontokan and other gambling games, making a little money
at cock-fighting, learning a Balinese song, discoursing with
the village ancients and burning holes in my palate with
their violently spiced food. I was an oddity, no doubt, but
a welcome enough honorary member of their community
for a few days.

The disclosure of my unmarried state flabbergasted
them. A bachelor in Central Bali is a young lad. The only
ones above the age of nineteen are either the more un-
presentable types of lunatic or lepers far gone in their
disease. A bachelor is a being of no account in the community, with no more rights than a child.

Had I stayed longer I suppose they would have made
an exception of me, and put down my bewildering bachelordom to the manifold incomprehensibilities of human creatures
not lucky enough to have been born in Bali. As it was, the
revelation shadowed the closing hours of my visit and I
wished fervently that I had not let fall the luckless admission.

I had not at that time read Mary Kingsley's useful advice to Victorian spinsters. " I may confide," said that redoubtable gentlewoman in a lecture, " to any spinster here present who feels inclined to take up the study of the African that she will be perpetually embarrassed by inquiries of ' Where is your husband ? ' Not ' Have you one ? ' or anything like that, which you could deal with, but ' Where is he ? ' I must warn her not to say she has not got one; I have tried that and it only leads to more appalling questions still. I think that it is more advisable to say you are searching for him, and then you locate him in the direction in which you wish to travel. This elicits help and sympathy."

I must, I decided for similar reasons, arrange for a wife to spare myself and my Toraja neighbours any recurrence of the misunderstanding and perplexity experienced in Bali. So when personal questions made their expected appearance during early days in La'bo I had my answers ready.

Yes, my wife was in England. Oh, yes, with my children. Three. All boys. Two at school, one too young, home with his mother. Yes, I should be glad to see them all again. Two years since I had seen them. Yes, it was true that I was no longer a soldier and could go home when I pleased, but I had come to Celebes first because the army would pay my passage home. If I rejoined my family first and came out to Celebes later I should have to pay much money for the ride in a ship or airplane.

You see how it grew. It wasn't just a case of one simple deception; almost daily new strands were added to the web of falsehood I had spun, and I was frankly nervous at the mass of detail I was obliged to memorise to avoid being caught out.

But my anxiety was not confined to the liar's fear of exposure. Much more distressing after a time was the compunction at deceiving Salu, a faithful husband and father of four sons, who took an affectionate interest in my invented family from the first and made kindly inquiries concerning them at the most frequent intervals. Nor, by the time that stage was reached, could I possibly have confessed my deception and its innocent origin to him. Though to be sure I was common clay beside his hero, Dr. van der Veen, he yet showed esteem for me and would naturally not have understood my motives, especially since (as I discovered too late) bachelordom was not unknown among the Torajas, and indeed regarded by many of them as an excellent idea, if you could get away with it.

To make matters worse, I inadvertently added to the imposture one day when I was trying to concentrate on writing a letter in French amid the excitement and questions of the smaller children, who had been given permission to rummage in a large box of odds and ends thrown together at the closing of my office in Batavia. Racking my brains to produce some adequate response to the eloquence of my correspondent (whose acquaintance I had made in the heady hours of the liberation of Paris and who had written, as usual, of *souvenirs impérissables*, *nuits inoubliables* and the like) I found fat Sipa waving a postcard photograph in my face and asking me to identify the sitter.

As a matter of fact, it was Miss Joan Fontaine, the movie actress, for whom a Madrasi clerk of mine had nourished a deep admiration. Whether the admiration had waned I do not know, but the photograph remained on the office partition when he was posted back to Singapore and had evidently been gathered up by the Chinese clerk who helped to clear the office on my departure.

" Oh, that's my wife," I said absently to Sipa, wondering once again why the most sincere of avowals always looked so false in French.

That did it. A few moments later a hastily collected group of neighbours were gazing with respect and admiration upon Miss Fontaine's lovely likeness.

The lie was getting out of hand.

Miss Fontaine goes over big with the La'bo playboys. " *Wah!* " sighs Masak. " How much age has she, Tuan ? "

I hope I am not guilty of ungallantry when I answer " Twenty-eight." I can hardly say less, since my firstborn's age has been fixed at ten and an implied marriage at under sixteen might surprise them in view of what I have told them of the lateness of Anglo-Saxon marriages.

" Her name is John," Lindung interpolates.

As Tambai holds the portrait up in the candlelight the small crowd in the doorway moves forward and the spell of silent tribute to exotic beauty is broken by a desperate outcry behind me. It seems that Barra, stepping forward for a nearer glimpse of my grass-widow, has pushed his cigarette into the ear of a piglet which has been drowsing in a plaited harness slung round the neck of an old man resting in the bungalow on his way back to Bunt'ao from market. Salu, appearing suddenly, exclaims in shocked tones at the affront offered to me in introducing swine into my personal apartments and all the casual callers melt away.

The game gets going again and is won by Manga, the nicest of the playboys. He gets six cigarettes and the others one each. In twenty minutes or so he will be sharing his six with the others. . . .

The second game is more fun.

There are no fewer than ten of us, three adults and seven children. Salu and Barra sit on either side of me, Barra looking noble in a new-style fillet made from a length of the red backing paper of a roll of film. Isak, the slender, soft-voiced son of Salu, sits at his father's side with his friend Siu on his other side. Siu is a nice child who fetches my mail every week from Rantepao post office. His nose in profile is practically non-existent and he has a sweet voice— in England he would be a cathedral soprano, or perhaps even a recording boy wonder. Both he and Isak have had their heads shaved recently on the orders of the schoolmaster.

Four boys who form a somewhat similar group to the
playboy quintet sit on the opposite side of the bedstead.
Duna, Sesa, Timbo and Massang. Sesa appears to be the
eldest, a boy of fourteen or so who circumcised the others
two years ago. From the first evening he has been a
faithful friend to us and he is an extremely nice youngster
altogether, thoughtful, hard working, well mannered and
gay.

Duna you know already. Massang is tall and very slim,
with an ethereal and melancholy face that suggests T.B.
Yesterday he borrowed a needle and thread from me, and I
found him afterwards squatting naked in the cookhouse,
trying to draw together the hopeless rags of his shorts. I
made him a present of one of the scarlet mailbags used
previously for my priority air despatches to Lord Louis
Mountbatten's headquarters, and to-day a Buginese woman
in the market has converted it into a pair of shorts on her
early model Singer. He usually looks more as though he
were taking part in a spiritualist séance than a rummy school,
but when luck comes his way he is liable to jump up with a
head-hunter's whoop. Massang is more constantly than the
others aware of the presence of souls, *bombos*, *batitongs*,
deata and other unseen creatures of the Toraja world, and
I have many interesting talks with him.

Timbo, Kandilli's groom, is apparently younger than the
others but has won his place in the group because of his
precocity. There is no more valuable member of the
rummy school than Timbo, for he is a born clown, and when
he is in the mood to entertain I go to bed with sides aching
from an evening of laughter. Popular with everybody, he
is an especial favourite of Salu's, and when later I suggested
engaging him and Massang as slaves for the last three
months of my stay Salu agreed at once. " We are always
happy when Timbo is in the house," he said. Timbo, too,
is thin, but very wiry. His black eyes seem almost to crackle
with lively intelligence and his dense disarray of shiny hair

always reminds me of an old man I knew in Bali who wore a fur wig.

Sulo, the last player, is rather an isolated figure. He is the son of Pong' Rantebambam's old age; a meek, wide-eyed child of twelve or so, with all the cares of a rich man's son. He is the only child in the village who seems to be at somebody's beck and call; the cliffs resound every hour to shouted summonses for him. Compared with most English children he is amazingly independent, but by comparison with the children of La'bo he is a down-trodden little serf. He also suffers now and then from grievous boils, coming and sobbing on my floor and thinking I can do something to help.

Barra, who prefers Thirty-Ones to rummy, has dealt out three matches to each player in a high-handed way. These take the place of the three sixpences customary in the army game. Most of us leave them lying before us, as the rules of the game require, but Duna, Massang and Timbo thrust theirs out of sight among their hair. When we play *vingt-et-un* this habit is a cause of delay, for they are never sure whether they are broke or merely hard up, holding up the game while their fingers delve and rootle in their not uninhabited coiffures.

I deal the cards.

This is evidently one of Timbo's evenings. He has been dealt a poor hand and reacts by hooding his head with his sarong, covering his face with his hands and filling the room with the desolation of the ceremonial weeping performed by women round the coffin at death-feasts. His miming is always miraculously exact, and Salu is soon wiping tears from his eyes with his skirt while I feel the familiar stitch starting in my side.

Sulo wins the round and at once asks whether in the event of his winning the game he might have three *golla-gollas* instead of three cigarettes. Like Isak and Siu, he does not smoke, observing the schoolmaster's veto which Sesa

ignores. Duna, Massang and Timbo, who only went to the
village school and left after a few years, smoke like chimneys
and are even now drawing tresses of Buginese tobacco from
the tin that is replenished each market day and wrapping
them deftly in scraps of my air edition *Spectator*. Normally
they light them at a candle flame, but at market to-day
Timbo has squandered twenty-five cents of the money I
gave him on a box of matches. This token of affluence he
brings out with an air, slowly striking a match and offering
it in turn to the others.

The next hand has more drama about it. As I pick up
the card Barra wants he crashes his fist on the bedstead,
and shouts "*Buaya!*" The word means "crocodile," but
it is used as an expletive with the meaning "scoundrel."
Mina, who has been nursing my left arm and gazing up at
me with adoration, raises the shrill tinkle of her tinny voice
in protest at this affront, her eyes darting fire at the impassive Barra. Then Sulo takes the card Timbo wants.

"*Bagera!*" exclaims Timbo.

"Timbo speaks Japanese, Tuan," Siu says. "*Bagera* is
one of their dirty words. They said it often at us."

"They said it to me, Tuan," says Massang, "when I
carried a soldier's box from Rantepao to Sangalla and then
asked for money. The soldier said '*Bagera!*' and hit my
head. I fell down and couldn't get up again."

"But the Nippons liked Timbo," Sesa puts in mischievously. "He went many times to their camp to sing
and make the officers laugh."

This is true. The Japanese had recognised the boy's gift
for mime and enjoyed his singing of Marakka songs. He
had given several command performances in Rantepao.

"The Nippons——" Timbo says with a frown, and goes
on to allege certain unprintable habits among his former
patrons, detailing the unprintable circumstances in which
he had made the discovery.

"They eat snakes, Tuan," Duna adds, and is obliged to

hop down from his chair to spit through the floor-boards in disgust.

"They are not circumcised and they made our people dig great holes every moon," Sesa says, the last in reference to the air-raid caves constructed everywhere on the orders of the nervous conquerors.

Lindung, Torri and Tu'ugun scramble up from their endless game of Snakes and Ladders at my feet to give a demonstration of Japanese foot-drill. Sipa, with his unfortunate sniff, is their officer. The noise brings in several silent wayfarers from the road.

The game is resumed, with Isak taking and maintaining the lead. He is an odd child, too prim for a Toraja. If you were asked to pick out the only Christian child present you would have no difficulty in distinguishing him. Though he must be younger than the sixteen Salu says he is, he already has a clerkly air about him and his words and gestures show a slightly spinsterish precision. All the same he is a very good-natured and conscientious lad, and I have said he may stay at the bungalow with his father as long as he likes.

The laconic impassivity characteristic of Western card-players is not to be observed amongst us.

"Kandel!" gloats Timbo over a good card. That word means "food," and its use as an ejaculation in moments of good fortune is perhaps a measure of the Torajas' close acquaintance with hunger.

Duna has a hopeless hand. He strikes himself passionately in the face.

Sulo groans despairingly over his receding chances of winning three golla-golla.

Massang suddenly leaps on to the bedstead in his scarlet shorts, yelling like a maniac over an eleventh-hour win.

Sesa is usually less demonstrative. Inured by seven years' schooling to sitting on seats, he will go for an hour without drawing his feet up on to the seat of his chair; the others, even high-school boys like Siu and Isak, never last that long.

As for those agreeable young yokels, Timbo, Duna and Massang, they can never keep their feet on the ground for more than a few moments. Their heels jerk up on to the seat and they rest their elbows on their high-bent knees. So does Barra. The smokers fidget more than the rest, for they are under the necessity of jumping like frogs to the floor every few minutes to spit with delicacy between the wide-spaced boards.

Massang wins and pokes his three prize Player's cigarettes into his hair. A cry rings through the night and they all start making fun of poor Sulo, once again pulled back on his tight leash. He departs meekly, and I hope he is out of earshot before Timbo delights us with his uncharitable mime of Pong' Rantebambam's querulous voice and graveyard cough.

While Salu goes to make my mug of coffee, Mina, who has gone to sleep in my lap still nursing my arm, is gently roused by Sesa and the enormous hat is balanced on her drowsy head.

Duna is at my elbow.

" I ask to go out, Tuan," he requests, " to find a girl." And when I nod he goes off with a friend of his called Riri. It may be that Duna's pretty regular surrenders to the promptings of Venus will break up the group of which he is a member, because Sesa, Massang and Timbo have only occasional adventures of that kind, at death-feasts and the like. Riri, a boy of fifteen, presumably performs valuable introductions into various finer details of the excitements of manhood.

Siu, always well mannered, asks my leave to go to his house for supper. Sesa asks the same, and I wish Mina good night. She can hardly stand for fatigue.

" Has Massang had his food ? " I ask.

Massang, with an arm round Timbo's thin shoulders, says simply and without self-pity, " We can't eat to-night, Tuan."

I feel sad and somehow humiliated, wondering how many in La'bo will go to sleep to-night with Hunger for a bed-mate, familiar since childhood and nothing to make a song about. The pleasant dignity with which the two boys accept bananas and the unfamiliar but appreciated bread and butter helps me not to feel too bad. . . .

One advantage of the bungalow's lack of modern sanitation is the necessity for going now and then into the garden, so that I can keep in touch with the night. There is usually something good to see or hear.

To-night a baby moon is lying on its back not far above the black horizon, not bright enough to dim the lightning flashes except in its near neighbourhood. There are no thunderclaps. The monsoon has fallen and the whole region of the air enclosing the village is utterly still.

But not silent. Apart from the quiet talk of a few way-farers returning from market there is the mysterious, persistent stridulation of the cicadas, an elemental resonance under the influence of which the air seems to contract and expand. This eldritch vibration more than anything else inspires the old fancy that I am standing on some far outpost star, witnessing the whole operation of the universe, the flying of the constellations, the roar of the great currents of ether, the whole articulation of the cosmic drift.

It is an experience which I have known at intervals all my life; but never since childhood so vividly as here in the magical nights of La'bo. In childhood it had a reality more intense than anything I now call reality, and there are no thrills nowadays to compare with the moments when I would lie in bed breathless with the dizzy velocities of Time and Space around me, happy like some exiled creature restored to its true element.

Now that I can observe and analyse my experiences, only the faintest shadows of the excitement ever visit me, shadows so faint that I can attempt to describe them only in the most obliquely allusive language. I have no idea what can be the explanation. At times I have wondered whether it could be some temporarily induced awareness of the operation of my physical system, as though my perceptive self, a vivid organ of microscopic size like one of the Toraja souls, were on tour round my anatomy, adrift amid the cataracts of blood and the labourings of the glands, rocked by the gigantic suspirations of the lungs and buffeted beneath the vibrations of the nerves, thrown into ecstasy by the earthquakes of muscles in their convulsions and the power of the sap and the mass-production plant of the belly.

I have heard, too, of pre-natal memory. Can it be that? Perhaps everybody has felt it. . . .

Coming down to earth, I make a pleasing discovery. Under the wide eaves outside Salu's window there is a little cloud of thin green light. It comes from a frilled fungus that has grown there, cream in the light of my torch but greenly incandescent in the darkness. Timbo and Massang are surprised at my interest in it.

A short while afterwards Massang calls me into the cookhouse to show me a long, thin centipede. He strikes it with his knife and at the same time Isak blows out the oil dip; but in the darkness the creature can still be seen, because where Massang has wounded it it is bleeding light. He stabs it again and more incandescence spurts from its coiling body. It takes an actual bisection to kill it and stains of greenish light are left on the boards of the platform.

By the time the next game begins Sesa has returned. Siu has said good night on leaving, but his place is now taken by Lelang.

I feel a smile breaking over my face as I start to write about Lelang. Most people grin when he is mentioned.

He is the village outlaw, though you would never think it to see his utter self-possession and the esteem with which he is surrounded. The fact is that he is only an outlaw from the newest Authority in the community—that is to say, the *guru*.

Lelang is a runaway from school and the *guru* is empowered, if he can catch him, to avenge this betrayal of Progress with severe corporal punishment. By that I mean a succession of blows on the head, Japanese fashion.

" Why did you stop going to school? " I asked the boy, who appears to be about eleven years old, shortly after our acquaintance began.

His clear eyes looked up at me very straight.

" Tuan *guru* every day *pukul-pukul-pukul*," he replied, raining blows on his head with his fists in illustration. And his candid glance added, as plainly as any words, " And I'm Lelang and I don't take that from anybody! "

During the hours of daylight he never dares to show himself on the road or near it. A week ago he risked it, and my younger visitors of the moment shouted themselves hoarse as they watched from my veranda the *guru's* swift but unsuccessful pursuit. I made a point of standing on the veranda when the breathless *guru* walked past the gate a few moments later and called a greeting to let him know that I had witnessed his loss of dignity and face. Whether this occasioned him any chagrin I do not know.

Yes, I am on Lelang's side in his feud with the schoolmaster. It is wrong of me to have taken up so definite a position without hearing the *guru's* side of the story, but I am of the opinion that the *gurus*, good men as most of them are, show too much arrogance to set a really good example to their charges. I know very well that if Lelang and the *guru* should chance to meet in the basket bungalow the boy will not be beaten here.

Once I went into my bedroom during a pause in the rather heavy labour of entertaining the *guru* and found

Lelang squatting composedly beside the camp-bed with only a yard of space and a basket partition between him and his enemy, looking at the illustrations to the Natural History of Selborne while he waited for the *guru's* departure. We exchanged grins.

I said to him when the schoolmaster had gone, " Five years more and you will be too big for the *guru* to beat."

Lelang raised his fine brows.

" No, Tuan. It is two moons since I ran away from school. After two more moons the *guru* will black my name out of his book and not seek me any more."

That was the rule, and before I left La'bo young Lelang was able to pass the *guru* on the school path without risk. . . .

He is a child of few words, but his silence and total self-possession amuse. His only trick is to mimic the call of the Muslims' goats in Makale. He does that well and the sound is a sort of nickname for him in the village. When he is seen coming the other children make goat noises, though none so well as he. His handsome square face, candid eyes and sturdy body all testify to strong and independent character.

(It is characteristic, incidentally, that his father does nothing to back up the *guru's* authority. Lelang is a Toraja child, accustomed to making his own decisions and judging for himself. His father is the clairvoyant Pong' Sakuru.)

Timbo, meanwhile, has embarked on a lengthy mime having to do with the domestic relations of a certain couple in the hamlet of Parrara. I miss the point of some of it, but so vivid is the miming that I can recognise at once the main problem of the ménage in question: the lady is far from having passed the enjoyment of the delights of the flesh and is not easily reconciled to the short commons provided by her very elderly husband. For five minutes Timbo has us in fits, as Mr. Pooter would have said.

It is rummy this time. Lelang has all the luck, though his calm features betray no excitement. Salu, still laughing

215

and wiping his eyes on his sarong skirt, is unable to concentrate and keeps rousing from a fit of weak laughter to realise a chance thrown away and sigh a mortified "*Wah!*" He has not recovered by the time Timbo sets him off again with an impression of the *Burakke* from Tokesan. His picture of the priest-priestess is consummate. With his sarong tucked in above his narrow chest like a woman, he minces along with a pansy wriggling of his shoulders, astoundingly like the odd figure that sidled past the gate just before sundown.

Only Massang is not amused. With possibly alarm as well as disapproval in his voice he speaks in rapid Toraja, as they do when they don't want me to understand. Without a very good grace Timbo desists. Evidently the *Burakke*, as a quasi-sacred personage, ought not to be mocked.

Lelang has heard from somebody that I had said there were no buffaloes in my country. When I confirm it he frowns.

" Then what happens when you die ? " he asks, as though not entirely convinced that people could die without bulls to take their leading part in the great rituals of death.

" They put us in boxes and bury us in the earth," I reply.

" And where do you go then ? " he asks.

While I hesitate, Salu intervenes with one of his unbecoming fits of primness. In brisk Toraja he ticks Lelang off for presuming to cross-examine a Christian so bluntly. Christians are, for Salu, the ruling class of the religious world and ignorance of, or lack of respect for, their beliefs are signs of unhappy heathen darkness. He does not, however, in the least abash Lelang and soon he is his genial self again, doubled up with laughter over Timbo's mime of me receiving the Controleur. It is so like a caricature of two *pukka sahibs* drinking together that I feel a twinge of uneasiness. The phonetic sketch of the English language sounds like nothing at all to me but scores a direct hit with Salu and Barra, reducing them almost to collapse.

Unfortunately, the prim mask descends again on poor Salu after a little while. A wild scream from the darkness outside the fence brings me half out of my chair with quite the wrong idea.

" It is only a girl, Tuan," Salu says with a tightened-up face, " playing with the men."

When Oberammergau comes in shortly afterwards he denies Barra's accusation of taradiddling behind our fence and provoking the squeal of feminine rapture that had disturbed us. His pious features and apostolic curls support his denial, but his reputation does not. Rante has come in, too, leaning with his air of poetic melancholy in a corner. Palimbong's writer, returning late from business in Rante-pao, looks in to collect the sleepy Torri.

The evening-long game of Snakes and Ladders breaks up. Sipa has left us much earlier to go and sup as usual with his rich kinsman Sulo. Lindung and Tu'ugun fold up the board, shut the dice and counters in their little box, sigh and draw their sarongs over their heads and fall suddenly asleep at our feet. Neither the loud oaths of the card-players nor Oberammergau's ribald song disturb them. And even when Timbo, obliged to leave the game for a moment, falls over a recumbent cocoon and with a kick shouts, " Sleep over there, Lindung! " the humble child merely crawls into a corner and is at once asleep again.

The quintet of playboys come trooping in from I don't know where to wish me good night. The room is so full that there is much ado in shutting the door, and shut it must be for it is cold to-night. Cigarettes are lighted up.

It is at moments like these that I sometimes recall the Dutch lady I met on my journey up-country from Makassar. The little armed convoy in which I was obliged to travel had halted for the night at Pare Pare and she was a fellow-guest in the rest-house there, a friendly lady of early middle age, the wife of an administrator in another part of the island.

When I told her of my plan for the next few months she looked doubtful.

" But will that be safe? " she asked, a reasonable enough question in an island where scattered bands of nationalist terrorists were murdering white men with some frequency. I told her that none of the terrorists had penetrated beyond the fringes of the Sadang Toraja country and that the Controleur of Makale had pronounced the areas I wished to visit safe.

" All the same," she sighed, " I don't like to think of anybody going and living all alone at a time like this."

" But I'm not going to be alone," I said. " I shall be living in a village."

" Yes, I know," she said, as though I had been splitting hairs. " But *really* all alone."

All alone! It would be going too far to suggest that the lady considered Salu and Barra and Lindung and the rest less than human; but she did obviously think that with only them and their like for company a man with a white skin would inevitably feel lonely and unfriended.

When I decided to write this book I considered for a time using that as an ironical title.

All Alone!

It has been dark for about three hours, so it must be past nine o'clock. Bed-time.

Lelang wins and runs off bleating into the night with his prize. He is safe on the road at this hour. The playboys shout and laugh as they slide about on the steep, muddy path up to Pong' Rantebambam's house, where they will sleep the night. Isak collects the cards, no longer very clean, though each player punctiliously washes his hands before we play, and packs them into their cases. A heaped-up ashtray is borne out by Timbo and emptied into the rubbish-pit. Chairs are piled on the old bedstead, for the room is now a dormitory and the floor-boards, spread with one or two thin woven mats, will be bed for a big party.

Outside a little gentle rain has begun to fall and a few frogs lift up their voices. A *silly-silly* flies over the bungalow roof, winking with her yellow light.

There is no sign of Duna.

When I go into the front room to collect the candle seven sarong-muffled forms lie side by side on the floor like climbers in an Alpine hut or guests in a medieval inn; Barra, Oberammergau, Sesa, Massang, Timbo, Tu'ugun and Lindung. Gathering up the stalagmites of guttered candle grease from the tin lids which serve as candlesticks, I place them beside the cigarette tin that contains all Lindung's small treasures. It is his delight to fashion exquisite little conical candles from waste grease.

"*Bongi melo*," I wish them all, and they echo the greeting in chorus.

Rante, by reason of his post as *ronda*, sleeps in the veranda room. I ask for *Sailo* and the *pa'suling to'dolo* as usual and bid him good night. Then good night to Salu and Isak in the room opposite mine.

For some minutes there are sounds of horseplay from the front room, but when my candle goes out Rante's flute fills the basket bungalow with the sweet grief of the golden past, and soon after it has sobbed into silence I am drowned in easy sleep.

X

WORK AND PLAY

" THEY are lazy," says the *Encyclopædia Britannica* of
the Torajas. " They are naturally lazy," declares the
British Government Manual of Netherlands India.

The Torajas are a moderately industrious people.

Sometimes as I watched my neighbours at work in La'bo
I would ask myself whether Anglo-Saxon labourers would
work as energetically with the thermometer above 80 degrees
Fahrenheit. I felt reasonably sure that they would not.

Of course, for most Torajas there is no regular eight-
hour day. The moons just before and after the rice harvest
are pretty easy times for rice-growing Torajas. They do a
fair amount of lounging then; they would be fools if they
didn't. When work is to be done I say they work hard; and
what is more, I say to hell with people who make patronising
generalisations in authoritative works of reference about
people it would seem they have never set eyes on.

A Toraja frequently begins his or her working life at
the age of three or four years. Little girls and boys are
the nursemaids of their baby brothers, sisters and cousins;
and I may add that they make a very good job of it. I never
once heard any of those little nursemaids speak crossly to
the heavy babies astride their hips, and nothing could have
been more contented than the happy-go-lucky babies who
practically never cried from one week's end to the other.

Pleasant pictures they made, the tiny nursemaids of
La'bo, bent almost at right angles—especially the little boys
—to support fat babies astride diminutive hips. Whenever
a troop of small children was seen in hurried movement,
whether toward two bulls that had started to fight or toward

the bungalow where Tuan Colonel had opened the *golla-golla* tin, the rear was likely to be brought up by one or two of those naked, right-angled scraps of eager humanity with cheerful and slightly raffish babies bouncing on their hips.

Little girls not employed in looking after smaller children help their mothers with the cooking, spinning and weaving, with water-fetching and the care of gardens. Little boys are buffalo grooms, the smaller ones looking after the calves and cows, and the boys who are nearly ripe caring for every need of the lordly bulls. Boys help in the ploughing and weeding of the rice-fields and boys and girls join in the planting and harvest.

School, of course, cuts across all this and is a disrupting influence on tribal life. I estimated that roughly a third of La'bo children went to school. Though education is free, the cost of the rather better clothes school children wear and the loss of the children's labour or earnings make school impossible for the poorest children.

Toraja children are conscientious workers. They are not expected to do the heaviest labour, but their standard of skill must be high. They do not play at helping daddy and mummy; they have to do their jobs properly. A ten-year-old Toraja boy is an excellent little handyman, as I can vouch from experience, and I have no doubt that his sister is just as accomplished in her different way. They are, moreover, in my opinion very quick to learn.

A fortnight after I had taken Timbo and Massang on to my establishment as supernumerary slaves, Salu was suddenly called home by the news that a young son was very sick with dysentery. I sent him off with a supply of sulfa-guanadine tablets and the reflection that I had reserves of eggs and tinned stuff to provide for easy camp cooking till he came back.

Returning late that afternoon from a death-feast in the hills, I was washing my hands and deciding on boiled eggs as the line of least resistance when I saw Timbo approaching a well-laid table with a steaming plate of soup. I said no more than "thank you," and sipped it, prepared for the worst. It was as good as Salu's.

A dish of fried chicken and calf's liver followed, with fried potatoes and steamed green beans. Delicious. Then hot macaroons and coffee.

I went out to the cookhouse and found the two boys roasting coffee beans, perched like dreaming birds on the edge of the table-top fire.

" I did not know Salu was educating you to cook," I said.

Apparently surprised that I should have made any comment, Massang said, " Ambe'na Isak did not educate us, Tuan. But we have seen him cook Tuan's food."

I asked myself what sort of show I should have put up when I was thirteen if I had suddenly been required to produce several dishes of exotic food, totally meaningless to me, which I had merely happened to see a cook preparing a few times.

Occasionally they cooked for me later. Except that Massang's macaroons were dryish and Timbo's coffee somehow no better than English hotel coffee, they fed me as well as Salu did.

Earlier than that I had been surprised in the same way the morning after a storm blew the bungalow roof off. It fell back again, but leaving a gap more than a foot wide all along the roof ridge, through which the moon shone. I was grumbling over the necessity for asking Chief Deppa for a labour squad to repair it when a dozen little boys from the village school, without any ado, began to swarm like monkeys all over the roof, which in half an hour they so effectively mended that it stood up to several violent storms without ever letting in a single drop of water.

These are the main divisions of work between the sexes among the South Torajas.

Men do all the work connected with building houses, roads and bridges. They erect fences. They dig and plant the vegetable gardens. They plough and otherwise prepare the fields for rice-planting and maintain the elaborate and delicate systems of terrace irrigation. They gather *tuak*. They gather firewood. They weave baskets. They carry the harvested rice to the granaries.

Boys help them in all these tasks.

Women cook and do the general housework. They care for babies and the sick. They spin and weave, make clothes and pots, and fetch water. They pound the rice to husk it, and they weed the gardens. They plant the rice. Young girls assist them.

In the markets men sell buffaloes, pigs, dogs, horses, oils, hats and knives. Women sell vegetables and fruit. The sale of *tuak*, chickens, rice, salt, pots, tobacco, *sireh* and coffee is shared.

The harvesting of the rice is shared by both sexes and all ages.

Round La'bo there is no uncultivated ground and the standard of rice culture is among the highest in all the Indies. It does not look like the homeland of a lazy people.

Nobody works in the rain. " It would make us sick, Tuan," Barra explained. I expect it would, if only because few Torajas have more clothes than those they stand up in, and if those are wet through as the evening chills descend there may be danger of respiratory disorder, for they sleep in their sarongs.

The government exacts most of its taxes in the form of work. Each year a Toraja between the ages of about eighteen and fifty must give fifty days' labour. Twenty-four of these are called *heerendienst*, and are usually served outside the man's own district, working on government projects such as the construction or maintenance of roads and big

bridges. Eighteen days are called *gemeentedienst* and take
the form of community work in his village, directed by the
village chief. Each man must work four days for the village
chief's own convenience, two days for the complex chief and
two days for the Ampulembang. Only for the last eight of
these days is food provided.

On payment of a certain sum (eighteen guilders, I believe)
a man is excused *heerendienst* for one year. I did not find
that these exactions were bitterly resented, as they are in
Java, though there is some murmuring against the *heerendienst*, since it is hard for the average villager to see that big
roads and bridges are of any value to him and his family.

Hunting is a form of work unknown in La'bo, where
there are no wild beasts larger than a wild cat, except for the
families of baboons on Sarira. In Pangala and most other
parts of the Torajalands away from the big rice valleys men
with dogs hunt the wild pig, the pig-deer, the *anoa* (a fierce
dwarf buffalo hardly bigger than a St. Bernard dog), and in
the warmer forests pythons that sometimes attain a length
of thirty feet. Spears are the normal weapons, and in the
district of Baoo game is driven into large nooses arranged
along the jungle paths.

It is not out of place to write a page or two on Toraja art
in a chapter devoted to work and play.

There is a whole world of difference between an artist
like Munu or Tambai and our Western conception of an
artist. We think of an artist as one who creates, who makes
an individual contribution to the beauty in the world by
expressing his personal vision of the world. But a Toraja
artist is no individualist, no originator. He is totally
objective, concerned only to pass on the traditional forms
of his art as pure as he received them.

Torajas at Home

An Artist

I suppose " craftsman " would be a better name for most savage artists. They are not concerned with winning personal reputations. They serve their art as a priest serves his religion, safeguarding the continuity of tradition, celebrating truths and forms already expressed.

In Bori I had an artist friend, Tambai. It was pleasant to sit on a corner of a granary platform, watching his cunning left hand carving the panels for the new house he had been commissioned to decorate. He was a strangely dedicated figure as he sat at work, his waist-long hair coiled round his head and bound with a narrow fillet, never uttering a word while the short knife in his left hand first sketched and then carved in relief the lovely designs on the black-painted panels at extraordinary speed. His inseparable friend Bulan often sat with him in silence, leaning drowsily against a pillar as he watched.

Tambai had no notion of himself as belonging to a class exalted above other skilled workers. He had no inkling of my conception of the artist and æsthetics. When I said his panels were *melo* he was pleased that I agreed with him, but we were using the word differently. I meant that the designs on the panels were to me things of beauty; he meant that the panels were pieces of good and faithful workmanship.

Nor did old So' Kadoya, whose house they were to adorn, see them as *melo* in my sense. To him they expressed power. I don't mean that he saw them as crude symbols of his wealth, though they were that in so far as only men of substance could afford the services of fine artists; I mean that the intangible quality about the designs was for him not æsthetic beauty but strength and invigoration, a virtue something akin to the strong soul and magical strength of the red *tabang* plants growing round the house.

It seemed to me that most Torajas had considerable feeling for form. The mud bulls modelled for me by the small children of La'bo were instinct with energy. But Western influences may well corrupt their gift.

One morning after a small crowd of Bori men had spent the evening at the bungalow there I found a cock carved in one of the roof posts, a vivid sketch of fewer than twenty careless knife-strokes. I inquired who had done it, for I wanted to see whether he could work with paint and paper, and, if so, commission him to do end-papers for this book; but they were afraid I was angry at the defacement of the roof post and the artist would not reveal himself.

The Ampulembang of Tikala, appealed to, assured me that there was a fine artist in one of his villages who could work on the cartridge paper I offered and he would order him to paint me the conventional cock and rising sun, as appear on the gable of most rice-barns. Alas, the artist had been school-trained, and I was brought, not the leaping vitality of the Toraja cock and the sun he brings back each morning with his song, but a pathetic daub, a realistic drawing of a cock with a pale lemon sun, the whole thing so anæmic that it repelled.

It was shocking to realise how quickly and completely a vigorous talent could be depraved.

Play is not so prominent a feature of Toraja life as it is of our own in the West. Toraja children have very few games in comparison with white children. That is chiefly because they are not banished into a world of childhood as our children are, but share as far as they can all the work and play of their elders.

Little girls in La'bo have no dolls and none of the small boys has a toy. The difference goes further, for there are no festivals for children there. No Christmas, of course, and no birthdays, since practically nobody can keep count of children's ages. Games of make-believe are very rare.

You would be mistaken, though, if you imagined that this made the lives of Toraja children grey and prosaic. I would say myself that it is our children who sometimes seem bored and elderly, and Toraja children who preserve the wonder and bright simplicity of childhood.

From their earliest days the children of La'bo are treated as human beings, not creatures separated by gulfs from adult life, not pets, not little slaves to be ruled by their parents' will, not little incompetents incapable of looking after themselves until well on in adolescence, not raw material to be wrought into such shapes as their parents choose and certainly not little underlings to be threatened and punished. The calm self-sufficiency and self-reliance of my smaller friends in La'bo was delightful, and no more detracted from their shining naïveté than did their thorough acquaintance with birth, sex-life and death.

Treated as responsible beings, they behave as such. Tu'ugun, aged seven or eight, himself negotiated with old Pong' Rantebambam his succession to Lameh as groom to Saleko, the most valuable bull in La'bo, bargaining for a new sarong as well as food for wages. Karrak and his sister went to live with an uncle whom they liked better than their father. Other La'bo children lived with grandparents or friends, pleasing themselves where they would make their homes.

Such children, gay and self-reliant, do not think much of make-believe, though once or twice I saw little boys strip and fight in the wet grass like bulls, crashing their flat-backed heads together until their necks looked like snapping off; and in Pangala I saw a few miniature rock-tombs cut out of a low sandstone cliff. But Toraja children have no need of make-believe, for the whole range of adult entertainment and play is open to them. If Anglo-Saxon children could go to dances, race-meetings and theatres I imagine they, too, would be less keen on make-believe.

Sisemba is the chief game in La'bo and round about. It is a contest and may be played as singles, doubles **or** anything up to 200 a-side. It is something like an inverted form of boxing, fighting with the feet and any blows with the hands rigidly barred.

The time for *sisemba* is after the rice harvest. Tournaments are held in open spaces everywhere during the harvest festivals, some of them small affairs with only a handful of boys or men fighting and others mass combats in which one village will challenge another. Only the males fight; the females look on.

The Toraja conception of the place of children in society is well illustrated by the shape of a *sisemba* tournament. Just as the smallest children have helped to gather the harvest, now the smallest male reapers have their parts to play in the harvest fights. It is they who open the show.

Tiny three-and four-year-old boys, naked and hand in hand, are drawn up in two opposing lines ten yards or so apart. They jig on one foot, kicking out derisively with the other, and doing their best to imitate the savage, taunting cries of their fathers and big brothers. At a signal they advance and engage, while proud fathers and mothers and grandparents watch the first budding of aggressiveness and endurance in the boy babies. Cheering and barracking are on a prodigious scale.

Then older children take the field, boys between five and ten, followed by the circumcised boys a few years older. By the time the ripe boys line up, those of thirteen to fifteen, the play is tough, for the ripe little girls looking on are not eager for timid lovers. The pace and excitement increase as pairs of youths challenge each other, and finally, in a hurricane of wild vitality, all the men of a village or hamlet line up to fight the team of another community.

I was not in Kesu for the rice harvest, so I never saw the big games so often described for me; but the Puang of Sangalla staged half an hour of *sisemba* on one day of his mother's death-feast. I found it more exciting than the bull-fights.

The fighters go into action in pairs. They fight hand in hand, because the most powerful kicks will overbalance the kicker unless he has a partner to hang on to. Before the start, the two rows of contestants insult and provoke each other with hair-raising invective and shakings of the leg. Then comes the advance and the clash, and the air is full of powerful legs whirling in prodigious arcs. One partner will stand with his legs well straddled while the other throws the whole weight of his body into the air, at the same time kicking out with every muscle of his massive leg. He comes to rest, having hurled himself in a semi-circle round the pivot of his partner, who then takes the next kick. That is the method, but in so dense a tangle of limbs and with the field of battle swaying and surging in all directions classical kicks as often as not come to nothing.

There are no finicking rules to restrict blows, except that they may not be delivered by anything but the foot. They may fall anywhere; indeed, one of the blows most tried for is one barred in any Anglo-Saxon sporting contest. In my effort to photograph the encounter I was suddenly enveloped by the shifting field of play, kicked on the funny-bone and pinned against a megalith under the nose of the plunging bull that was tethered to it.

Salu said it was a poor fight, but a few teeth were lost and more blood shed than in the bull-fights.

" In the moon of the harvest many legs are broken," he said. " There is much work for Dr. Goslinga then."

" In the days before the Company," said deaf So' Sampe, using the old-fashioned Indonesian name for the rule of the Dutch, derived from the distant days when it was the Dutch East India Company, " there was *sibamba* also after the cutting of the rice. The Company forced us to give it up, so now our ripe boys must grow up like women."

The *sibamba* game had evidently some affinity with the

initiation ordeals through which the boys of early societies in many parts of the world had to pass at puberty. It was a form of fighting with wooden clubs, no blows barred, with bull-hide shields carried in the left hand for protection. The Dutch District Officer abolished it at the same time as head-hunting was forbidden. It came under the heading of bloodshed, I suppose, for naturally blood flowed freely on such occasions and there were even rare deaths.

Another dearly loved sport now almost abolished is cock-fighting. There were always gusty sighs when I told Toraja friends how in Bali I had seen cock-fighting nearly every day, permitted by the government, and when I added that gambling went on openly everywhere daily they came to the conclusion that Bali must indeed be the last paradise.

Only on the occasion of the largest death-feasts, and, I believe, the harvest festivals, will the Controleur relax for one or two days the stringent prohibition of cock-fighting. When on the fifth day of the death-feast at Menkendek a day's cock-fighting was permitted, crowds of Torajas assembled on foot from places twenty, thirty and even forty miles away. No non-Torajas are allowed to bet on such occasions, and the Controleur asked me to abstain for form's sake, though the discrimination had been introduced solely to prevent the exploitation by the artful Bugis people of the Torajas' headlong gambling passion.

When I recalled my pleasant hours of gambling in Manokayana village among the friendly Balinese I could not help wishing that the ban on Toraja gambling had never been imposed. It seems, though, that the circumstances were not identical. For all the Balinese love of gambling, they do not plunge with such immoderation that the economic life of the community loses its balance; and that, I was told, was what happened among the Torajas thirty years ago. It is probable that puritan resentment at the pleasure gambling gave played its part in the pressure which ended in its virtual abolition; but I heard several tales of livelihoods lost and families reduced to beggary in a few hours of wild dicing, card-playing or cock-fighting. Legislation to moderate rather than stamp out this ruling passion obviously presents complicated problems.

If some invader had conquered England and banned cricket and association football except for one or two matches a year you would expect record crowds at those matches; so there is no cause for wonder at that great trek to Men-kendek. You would also expect a number of illegal games to take place in remoter parts and, just as naturally, illegal gambling and cock-fighting take place in the forests and on certain cliff ledges of the Toraja country. Once I innocently alarmed an outlaw card party on the slopes of Sarira, sur-prising their youthful outposts and shortly afterwards being obliged to ignore a dirty King of Diamonds and another card that had been dropped under a bush in hurried flight. These illicit games are no secret to most of the villagers. Women make food and hover near till the gamblers should be hungry, for the winners are in a mood to pay good prices.

Their favourite card game is a simple affair, a little like *vingt-et-un*. Their dice have the numbers 1, 2 and 4, but the other three faces show formal designs.

Bull-fights delight the heart of every Toraja. Though the first clash of horns is undeniably dramatic and the stance of two clinching bulls is a noble spectacle, the combat is almost invariably so short, often no longer than the whirlwind death encounters of the game-cocks, and usually end, unlike the cock-fights, so tamely, that they often seemed to me prodigies of anti-climax. It appears, however, that they will continue to entrance generations of Torajas for many years to come.

On top of bull-fights, and in place of the cock-fighting they have taken away, the whites offer the Torajas football. Among the most sophisticated young Torajas the association game is popular, but since every level piece of ground bigger

than a billiard table is planted with rice the chances of
playing are severely restricted outside the capital villages
of Rantepao, Makale and Tondon-Pangala. The little boys
who played it with a wicker ball round the bungalow showed
a tendency to use a number of *sisemba* kicks in attack and
defence. But that is the Toraja's instinctive gesture of
aggression; on the rare occasions when I saw boys fighting
it was always with their feet. Those, incidentally, were the
only times I overheard invective in earnest. I remember only
"*Baratitik!*" (" Be a dwarf! ") and " *Ta'bollo!* " ("Have
the dysentery! ").

The supreme traditional sport of the Torajas was war.

Sentimental nonsense has been written about preliterate
societies with traditions of war and head-hunting. I used to
picture all such societies as permanently dominated by
numbing fear till the white man's conquest and pacification
raised a dark cloud from tribal life. In a few weak or
cowardly tribes that may have happened, but in the majority
of cases the prohibition of war is unanimously regretted
among the tribesfolk.

In his pleasant portrait of the free, unpacified head-
hunters of Assam, *The Naked Nagas*, the Austrian anthro-
pologist von Fürer-Haimendorf compares the impression
made on the community by the loss of a villager's head to
the impression made on us by the news of a fatal traffic
accident. None of us is thrown into a state of alarm by news
of a road accident because we all believe we know how to
avoid the dangers of the road; in the same way the Naga
villagers' fun is not spoilt by the occasional loss of a careless
fellow-villager's head.

We should be wrong if we imagined the Torajas of fifty
years ago saddened by their frequent wars or in the grip of
fears from which they welcomed release. It is, of course,
stupid to use the word " war," now that it has for us the

connotations of mass slaughter and overwhelming evil
attendant upon our own wars. The old Toraja wars were
for the youths of the tribe formal tests of manhood and for
their fellow-tribesmen and women occasions of festival. The
taking of heads also held an important place in the structure
of their religious beliefs.

It is probably true that the unforgettable quickening of
personal and community life that transformed the England
of 1940 was testimony more to our mismanagement of our
lives in times of peace than to any vivifying virtue possessed
by war. But for a simple society like that of the Torajas of
yesterday it seems to me probable that mild and frequent
experience of such stimuli, backed by no deadlier dangers
than surround ourselves in times of peace, was good rather
than bad.

XI

PATROLI

I SHALL always be grateful to Dr. Goslinga for his invitation to me to join the *patroli* which he and a party were about to make into the wild country south-west of Makale. Though my main plan had been to settle down and get to know some of my neighbours, I had always hoped to make one expedition into remoter parts.

The doctor came to me one day with the news that he and representatives of the government were shortly to spend eight days travelling through the mountains to regions unvisited by white men since the Japanese invasion in 1942, making contact with the wild tribes of Baoo, Bua Kayu, Simbuang, Mapa and Balepe. A main reason for the *patroli* was the introduction of iodised salt to those tribes afflicted with a high incidence of goitre, due to deficiencies in the drinking water.

"We will travel on horseback," the doctor told me, kindly adding, "you can have one of my horses."

I am no equestrian. Moreover, I was brought up to believe that stallions were beasts of uncertain and formidable temper, like bulls, only more so; and stallions are the only horses ridden in the Torajalands. It might not, then, be fun all the way, I told myself, but I accepted the invitation gratefully. Two mornings later I rose in the dark and a jeep called at sunrise to take me to Makale.

I suppose Makale may quite possibly be the only place in the world where you can see men playing billiards at seven o'clock in the morning. Small tables have been installed in two open shacks out towards the football field and the forsaken Japanese brothel, and young men with the

seediness of cities about them sprawl under the sick glare
of pressure lamps playing a very poor game. That strikes a
squalid note, however, and Makale is anything but squalid.
The capital village of the South Torajas is built round a
beautiful lake which reflects the trim white bungalow of the
Controleur, the pleasant rest-house on a hill-top, the church
that looks as though it had strayed ten thousand miles from
a Swiss village, the long white high-school buildings and a
dancing skyline of encircling crags. There are spotlessly
white government offices of miniature size, a neat little jail,
several schools, a clean Roman Catholic presbytery and a
dirty tin mosque (for Islam has reached as far and the
Muslims' goats flourish side by side with the Torajas'
beloved pigs), a dozen Chinese shops, a tiny hospital, the
residence and office of the Puang of Makale, a very large
market place, a barracks and a military workshop. At this
last we halted, for we could almost see the air through our
worn tyres, and that was not the jeep's only weakness. An
Ambonese soldier mechanic, with two superlatively supple
Toraja boys to assist him, got to work on it while I wandered
round the lake.

Menadonese drill sergeants were shouting orders in
Dutch to Javanese, Timorese and Papuan soldiers who were
doing English army foot-drill in American uniforms.
Strangely enough, the result was not at all bad. Little
children were bathing in the lake and helping Toraja
soldiers to wash a truck. A flock of white geese ambled
about the tiny green island in the lake. Outside their own
school, pale Chinese boys and girls with almond-leaf eyes
played a noisy game.

By the time we left the capital several choirs of sweet
schoolchildren's voices were singing their morning assembly
hymn. The sun rose late over the high, wooded mountains
that shut the village in. Along the narrow road to Rembon,
where the horses and horse-boys awaited us, there were
many travellers, for it was Rembon market day. In the

small polyclinic there we found the young *mantri* giving yaws injections to patients attending the market. Stacked in his surgery were long boxes and thick bamboo pipes of the salt that was to be distributed to the goitre areas.

In the rather dispiriting way in which most occasions start off in the Torajalands we found ourselves the centre of an incomplete chaos. Not all the horses had appeared and there was no sign of the Ampulembang of Ulu Salu and Malimbong, who was to accompany us as Deputy Minister of Health, so to speak, of the new government. Mr. Kollewijn, the new young Assistant Controleur, was there, and so was Lete, a Toraja assistant of the Controleur's whom I knew and liked very much.

A large disarray of baggage lay in an open space with a number of porters looking irresolutely at it. But all at once they unsheathed their knives and attacked a small bamboo grove close by, producing in a few moments several stout shoulder-poles and yards of tough bamboo rope. Our non-descript belongings, together with the medical supplies, cooking-pots and rations, were neatly tied up and balanced upon brown shoulders, and the file of good-natured tribesmen left the road to turn south along a narrow path deep in mud.

I and the little bay stallion assigned to me had been eyeing each other for some minutes and now our partnership was due to begin. He was a pretty creature, with a jaunty boyishness in place of the touchy majesty I expect of stallions. A nice horse-boy by the name of Sesa introduced him as Ronni and held him while I mounted, telling myself that so long as you didn't want to show off there was nothing to riding a horse; you just sat down on it while it carried you to your destination.

So it proved. Ronni was an admirable little beast, mild and good tempered like all Torajas, and though he must have thought me a curious rider at those times when I was glad to be the only member of the party with a camera, we quickly made friends and never fell out.

Toraja horses, like Toraja people, climb faster than they descend or go on the level. They attack a climb with bounce and sparkle; on the level they dawdle abstractedly; down descents they creep like old women on a frozen path. Nothing could have suited me better than such a mount on the *patroli*, for I should have found the steep ascents in the hot sunshine a sore trial on foot, but I was only too glad to ease my cramped thighs by leading my beast down the descents and along the rather infrequent stretches of level path.

" A good horse," I remarked to Sesa after a few miles.

" He is better if you beat him, Tuan," the boy advised.

This, though, I was disinclined to do, even when Ronni treated the path as a running buffet and we got left far behind. No words of mine, however, whether coaxing, peremptory or violent, had any effect on him, and a switch, not often used with severity, is the Toraja substitute for training; so when we dawdled so far behind that I feared we might get lost in the empty immensities of the valleys we had entered, I would flourish a spray of leaves a few inches from Ronni's face. The next moment I would be hanging on earnestly as he broke into a short-lived canter.

By noon we were threading our way like ants through a deep, sun-brimmed primeval valley littered with boulders the size of Odeon cinemas. For miles there was no sign of man. A lonely raven on a crag watched us pass below him with an offensive lack of interest.

The Ampulembang of Ulu Salu and Malimbong, a young man with a plump, friendly face and a beautiful petunia silk sarong, had soon overtaken us, riding a handsome little piebald which took advantage of a halt to chew and swallow with relish several mouthfuls of soil.

I said to the prince, " Tuan *parenge*, your horse is eating dirt."

"Yes, Tuan, he eats dirt," he answered complacently. He added, with a frown, "Sometimes he is wicked and eats red soil. It makes his belly ache."

The Ampulembang, Kollewijn, Lete and I were the only riders with saddles. I had the doctor's saddle, while he, protesting that he liked nothing better, rode on a large kapok-stuffed cushion. His young Christian Toraja assistant, Julianus, rode a little white stallion, using as a saddle a cushion so wide and overstuffed that his short brown legs stuck out horizontally, wide open.

When we resumed our journey after an hour's halt in a tiny village called Palesan we were joined by our escort, three Toraja mounted policemen with tommy-guns, singing dirges in a contented and abstracted manner. The golden Sadang river, deep and calm between Rantepao and Makale, was now a raging torrent below us, roaring down its steep bed, southbound.

I realised when the first warm drops of rain began to fall that I had not seen the porter who was carrying my waterproof for two hours or more. For myself I did not mind, but inevitably the three hours of heavy rain that followed fogged films and damaged both cameras, with the result that from the whole *patroli* I brought back not one good picture.

The rain was spectacular, like the final collapse of the skies. The steep mountain we had started to climb retreated into mist and a thousand new torrents rose to swell the roar of the tributaries plunging down to the Sadang 1,500 feet below. After only ten minutes we resembled Kinglake and his party entering Constantinople. "On we went, dripping and sloshing, and looking very like men that had been turned back by the Royal Humane Society for being incurably drowned."

It was quite impossible to ride up the steep, streaming slopes and at times it looked as though we couldn't even drag our horses up. But getting down the other side was worse, for though the going was less arduous for the humans, the horses were pitifully nervous on the wide expanses of wet, soapy rock over which their unshod hooves slipped wildly.

That is another thing about Toraja horses—their sure-footedness. This sure-footedness can be implicitly relied on, but that must not be taken to mean that they do not slip. They slip all the time, but all the time they recover themselves. It is not always reassuring at the time.

To ride a Toraja stallion over one of the remoter Toraja bridges gives an added kick to life when you reach the other side. The bridge will probably span a gorge of considerable depth, with rocks and a torrent at the bottom. It will be built of bamboo throughout, with a floor of plaited flattened bamboo, probably in an unimpressive state of repair. Your horse's first step sets the whole structure in motion, though if there is any wind it may already have been swinging gently when you reached it. As I said, the horse's first step sends a wave of motion across the bridge; when this reaches the far side it turns round and comes back, meeting the later waves set up by your horse's advance and combining with them in a rather fugal way to bring about a complicated system of stress and agitation. Quite soon your horse slips badly, one hoof sliding to the very edge while the others plunge a good deal to re-establish balance. All this communicates exciting lateral movement to the bridge and if you are no hardier than I, you will begin to wonder why you hadn't sacrificed dignity and walked across.

There is worse to come, however. You will have assumed that the horsemen behind you would not start to cross the flimsy bridge until you had safely reached the other side, but if the other horsemen are Torajas they certainly will, humming a careless elegy. Refusing to look down (as if that helped!) you go over in your mind your estimate of the drop below and perhaps of the height of the hand-rail which, however flexible, might have lent an illusion of support if you had walked. Having already spent so much time on the bridge, you wonder why the other end is still so far off. And why is that confounded Toraja crowding up behind you and hooting to catch the echo from the cliff opposite? If you're like me you will feel obliged to hoot too, and toss your head in a carefree way. By now there are probably three horses and riders on the bridge and you are bobbing so violently, both laterally and vertically, that you can't focus your eyes properly on the end of the bridge.

And then you are on the path again, talking affectionately to your horse, gulping in the scented air and blissfully aware of the virgin loveliness of the day. . . .

As we reached the foot of the mountain at last, the rain stopped and we rode through rolling, park-like country in the dusk to Bua Kayu's capital. Under a small grove of thorns I saw a tomb, richly carved and coloured. I was chilled and soaked to the skin, and when at last I dismounted outside the little *baruga* of Lewon I was so cramped that I fell on to my knees in a helpless and humiliating manner.

I was by now on good terms with Ronni, and I had left behind me my morning uneasiness over our relationship. All the same, the day's experience had confirmed my suspicion that I was not a born horseman. It was all very well for Montaigne to exclaim so rapturously, " I should chuse to weare out my life with my bum in the saddle, ever riding." That was just another quotation I couldn't borrow for my diary.

There are few fresh morning transports to rival the contentment of recovery from physical exhaustion. An hour after our arrival at Lewon we were lounging in a state of happiness on the rough rest-house veranda, drinking strong coffee while our horses ate their way through breast-high heaps of maize leaves and cooks and porters drifted round half a dozen fires preparing supper. The candlelight fell

Basket Bungalow and Bathing Booth

Boar Hunter of Baoo

pleasantly on the row of saddles thrown astride the veranda rail and on the august face of old Bombineh, Ampulembang of Bua Kayu and Rano, who had been there to greet us on our arrival. In 1906 Bombineh fought the Dutch under the war chief Saruran, brother of the last warrior hero Pong' Tiku. For his share in the Torajas' last resistance he had been banished to the island of Buton for three years, after which the Dutch, with the moderation and wisdom they have frequently shown in their dealings with the Torajas, confirmed him in his petty chieftainship and approved his subsequent election to higher positions among his tribesmen. He had been the paramount chief of Bua Kayu and Rano for many years now.

The *baruga* stood on a steep, forest-clad hillside and the air about it was full of the song of falling waters. By the gate was a dark grotto in which we had bathed our stiff, chilled limbs under a gush of tepid water. A heap of young coconuts from which we had drunk the delicious milk lay in a corner. The Parenge Ulu Salu had changed into a polo sweater and wide trousers of pink flowered print. The three policemen had laid aside their arms and American army uniforms and now willowed about unrecognisably in heliotrope and cyclamen sarongs.

A large amount of good food on a really empty stomach is the way I like best to eat. Rice with fowls presented by Bombineh was very good that night. The little stallions neighed and indulged, appropriately enough, in a good deal of horse-play. The thought of the trek to Baoo next day was no longer the thing of dread it had been a short time earlier.

I always sleep well, but there was something sweeter than usual about that night's rest. Rising at sunrise, I found Julianus going into action on the veranda. A table had been furnished with many neat rows of medicines and drugs in tins and bottles; instruments lay in trays of water, sterilising over spirit flames; a chair was set for the doctor and a curtain of black waving hair fell over Juli's face as he made up small packets of tablets from a huge bottle of atebrine.

When I went to the grotto for my bath I had to pick my way through a crowd of early patients and pass by a sheaf of spears beside the gate. Returning from the bath, I found the stack of spears denser, for the hillmen were arriving all the time. Bombineh had decided that so big a meeting of his people would provide a good opportunity for a large-scale boar-hunt, so the men had been bidden to bring their weapons.

By the time the doctor was ready to start there were several hundreds of patients round and under the bungalow, the men and boys in front of the veranda and underneath the floor, the women and girls round the sides and back. There were more than a hundred goitres, and these patients were examined first and told to stay and hear the words of the Ampulembang of Ulu Salu. The next group of sufferers were the victims of chronic malaria. Their lives were weary with anæmia and painfully enlarged spleen. A supply of medicine during the few preceding years could have preserved their health, but the occupying Japanese authorities had allowed the people no medicine of any kind.

Dr. Goslinga directed my hand to a swelling below the waist of a thin, listless youth. " Feel that spleen," he said.

Even from my careful touch the swollen flesh flinched. The swelling was as hard as a bone.

" And look at that," the doctor went on, drawing down the lower lid of the lad's eye. It was as white as death inside. " Amazing that he can walk about."

I felt the helpless distress and irrational shame of my own good health that such situations inspire. It was a feeling that was to grow painfully familiar during that week. . . .

A few gruesome wounds were next displayed. I could feel happier about them, knowing the swift response of Toraja flesh to sulfa drugs. The trachoma sufferers inspired less hope; their sickness, too, could be cured if only they would make the long, regular mountain journeys to the Rembon clinic for the simple, agonising treatment that could save them from ultimate blindness; but unless a remedy gives early evidence of efficacy, Torajas will seldom persevere with treatment if not under supervision.

Two orderly groups, of schoolgirls and schoolboys respectively, arrived for dysentery inoculations. Some had further treatment for individual sickness and the young *guru* was given a stock of a few main medicaments.

Julianus, meanwhile, was dealing with the smallest sufferers from scabies, the treatment for which was so simple that I lent him a hand. With gentle briskness he took a naked baby or toddler and tucked it under his arm while a horse-boy poured into his hands an oily lotion from a large can. With this he firmly and swiftly massaged the small body while the mother clasped her hands in anxiety lest the oily hands should lose their grip.

One charming little girl of about two years delighted us all with the expression of horror that came over her face when she realised the liberties Juli was taking with her attractive nudity. A dimpled arm rose and she slapped his face with outraged violence. We all laughed gently together, and for the hundredth time I reflected how quickly one felt at home in a Toraja crowd.

But the main event of the morning, considered as a festival (which, as I must have said before, is the way Torajas like to consider everything, if possible), was the interlude of dentistry. The moment the doctor was seen to be armed with a formidable pair of dental forceps and candidates for extractions were called forward the whole crowd gathered closer. The veranda rails became heavily massed and servants and policemen of our party clustered in the doorway, those behind clasping their arms 'round the necks of those in front.

After the third extraction I began to time the doctor on

the Controleur Aspirant's watch. The average time for the next four patients was thirty-five seconds.

This was heroic dental surgery. No cocaine or gas. But the patients did not seem to mind. What they minded was having to sit on a chair while being treated. They were *tida biasa* to sit on chairs, and several refused nervously. To sit in an unaccustomed chair while white men stood made them bashful, and when the doctor insisted amiably they complied with hesitation, feeling an arc light of unfamiliar conspicuousness upon them as they gingerly lowered naked rumps on to the rough wooden seat. Usually their knife scabbards got caught in the arms to increase their confusion. Then while Juli, nimble in a white shirt and yellow-striped shorts, darted about on stout little legs and bare feet preparing cotton swabs, the doctor asked the patient to indicate the tooth he wanted to be rid of. Next moment a thrill went through the crowd as the steel forceps gripped and the doctor's biceps knotted. A slight convulsive movement from the brown man in the chair, a tight hooking of the mud-caked toes, and the tooth was falling from the forceps' steel jaws into the half husk of a coconut by Juli's feet into which the other extracted teeth and discarded swabs and dressings had been thrown. Starting up from the chair, the patient was handed a swab by Juli to bite on and he moved away, blinking and spitting a stream of scarlet over the veranda rail.

Only one extraction provided the crowd with the thrill they had been waiting for. A molar broke off, and the excavation of its roots made considerable demands on the doctor's skill and the patient's endurance. For more than a minute the white man wrenched and twisted at the forceps while the brown man's belly tightened and his fingers hooked agonisingly round the chair arm. When a faint groan escaped him and he kicked out his broad feet in agony the spellbound crowd roared with appreciative laughter. Babies were held up to watch the struggle, and

244

when at last Dr. Goslinga displayed two scarlet-fanged roots a throaty "*Oo-ah!*" rose from the spectators.

The doctor and Julianus had been working at full pressure for four hours, but when the last patient had been attended to and the crowd gathered to hear the Ampulembang of Ulu Salu tell them about the salt that would save their children from developing goitres and halt the growth of goitres already appearing, Juli still had to face the job of packing up the array of medicines and instruments in the many boxes and tins ready for the porters to carry to Baoo. Assisted by the doctor's servant, he got it done in thirty minutes.

We talked for a while with a grave and handsome young woman whose baby was sick. Her husband, a Christian Toraja evangelist, had been murdered by Indonesian nationalists in Masamba a few weeks earlier. " It is difficult now," she sighed. . . .

The hornbill Lete shot soon after we started on our way to Baoo was a monster of ugliness and a miracle of beauty. The ugliness was the fault of the superstructure of hollow crimson horn that rose above the creature's huge buttercup beak, a grotesque disfigurement for which I can imagine no good reason, though I expect there is one. The gloss on its black body and white tail was dazzling in the noon sun, and there were never blues more vivid than the two, Oxford and Cambridge, that glowed in the absurd wattles at its throat.

" *Alo*, Tuan," Sesa told me, pointing and speaking slowly in a told-to-the-children tone.

" Can you eat *alo*? " I asked him.

" Yes, Tuan," he said. " It is good."

Our way led us for several miles along the west bank of the galloping Sadang. Twice we had to ford tributaries because the guides told us the bridges were unsafe, and when a Toraja declares a bridge unsafe I take it to mean that it will collapse for sure under anything heavier than a greyhound. I indulged Ronni in his predilection for making a non-stop picnic lunch of the trip, for it was pleasant to lose the party and amble alone for miles amid hills and forest utterly empty of any sign of human visitation.

Once I mounted a ridge and looked down upon a great expanse of forest and for the first time saw the birds of the region to effect, for I looked down on them as they flew through the sunshine above the blossom-starred tree-tops instead of seeing only their silhouettes against the sun. The orioles were comets of living gold; there were long-tailed cuckoos of shining black and white, crimson and green parrots and a host of smaller jewelled creatures flashing through the primordial sunlight below me. At my side a vivid blue pea-flower climbed, its blossoms visited in her shy, hovering flight by a little cream velvet butterfly with carmine roundels. We had lost a good deal of height since leaving Makale and the air here was thicker, warm and sumptuous like the scent of gorse flowers.

With the aching regret that recurred so frequently, I pictured the happiness it would have been to have visited that land in the years of youth, when the first bright apprehensions were undimmed, and to be in love with the world and its life was a day-long rapture and not a faint and fleeting mood. With middle age not far ahead there is nothing to be done except count one's blessings, and a blessing it was to have set foot there, even though one had arrived twenty years late.

When we talked it over afterwards, Kollewijn, the young Controleur Aspirant recently arrived from Holland, agreed with me that of all our halts on the *patroli* that at the tiny rest-house at Baoo was the most delightful.

Picture the confluence of two great highland torrents

against a high background of lavender-coloured castellated
mountains—a skyline like broken bottles, as T. E. Lawrence
would have said. A steep mountainside plunges down to
the joint river, hesitating at the last moment in a narrow
beach of boulders and gently sloping floors of grey rock.
On a little ledge twelve feet above the tortured currents of
golden water stands the *baruga*, tiny, primitive, half ruined.
Forest all along the opposite bank and a lonely canoe moored
there, just a tree-trunk hollowed out and fitted with a single
rough outrigger. No man nor dwelling to be seen anywhere
in all that immensity. Hold your breath and you can hear
the roar of an even greater river, for the newly-formed
torrent sweeping past the *baruga* throws itself into the
Sadang only two hundred yards downstream.

That lonely meeting of the waters was our camp for two
nights. I discovered a childish pleasure in the fact that I
was the only Englishman ever to have seen it.

It was hot at Baoo, because we were no more than five
hundred feet above the sea. That is the lowest point in the
Torajalands. It is warm enough for crocodiles to live beside
these rivers, and a man had been devoured by one in the
spot where I shaved each morning—but that was several
years ago. The crocodiles are few and I didn't see one.
They and the pythons living in the forest are hunted by the
few shy tribesmen inhabiting the hillsides, who sell their
skins to Chinese merchants at markets far across the
mountains.

We were met by a humble young man who told us he was
the acting Ampulembang. " Because our Ampulembang is
in prison in Makale," he explained.

I asked why.

" He listened to the Nationalists, Tuan, and let them
come here. They were bad men. They murdered some of
our people." When I frowned at the thought of the seedy
intrigues of the Nationalist leaders in Java disturbing the
peace of these innocent valleys, he added reassuringly,

" Your policemen will find none now. They have all gone."

It was just in case they had not that the escort had been sent with us.

After supper, which was complicated by a multitude of tiny beetles that fell into the coffee and rained upon the rice like black sequins, I went out and stood by the river in the warm, sumptuous darkness. The waning moon had not risen, but there were rents in the clouds through which archipelagos of yellow stars poured a faint, haunted light. With the coming of darkness the mountains seemed to have grown higher and closed in upon us; I had to lift my head as well as my eyes to see their long embattled line, like a black diadem against the stars.

A group of servants and porters surrounded a man who was drying the head of the hornbill in the smoke of a small fire. A bamboo tube had been thrust up the neck and the vividness of plumage, horn and wattles was dimmed in the blue smoke. I could not help reflecting that the head of a hornbill, carefully preserved, is worn by the youths of many tribes, from Assam to New Guinea, to show that they have recently taken their first human head. . . .

Marura, appearing silently out of the darkness, told me that the hornbill's head was worn in a fertility dance. He was a quiet, shock-headed boy from the doctor's household, who was our cook for the journey. The superior, Christian way in which he spoke of the head broke the spell of flesh-creeping fantasy in which I had been indulging.

Our two mornings at Baoo were warmer than I had been accustomed to in recent weeks. There was a touch of honeymoon languor about rising and drifting down to the rapids of the Masupu river to find the two half-submerged boulders which I used as bathroom fittings, one a support for my mirror, the other a seat as I shaved.

After Dr. Goslinga had returned with his Bible from a

Sunday morning meditation in the steep solitudes above the river and we had eaten fried eggs for breakfast (gruesomely cold, as usual) we set out for the primitive village which serves the district of Baoo for a capital. This entailed crossing the river in the dugout canoe, a small adventure in its way, for the savage currents made it necessary to cross in an irregular arc, shooting suddenly down steep little lanes in the wild waters and climbing painfully towards the beach opposite the *baruga*. Our horses swam well, following the canoe with dramatic, despairing eyes just above the golden flood surface.

A narrow path led us up through torrid forest along the west bank of the Sadang, which pursued its headlong flight southwards three hundred feet below us. Now and then we passed through gates in fences built to protect gardens of maize and cotton from wild pigs, but each acre of cultivation was surrounded by square miles of jungle. I was still seeing new varieties of butterfly almost every hour.

I rode with Kollewijn, who was even more of a newcomer to the East and the Torajalands than I was. But the five-year University course through which a young Dutchman must go before he can secure an appointment as a junior civil officer in Indonesia had sent him out equipped with a thorough knowledge of the Malay language and a full acquaintance with the history, ethnology and complicated traditions of law and religion of the Indonesian archipelago. You would have thought he had served several years as an administrator already.

The village, which we reached after forty minutes' riding, was a poor, humble little place, a pigmy village of tiny cabins clustered along narrow, boulder-paved lanes on a hillock top, the whole smaller than a cricket pitch. Only on one hut was there any trace of traditional ornamentation and that was of childish roughness and uncoloured.

I often thought afterwards of the *guru* there. He was a youth of about twenty, yellow and wasted with chronic

249

malaria, and so lonely that you saw his loneliness as though
it had been a great scar on his face.

" It is difficult here, Tuan, difficult," he sighed to me
after the party had inspected his hut-school outside the
village. He moved close and held my hand after he had
shaken it. " Difficult, Tuan."

" Tuan is from whence? " I asked.

From Rante Bua, he told me, a district several days'
journey from Baoo. He fixed his eyes on my face in childish
expectancy, as though I could help.

" Tuan has no wife? " I asked.

" I cannot marry here," he said, looking round him with
tolerant scorn, as though I had suggested the impossible.
His education and conversion to Christianity had removed
him far from the humble folk of Baoo.

" The last *guru* here ran away," Lete told me when I
spoke of the poor exile later. " It is difficult here, always
alone."

I felt an uneasy twinge as I said good-bye in the afternoon.
The *guru* stood on a boulder as we rode away, looking like a
sick child in hospital watching its parents leave the ward on
visitors' day. I wonder whether he is still there, waging
his daily and nightly battle with sickness, loneliness and
bachelordom. Or has he run away at last, like his pre-
decessor, or been moved to a more congenial post, handing
over Baoo school to a healthy married man?

Under the wide eaves of the village's largest hut Juli had
unpacked his medical stores, working at speed like a cheap-
jack setting up his market stall. Among the two hundred
local people who had come for treatment or just to look on
I saw many sufferers from goitre, and the doctor grouped
half a dozen of the more spectacular cases for me to photograph for use as an illustration to the monograph he intended
to write on goitre and cretinism among the Sadang Torajas.

They were a friendly, good-natured lot, as Torajas are everywhere. They gave us young coconuts to drink and roasted corn. In looks they were definitely inferior to the people of the Rantepao-Makale region, but they had sound, rich skins, unmarked by the subcutaneous scars of boils that are frequent in those more civilised parts. They all wore good white cotton cloth, too, of a fineness seldom seen in La'bo.

Noon was very hot. While the Ampulembang of Ulu Salu told them about the salt that prevented goitre, Dr. Goslinga prepared in a bowl an example of the ration that each individual should get every month and showed it round. "The village chiefs might want to keep back more than their share for their families," he remarked to me. " I want them all to know what they should get, so as to stop that."

It was strange to watch the total lack of self-consciousness among the goitre sufferers. An old dame gossiped away, making what appeared to be lively comments on our party, as though she had never realised the enormous multiple growth under her chin which gave her the appearance of having half swallowed three Jaffa oranges. A young boy with a fine face above a horribly swollen throat was the leader of a group of normal playmates, laughing and carefree.

While Juli packed away the dispensary an election was held. A hamlet in the mountains was in need of a new chief, the old one having reached an age at which it was thought best that he should retire. Thirty men, all the grown men there were in the hamlet, had come down to elect the new chief before the visiting representatives of the government.

The proceedings were vastly more free and democratic than elections ever are in the eastern half of Europe nowadays. The thirty men assembled in a far corner of the village and then advanced one by one to utter the name of their chosen candidate across the bench behind which sat the Controleur Aspirant, Lete and the Ampulembang with recording lists.

"I want whichever one the others voted for," one old man said hoarsely into Lete's ear. When he was told that the votes of the others were secret and he must make his own choice he said, "Then I ask for Sangan. He is old enough."

The result, when the last villager had recorded his vote, turned out to have an Eastern Europe complexion. Sangan had received thirty-one votes and his opponent only one, the one he had himself recorded. Sangan would have had my vote, too. He was an alert, vigorous-looking man with strong hands and a handsome profile. He would have won promotion in any community, I think. His opponent was an apologetic nonentity.

The thick, warm air made us all sleepy and it was that, I think, that almost killed the doctor a few minutes after we left the village. A little crowd of people had assembled on the opposite bank of the Sadang to hold another election. There was a dugout canoe to ferry our party over, but the doctor, yawning, said he would swim across. A few seconds later he entered the water and was immediately swept downstream by a violent current. Feeling that the doctor knew more than I about his strength as a swimmer I was not alarmed at first, but when Julianus began shouting orders to the canoe-man I realised that the situation might be as bad as it looked.

The canoe shot downstream, but the flaxen head now in midstream was far ahead of it. I had the dazed feeling of having been jerked violently out of a deep sleep. Swimmer and canoe were being swept out of sight when we saw a cross-current suddenly throw the doctor at an angle towards the opposite shore, a current through which he could make headway. Thirty seconds later he climbed ashore two hundred and fifty yards downstream from us.

"It was close," he admitted later that afternoon. . . .

Back at the *baruga* a small crowd waited patiently to see him. I recognised some as having been there early in the morning, for whom the dispensary could not be opened before we crossed the river; but cheerful waiting for many hours is characteristic of the Torajas.

Dakopa!—wait! The word was freely used by Juli and the doctor during the trip. *Dakopa!* And with the utmost good nature, inquirers and sufferers would get down on their hunkers to wait for anything up to twelve hours.

Dr. Goslinga, moving among them while once again Juli opened up the dispensary, was a well-remembered friend to many. His quiet voice, speaking fluent Toraja, his excellent manner that was the absence of a manner, his grave simplicity, were most agreeable to witness. There was an easy fatherliness about his heavy figure, bare-legged astride his white horse or bending over a wide-eyed sick child, and however painful one's doubts concerning the all-destroying impact of Western civilisation upon what is valuable and seemly in traditional Toraja life, one was at least thankful for the intervention of Western medicine and its representative in the South Torajalands.

For supper we had a pig, presented by the young *locum tenens* Ampulembang. The *satai*—chunks of pork speared on thin sticks and toasted—were good, but I was less happy about the pig's head which was set down boiled before my plate, blanched but sneering arrogantly. Poor Marura was even less happy, for though he had been a Christian now for many years he had been a Muslim as a child, and his enduring disgust at the thought and smell of pork had made the cooking of our gift an ordeal.

We left before moonset in the morning, for the day would be a long one and it was necessary to let the porters get away to an early start. As we climbed the first stretch, night lingered in the deep Sadang valley while the first red sunbeams struck the crenellated line of the mountain-tops and spilled slowly down their slopes like smouldering lava.

For two hours we climbed the steep path down which we had come two days earlier. Ronni, fresh after almost a whole day's rest, soared like a bird and only began to dawdle when we had passed the summit and moved along level avenues of giant aloes above a deep abyss full of dazzling white cloud. My nose and forearms flinched from the violence of the sun and I wondered what the noonday would be like.

The great boar-hunt of the men of Bua Kayu and Rano, begun at our departure three days before, was still in full swing. From the dizzy slopes above us, as we descended once more to the Sadang, came the echoes of breathless barking and the wild cries that are a little like the laughter of hysterical women. Spearmen crouched at intervals along our path, ready for any pig that might break out of the forest.

We broke our march to rest at the telegraph office at Bua Kayu. As might be expected of a line that stretches across so many miles of wilderness and crag, it is frequently out of order. It was out of order that morning. The grave young operator who came out of the tiny hut, glistening with sweat from head to foot, told us he had spent more than an hour in vain attempts to call Makale.

" *Sa'tengah mati*, Tuan," he said to me, and half dead he looked with the sweat-drops falling from his eyebrows on to his long eyelashes. I was in a similar condition. For an hour I had not used my camera because of the perspiration that splashed into the reflex viewfinder whenever I looked into it.

I started off up the track to Mapa with Julianus.

" Where did Juli get his training? " I asked him.

" Some with the doctor in the hospital at Rantepao," he told me, " and some at college in Java. I got my diploma in Makassar."

When Dr. Goslinga told me later that Juli had been placed first in his year, I asked him whether he thought the boy had it in him to take a medical degree if the chance came his way.

" I am quite sure that he could," was the doctor's reply. That was one of the times when I wished I had some money. A few hundred pounds or dollars to give the Torajas their first Toraja doctor—that would be money well spent; and since this book may come into the hands of some good reader with money, I make the suggestion here. An *adventure* to be able to spend money in that way.

If you stand with your eyes closed in the forests of the Sadang valleys you can almost believe yourself inside a very warm factory in which a huge plant is making immense quantities of delicately scented goods. This is because of the uproar produced by great numbers of unseen cicadas. For their size, these insects must surely be the noisiest form of life.

The ceaseless whirrings and vibrations set up by the Indonesian cicada is apparently a non-stop performance, day and night, except during rain. It hides in small crannies in banks and tree-trunks, and when you approach its hiding-place it will relapse into silence, the pulse of its din falling and slowing just like a turned-off machine. Sometimes the intolerable piling up of tension as one after another joins the chorus at short range induces a sort of aural panic.

By the time we had climbed up to the maize-fields of Mapa (Mapak may be a better spelling), dotted with the tiny thatched shelters of the garden-keepers, I was given over to voluptuous daydreams of food and drink. It was like the old climbing days when similar visions, lascivious in their intensity, had occupied so many hours of the final descents.

Stumbling along dipping, boulder-strewn tracks, leading Ronni and indulging him whenever he paused at a tuft of likely-looking grass, my face and hands burning fiercely and my belly concave, I stared ahead and over and over again imagined myself taking my seat in Ah Ho's friendly little restaurant, striving to make up my mind while tough Ling wiped the bare wooden table and reeled off a list of matchless Cantonese delicacies. " Hallo, sir, what you want? Flied slimps, flied plawns, flied lice, sharksfin soup an' clab meat, galoupa, boiled duck an' honey-ginger sauce, flogs' legs, birdsnest an' walnut. . . ." It is easy enough when you sit at a table supplied by a Cantonese cook to appreciate the dictionary definition of the word " Celestial: " an inhabitant of heaven or China.

And then we were at the *baruga* of Mapa, with Julianus once again unpacking the two huge tins marked WELFARE BISCUITS, and setting the medicines, dressings and instruments out in sparkling array while the smoke of many cooking fires—our fire, the Ampulembang and Lete's fire, the porters' fire, the policemens' fire—curled up through the floor-boards and made us cough as we drank the fresh coconut water the villagers brought us. I was glad to see Ronni led to a heap of maize leaves that reached up to his nose.

All round us was another, yet somehow the same, friendly crowd of quiet, wholesome Toraja folk. Their leader, however, was below standard. The Ampulembang of Mapa was a handsome young man of patently dull wits. As Lete explained how the iodised salt should be collected and stored, he frowned in deep concentration, and made wandering notes on a tiny bit of paper. Again and again he asked for simple directions to be repeated.

In the failing light the doctor and Julianus ministered to a large crowd of mountain folk, while I felt almost too tired to leave my chair. When I did, I was so stiff that I lurched and cracked my head against a hanging lantern. The porters who saw this mishap roared with hearty laughter in the pleasant, uninhibited way of Torajas, whereupon the doctor told me about an eminent missionary who was paying his first visit to a centre of Christian conversion in the Torajalands. He travelled in a car, the warmth of which had made him sleepy. When the car drew up abruptly at the little church outside which the faithful from near and far were waiting to receive him, he woke with a sudden start, on seeing which the crowd broke into a hoot of laughter. He was civilised enough to enjoy the reception.

For myself, I always enjoyed the frank, family-circle laughter with which they greet any minor mishap or droll inadvertency on the part of anybody, whatever his rank.

Most of the next day, which again started for us in moon and starlight, took us through high landscapes that represented Nature nude and relaxed in an amplitude of curves under the equatorial sun's hot gaze. It was astonishing to find miniature settlements of human beings dotted at vast intervals amid those high wastes, and somehow preposterous to pass twice beneath the festoons of the telephone wire which struggled indefatigably across the ranges to Simbuang.

Most of the slopes and summits were covered with thin, exhausted-looking grass, but there were a few woods and some towering slopes and cliffs of smooth rock, with august waterfalls. Several times we passed over high, thatched bridges, and there was one magnificent steel suspension bridge set in a desolate valley across the Masupu, the fine river beside which we had camped at Baoo.

I remember a lonely house we passed that had the year's maize crop stacked neatly up the outer walls, obscuring them completely. Then there was a high crag village, neatly built of rounded boulders on which stood ten wooden cabins, where we found the strongest and sturdiest Torajas I had ever seen. One man, easy and slightly quizzical in his acceptance of us, was a creature of golden magnificence who recalled to me the first Rajah Brooke's description of a pirate chieftain of Borneo: " The Sun was as fine a young man as the eye could wish to rest upon; straight, elegantly yet strongly made, with a chest and neck, and head set on them, which might serve Apollo; legs far better than his of Belvedere."

The village of Makkodo, over the summit of the last

mountain range, I remember for quite another figure. Reyu was not a bit like Apollo. He was sent for after the doctor had had a few words with the chief, and I was asked to be ready to take a photograph.

" I think we will see a cretin now," the doctor said.

For his monograph the doctor needed information on deaf-mutes, mental defectives and cretins, all of which are likely to be found in communities of goitre sufferers. So far we had not seen a real cretin, though there had been a deaf and dumb dwarf girl at Baoo and a mild young idiot called Ebang at Mapa. The parents of such unhappy creatures are naturally enough reluctant to exhibit them.

" Reyu comes," the tough little chief said at last, and we saw him approaching down the steep mountain track.

He was a sorry soul, big-headed and pot-bellied, moving on thin, oddly-jointed legs with the help of a tall staff. With much ado he was composed on a grassy bank, the thin legs giving and dipping strangely as he took off his wide banana-leaf hat and set down his staff. The man who accompanied him helped him with friendly words.

I could see at once that Reyu was not quite what we sought, a true cretin, for Dr. Goslinga had shown me in a book Fodéré's classic description, which includes ". . . *un visage muet, semblable à ces vieilles pièces de monnaie, dont l'usage a effacé l'empreinte.*" Reyu's face was not like that. He was an individual and his little eyes could express pleasure, trust and good will.

" You are not afraid, are you? " the doctor began.

Reyu looked up with a trustfulness that made his eyes somehow unforgetable. He understood most of the doctor's questions and directions, which were helpfully repeated in chorus by the crowd whenever he hesitated. His poor knees were tapped to test his defective involuntary reactions, his large belly was palpated, his muddy feet examined. I had

258

taken him for a young lad, but from what his old father said it appeared that he was about thirty.

While the doctor made notes of his examination I took Reyu's photograph. Every time I looked up I found his eyes on me, waiting for me to smile. The moment I did, his small eyes creased and his mouthful of teeth flashed in an affectionate response, while all the time his thin, crooked fingers scratched wanderingly at his temple.

When all was over he gathered up his staff, balanced the pointed banana-leaf hat on his swollen head and trudged slowly on weak knees up the hill path, moving against a background of the cruel mountains that had doomed him to be born an idiot by feeding his mother starved water while she carried him.

Poor Reyu. . . .

Journey's end for that day was Sima, the capital village of the district of Simbuang. Sima was high and cold, with a big *baruga* that had formerly been a hospital and a Christian church built in the style of a Toraja house beside it. A hedge of pink European roses was blooming between them. We arrived late and soon went shivering to bed, while the Indian Nightingale, dreaded as a bird of ill-omen in many parts of Celebes, threw his loud, spectral cries into the chill night.

Next day was one of steady toil for the doctor and Julianus. As the sun's clear face rose above a grey peak to dispel the cold of night Juli was already furnishing a dispensary under the wide *baruga* eaves. The Ampulembang of Simbuang's steward, wearing a high, fringed *poteh* to show that he was a mourner for a person not yet in his tomb, waited upon us with a silver tray of coffee-cups and a dish of puff-cakes. A bath was an ordeal in the hillside grotto, where scores of ravenous giant mosquitoes attacked the moment you were naked, driving you to the verge of panic.

259

While waiting for breakfast I went across to the church. It should have been a doubly sacred place for the three hundred Christians of Simbuang district, for the Cross took its place among the emblems of Toraja power and veneration—the horned mask of the bull over the door and the cock supreme above the long boat-shaped roof as a weather vane. Inside was a fine example of the beautiful traditional Toraja representation of the sun, surmounted by a Toraja translation of the words, " I am the Light of the World."

There was a green lawn round the long brown ark that is Simbuang's cathedral, with a vivid bougainvillea before the door. The air was very sweet. A poor distraught woman was wandering along the path beyond the church, weeping and occasionally throwing back her head to apostrophise the vivid sky. She stumbled along, moaning, as though lashes were falling across her back.

" Yesterday her son died," a grave schoolboy told me. " Seven days since he came back from a journey, strong and lively and eating much. Then he had the sickness of bloody dung and last night he died. She is mad to-day because she does not know where he has gone."

I reflected that if we had come two days earlier we could have saved the young man's life. . . .

Our doctors' waiting-rooms are not among the gayer social meeting-places, but things are different in the Torajalands. " Make a festival of everything," is the motto there. Let's go down the valley to the doctor and see if he can do away with that old sore on father's foot, and pull out the tooth that gives me hell so many nights. Maybe he can cure that tiresome itch between little Seba's legs as well, and we'll take a couple of small bamboo tubes in case he's giving away any medicine. It'll make a nice day out and everybody's sure to be there! That's how it goes in the outer territories of the Torajas, and I suppose that if we in the West could watch our fellow-sufferers examined and treated as we waited our turn the tedium of dispensaries, surgeries and consulting-rooms would vanish.

It is worth going along to see the doctor in the Toraja country even if there's nothing the matter with you. Alas, far too many of the good folk of Simbuang have things the matter with them, often things that can weaken and disable and blind although cheap and easy cures for them have long been known. This poor schoolgirl, her eyes weeping and already half closed with trachoma that will probably blind her completely in a few more years; that fine youth with the rot of frambœsea already eating into the root of his manhood; that couple with goitre whose next child may be deaf and dumb or half-witted: none of it need happen. A few shillings worth of drugs and no more skill than I have myself could save them all. But there is no hospital now, and the doctor comes to Simbuang for only a few hours every year. I had to sigh again at the thought of the blessings I could bring to these valleys if I were not penniless. What a wonderful way of laying out a little money, to reopen the *baruga* as a hospital and hire a doctor to work there!

It was a day of sparkling gaiety, staunch good nature and black tragedy. The doctor and Juli worked at full pressure for more than eight hours, the doctor in shorts and a pyjama jacket that split all down the back with the tough tempo of the morning. His gentle, unassuming strength and authority, his quiet humour and unhasty speed, were as delightful to watch as the good humour, excitement and *naïveté* of his patients.

As for Julianus, he was a little dynamo, as busy and brisk, as wholesome and charming, as a mother wren with a dozen young to feed. His strong little hands flashed from wound to bandage, from surgical plaster to scabies-scaled baby thighs, from swab to hypodermic. His strong white teeth bit savagely at a cork stopper while a hand wrenched the bottle free and poured a week's medicine into an old woman's bamboo container. The warm mud spurted up between his wide-spaced toes as he hurried round, distributing little screws of paper torn from Japanese military manuals containing enough atebrine tablets for a course of malaria treatment. The long waving black hair fell over his eyes as he passed nimbly down a row of patients lined up with their mouths open, dropping a dose of tonic from a large bottle in each mouth as he went and looking more than ever like a mother wren.

He looked hardly more than a child, but was somewhere in his twenties. One of the nicest people I've known.

It goes without saying that the necessarily incomplete and makeshift nature of his work on such occasions is a sorrow to the doctor. Without growing reconciled to it he has, however, perforce grown used to it through his many years as the only doctor among more than 200,000 tribesmen. During the war he suffered harder frustration in Japanese internment camps, where he was allowed virtually no medicines to treat his sick fellow-prisoners.

The frustrations of a doctor among such simple people are easily appreciated. Sufferers past curing are brought to him again and again, but he seldom has the luck to encounter diseases in their vulnerable youth. Courses of treatment that do not yield early or striking results are seldom persisted in, unless the patient can be kept under observation. The amount of responsibility he can safely delegate to the orderlies who assist him is always a problem, and year by year cherished schemes for improved medical services have to be postponed or curtailed

There is, however, endless inspiration in the volume of solid, beneficial work that can be done There is consolation in freedom from the fate of so many doctors at home, who spend time and energy in keeping old, unhappy, finished people alive or striving to heal with medicine the horde of mean and seedy psychological ills characteristic of our warped and overstrained civilisation.

For hours the crowd grew. Shy people from the higher mountain slopes. The commanding Ampulembang with his pock-marked face and gold teeth. Sixty school children, the boys' heads shaven, the little girls with wild gipsy locks, all chorusing a harsh, military *"Tabe, Tuan-Tuan!"* and softening to gentle curiosity afterwards. Vaccinations, inoculations, tooth extractions, scabies lotion applications, wound dressings, yaws injections, distribution of pills and medicine . . . until the sun went down the pace never slackened. One or two sick ones were urged to make the long, hard journey to Makale, where they would be received in the little hospital. For a few nothing at all could be done.

One of these last was a young woman brought on a litter borne by her husband and a kinsman. Her weakness was so extreme that you held your breath as you looked at her. The humble, sweating husband replied to the questions his wife was too exhausted to answer. They were expecting too much; that was at once plain.

" Rheumatic fever," Dr. Goslinga told me, and he quoted an English authority's observation: " It licks at the joints, but bites at the heart."

That poor mountain woman's heart had been all but bitten out. The doctor sighed. The journey to Makale or Rantepao, where in any case there was little that could be done for her, would almost certainly kill her. He gave the husband some vitamin pills so that they should not go home empty-handed.

And last of all, when the sun was down and the crowd gone and we were ready for supper, the quiet man who had sat all day apart under the rose hedge came forward.

" It is always the same," the doctor said to me. " The lepers are always ashamed. They like to come alone."

He was a good-looking man, with deep, intelligent brown eyes and a length of creeper binding his long black hair.

With a splinter of bamboo he was scraping roughly at a deep hole in the sole of his foot, excavating a quantity of black detritus. There was obviously no feeling left in that part of his body. The doctor showed me his hands, with their swollen and almost black knuckles and wristbones. For him there was little hope, either.

The white man invited him to his leper hospital at Rantepao, without holding out any bright hopes. To me he said that of seven lepers he had believed cured and sent back to their homes on the coming of the Japanese, two had died of leprosy before the Japanese surrender, and every one of the remaining five had been reinfected.

With an inconclusive, apologetic smile the leper went slowly away down the path by the roses.

We had reached the farthest point of the *patroli*. At first light in the morning we turned back. Lete bought a bouncing black and white puppy, which wailed dismally with homesickness as he was carried high into the mountains above his native valley. We met the poor bereaved mother again, stumbling through diadem bracken and white azaleas, calling upon us and the cliffs and the waterfalls and the chestnut cuckoos to give back her son.

Back at Makkodo the tough little *kepala* who looked like a Tartar chieftain awaited us with three or four score of his tribe. We had breakfast of fried rice and part of the pig the Prince of Simbuang had given us (poor Marura!) in the delightful miniature *baruga*, with doors only five feet high, floors and walls of heavy rough-hewn timber, the carved mask of some indeterminate beast above the entrance and not a single nail from roof-tree to piles.

Reyu was there, ready with a wide smile whenever I turned his way, and a portly small boy who wore his rough sarong like a toga, with all the dignity of a Roman senator. His smile was amusing and I was instrumental in getting him some of the rose-pink cough medicine he had set his heart on as well as the malaria pills he needed. (Numbers of patients would point out their preferences among the rows of medicaments. Worms might be their trouble, but if lung tonic looked nice it was lung tonic they wanted.)

The lovely pre-Raphaelite girl whose profile I had recorded on a film that had later jammed in the camera did not turn up again, to my great disappointment. There were two men wearing hats carved out of solid blocks of wood; they were light and took three days to make, so they told me. Some tribesmen wanted the dried hornbill's head that nodded above one of the porters' packs. They seemed to hold it in considerable reverence and wanted it badly.

Juli, lancing the tiny poisoned thumb of a small girl who reminded me of Mina, could not avoid hurting her for all his skill and gentleness. He smiled understandingly while she screamed and beat his face, and her diminutive, stamping feet raised a little cloud of dust.

Up over the summit again and down into the great valley of waterfalls to cross the wide, runaway river, with my cameras clutched to my breast and my feet held parallel with Ronni's wild eyes, while Sesa, stripped naked, led us safely through the deep rapids. On the other side I shaved and bathed, having funked the man-eating mosquitoes of the Sima grotto before our early start.

Balepe (which means " cockroach ") was our halt for the night, its capital village set on cliff-tops high above a majestic western landscape. A cold wind tore the banana leaves to tatters and gave the cream pampas plumes no rest. By lamplight the doctor and Juli went to work again, patient with the patient crowd of sick tribes-people. Two slaves brought a squealing pig lashed to a bamboo pole, the gift of the Ampulembang of Balepe, and the unhappy Marura, sick and revolted, set faithfully about cutting it up as soon as it was dispatched and cooking our share.

As we drank milky *tuak* with the friendly *parenge*, he told us how he had been obliged to stand behind the officer's chair when a Japanese patrol visited the district, helping him to the food and wine looted from him and his people.

Our last night in the mountains was hardly enough to restore our energy for the long, final stretch to Rembon. I remember little of the grilling up-and-down journey, and Dr. Goslinga, who had worked for long hours day after day while I sat idly by, looked all-in. But the admirable, the almost incredible Julianus seemed as fresh as a daisy, singing as he strode on fast, nimble feet up and down the steep, cruel paths or balanced with feet a yard and a half apart on the great mattress surmounting his dirty white horse.

It was over at last, perhaps the best of all the journeys of my life. Good-bye, Ronni, staunch little beast. Good-bye, nice Sesa and poor, bilious Marura. Good-bye, patient porters, changing almost daily and always remaining anonymous. Good-bye, for the moment, to the doctor; to young Kollewijn, who is lucky to share in the administration of such good people; to the pleasant young Toraja leaders, Lete and the Ampulembang of Ulu Salu; to the carefree, singing policemen, too. Good-bye to those mountains and valleys of Eden and may God bless and prosper the good folk who live among them.

"And good-bye, Juli," I said. "It has been good."

A smile flashed across his thin, alert face.

"Seven days—three pigs, Tuan!" he grinned.

For a Toraja there could hardly be greater approbation.

XII

THEIR BETTERS

OF Toraja society the *Encyclopædia Britannica* reports that there are no social distinctions and no tribal chiefs. "There are no social distinctions and no tribal chiefs," echoes the *British Government Manual of Netherlands India*; or is it, perhaps, that the former echoes the latter?

South Toraja society is grouped into four main castes. First come the *puangs*, a very small caste which has for some centuries provided the tribal chiefs of the three districts of Sangalla, Makale and Menkendek. Below them come the *to'madika* and *to'parenge*, from which caste the present *ampulembangs* are drawn. Next there are the *to'makaka*, gentry and yeomen whose forebears were sometimes freed bondsmen. The lowest caste is the great mass of *kaunans*, who include the slaves freed forty years ago by the Dutch.

A reigning *puang* must always, of course, be a man of *puang* rank, but he need not be a full *puang* (that is to say, one whose parents were both of royal rank) and he need not necessarily be a son of the preceding Puang. Within limits he is an elected chief.

It is not known, for instance, who will be the next Puang of Sangalla. So' Rinding, the present Puang, has three sons, of whom the two elder ones are definitely out of the running for the succession. Popang, the eldest, offended against Toraja morality by committing adultery with a married woman and later divorced his wife without paying the customary indemnity of twenty-four bulls required of men of his class. He served six months in Makale jail for his misdeeds and is now married to a beautiful school teacher.

Popang can never be Puang of Sangalla. No more can his brother Palayukan, who has also done six months in the prison at Makale. He lost his temper and struck a slave, knocking out some of his teeth. Evil temper is regarded with horror by the Torajas, and there can now be no question of his succeeding his father.

The *Puang Lolo* of Sangalla, the " Young Puang," is an agreeable and good-looking man, the spitting image of my Sergeant Ashwell in the 94th, but a little dull-witted according to some of the local gentry. Whether he was, in fact, the Puang's son I never discovered. Certainly he was not a legitimate son. " A woman gave him to me, Tuan," the old Puang told me, but whether the implication was that he had enjoyed a casual relationship with the woman I could not decide. I took it for granted at first that Sergeant Ashwell (as I called him, for I had difficulty in pronouncing his name) would become the next Puang, but I became aware of tension when I mentioned this assumption one day. He smiled without saying anything, but the smith and certain other artisans and slaves of the princely household collected round me and said emphatically that yes, he would be the Puang and any other proposal was bad. " He will be our Puang, Tuan! "

Others, including Kalasuso, told me that the Puang's third son, he who was slapped down by Peter Palinggi in a tribal fight at school, was considered to be shaping well as a future Puang. He is, moreover, the only candidate whose mother was also of *puang* rank. I was favourably impressed by him. He is modest, sturdy and balanced, and should make a good Puang. In fact, I should have been better pleased if he had slapped down Peter Palinggi.

The Puang of Sangalla, a stout old gentleman in his sixties, is the leading Toraja personage. His shrewdness

and unusual intelligence are not particularly evident at a
first encounter; they were not, at least, to me.

News that he was ill postponed my first call on him. Then
I heard that a little boy in Sangalla had dreamed that a
certain leaf, applied to the Puang's lumbago (if that is what
it was) would bring strong relief. A little later news came
that a wizard, with the assistance of the child who had
dreamed, had succeeded in finding the magical leaf and
that it had worked a cure.

The old man did not, however, look so good when Dr.
Goslinga and I called on him shortly afterwards. Wrapped
in a black robe, he received us for only a few moments,
pleading indisposition. I was disappointed, but he was
himself again when I went to pay my respects to the body
of his mother. He also was visiting the cliff-top house of the
dead princess and advanced to greet me through the violet
smoke rising from the fires over which the departed lady's
luncheon was cooking. The long nails of his thumb and
little finger, marks of high rank, cut into my flesh as we
shook hands. He was wearing an amethyst shirt, a black
sarong and one of those pink knitted helmets very small
European children wear in cold weather. He was fat, the
only really fat Toraja I ever saw, with enormous broad feet
and hands and *café-au-lait* eyes splayed outwards. He looked
as though he had done himself rather too well for forty years
or more.

Under one rice-barn a goldsmith was preparing gold leaf
to decorate the coffin for the death-feast, the date of which
I hastened to inquire from the Puang, receiving another of
the long series of vague answers I was growing used to. I
sat with him on the platform before the big house, and
Sergeant Ashwell, who is the local complex chief and acts
as the Puang's deputy, joined us shortly afterwards, wearing
a handsome beaded *poteh* round his crisply waving hair.
Conversation was easy once I got used to the Puang's swift
transitions from subject to unrelated subject. He addressed

me throughout as *Tuan besar*, literally "Big Sir," an extremely polite form of address. His voice was as fat as his figure and I kept wishing he would clear his throat.

In England had we rice, buffaloes, coconuts, pigs? In the war had the *tuan besar* fought in airplanes or on the earth? When the *tuan besar* had finished taking photographs of the Toraja country would he present him with one of his Kodaks? As English pigs were so much bigger and more prolific than Toraja swine would the *tuan besar* be good enough to send him an English he-pig in an airplane on his return? In that way the Sangalla she-pigs would farrow larger families of bigger pigs. Which were largest, the pigs of England, Holland, America or Australia? The people of Islam were truly bad people; in what countries outside Indonesia and Arabia were they to be found? And what was the English name for these (my field-glasses)? Feedassen? Indeed! *Wah*, his house was only a few steps away! And how many kilometres into the sky could the feedassen see? Ah! Was there much rice in Russia? Maize, then? Why were there no coconuts in Canada? *So* cold? Cold could *kill* a man? How old was the *tuan besar*? Ah, young. Young. He was old. Sixty-four years. He had been Puang for forty years. Could the *tuan besar* send a black he-pig in an airplane from England? Why had the *tuan besar* not brought his airplane with him? . . .

Under the house at our backs was tethered the fat black bull which on the night of the old noblewoman's death three years previously had been renamed Tandirapasan and tied there, to remain there through the moons and years until the days of the final death-feast, and to be sacrificed last of all the sacrificial bulls just as the coffin was finally carried from the feast-field to the tomb. Now he had only a few more weeks to live. And in the house above waited the *to'ma'aparandan*, who kept a similar vigil. She greeted me shortly afterwards, her pale face unsmiling under a fringed black *poteh*. She was the dead lady's daughter and could not leave her mother's body, any more than the dedicated bull Tandirapasan could leave the shelter of the house, until the time came for the progress to the tomb.

The Puang's mother was enclosed in a cylindrical coffin covered with lilac silk and decorated with silver. The pale *to'ma'aparandan* crouched beside it. Slaves lifted several smouldering black bamboo tubes from the fires and followed us up into the house, where Sergeant Ashwell split the bamboos open with his sword. Chopped pork and vegetables were collected from them in silver bowls and the black-shawled recluse presented them gravely to the lilac cylinder.

A wizard said a prayer and we were all silent for a moment, and then, rather disconcertingly, the bowls were withdrawn and the luncheon the dead princess had declined was tipped on to china plates and handed to the Puang and me. We sat together on a bunk in one of the two tiny end chambers of the house, our legs dangling as we swallowed the cubes of fat pork. A score of the corpse's slaves and attendants, some of them roused from sleep, shared the remainder of the meal.

A silly but amusing old man I thought the Puang that first day, but on subsequent occasions I found him keen-witted and to the point. He has long enjoyed a high reputation as a diplomat and he was for years the leader of the Torajas in their negotiations with the Dutch and with the coastal rajahs of whom the South Torajas were, until recently, to some extent vassals. He is not a Christian, though he has, so I was told, made prolonged examination of the Christian dogma, putting shrewd questions to those who sought to convert him. By a very large proportion of South Torajas he is regarded as the chief repository of Toraja tradition.

He seemed to me to add up to a great deal more than the two other Puangs put together. Andilolo, Puang of Makale, is young, small and Christian. He always wears Western dress, so that on one state occasion I mistook him for somebody's chauffeur. I never knew him very well, so my rather poor opinion of him may be entirely mistaken.

I met the Puang of Menkendek only once. He has the appearance of an autocrat. By a missionary I was told that he " had been " a Christian.

The castes of the *to'madika* and the *to'parenge* have differences between them not easily perceptible to Western minds. Members are said to owe their rank to the circumstance of their ancestors having been the first family to settle in a new locality. The first house in a hitherto uninhabited place became the *tongkonan*, the temple of the community that later grew round it and the scene of many ceremonies, and the head of that household was thereafter the local leader and interpreter in all matters of *adat*—that is, of all questions concerning custom, tradition and tribal law.

In recent years the South Torajalands have been divided into twenty-nine districts, each of which is represented in the government of the province by an Ampoe Lembang (or Ampulembang, as I have ventured to Anglicise it), a title invented by the Dutch. The *parenge* of each district is normally the Ampulembang. In certain instances one Ampulembang may represent two districts. Sangalla, Makale and Menkendek are, of course, represented by their Puangs.

I did not like our representative in La'bo, who was Sesa Tandirerung, Ampulembang of Kesu. He was a rich little man with two wives, a long row of rice-barns, enormous rice-fields and fish-ponds, and a great herd of bulls. He was a Christian, a miser and something of an oppressor. His district was one of the richest of all.

A much more pleasant person was Tira Kombolangi (the Builder of Heaven), Ampulembang of Tikala. I would not

Loedia

Left to Right: Friend, Acquaintance, Stranger

call him open-handed, but his personality was agreeable and I enjoyed his visits to me and mine to him. The very wealthy young Ampulembang of Nanggala, with the long hair and romantic profile of a stage Bohemian, was a welcome visitor, and I enjoyed my acquaintance with the Ampulembang of Ulu Salu and Malimbong. But outstanding among them all was Sarungu, Ampulembang of Pangala, a man of powerful personality, keen intelligence and delightful humour.

The alpine road this admirable ruler built before the war to link his district with Tikala and Rantepao is a most impressive achievement. It was hardly finished when the Japanese came. As soon as the news was confirmed, he ordered his men to destroy the bridges and concentrate secret dumps of wood in the forest. To the Japanese he played the rôle of a weak ruler, unable to ensure his people's compliance with their orders. His men had all fled into the forest, he would say; there were none at hand to fell and prepare all the timber they demanded. When the Japanese surrendered, the men of Pangala re-erected the bridges to link up the daring road which no Japanese vehicle had ever been able to use.

Sarungu's strong, deeply pock-marked face would shine with animation as he talked, mimicking the exasperation of the Japanese officers and N.C.O.s who found it so difficult to exploit Pangala as they had planned. He told me of the ceremony of homage planned by the Japanese to Pong' Tiku, hero of the Torajas' last resistance to the Dutch and a member of Sarungu's family. The warrior's tomb is not far from the capital village of Pangala, guarded by a swarm of ferocious bees. This heavy-footed effort to win the favour of the subjected was no more successful than other efforts of occupying forces to ingratiate themselves with the population: the Germans in Prague, for example, or the Russians in Berlin. And for the same reason: because the occupying forces were stealing all their food. The men of

Pangala honour the memory of Pong' Tiku, but they feared, despised and distrusted the Japanese too much to want to pay homage at his tomb in their company. The occasion was a flop.

Sarungu was one of the earliest Toraja *gurus* and later the chief of a village complex. He, like the Prince of Menkendek, *was* a Christian; but he incurred the displeasure of the missionaries when he decided to have two wives. The Prince of Kesu is tolerated in the Christian fold with his two wives because, a representative of the missions told me, the *adat* of Kesu permits plural marriage; but the *adat* of Pangala forbids polygamy, and the white missionaries decided they were justified in imposing a ban amounting to semi-excommunication upon Pangala's prince. He thereupon declared that he would not tolerate interference with his private life and that he would permanently cut himself off from the faith to which he had been converted. He has not, however, returned to the faith of his fathers.

Kalasuso, the Ampulembang of Bunt'ao, I liked very much. He is not one of the strongest Toraja rulers, but there can be no doubt about his sincerity, his devotion and his hard work. Indeed, it seemed to me that all the Ampulembangs I knew worked hard, particularly those holding high positions in the new scheme of Toraja government, about which it is time I said a few words.

Before the war Dutch rule in the South Torajalands was, strictly speaking, neither direct nor indirect. In effect it was direct, but so far as possible law was administered through the chiefs, and the ancient loyalties of the people to the various princely houses was undisturbed. This did not always suit the Torajas, however, for some of their chiefs were vassals of the Kings of Luwu, hated Muslim Buginese rulers who lived on the coast. It irked them to receive the most reasonable orders when they were signed by their ancient enemies and oppressors, from whose depredations the coming of the Dutch had delivered them.

Now that is ended.

The South Torajalands are now a tiny and remote unit of East Indonesia, the new dominion which comprises Celebes, Bali and the other Lesser Sunda Islands and the Moluccas, with its Balinese president and its parliament in Makassar. The rôle of the Dutch is now that of partner, and during my stay in Celebes the Controleur of Makale, Mr. J. M. van Lijf, was completing his important task of building up a new administration for the province in partnership with the princes and the people's chiefs. From what I could see he had already won a large measure of success in his enterprise.

The effective instrument of the government of the South Torajas is now the *tongkonan adat*, which is largely his creation. *Tongkonan* properly means a tribal house or temple; *adat* is the massed wisdom, custom, belief and law of the race. The *tongkonan adat* is an assembly comprising the three Puangs and the Ampulembangs of Pangala, Tikala, Nanggala, Kesu, Mandandan, Ulu Salu and Bua Kayu. This council of ten, advised by the Controleur, is a sort of cabinet, with certain individuals undertaking leadership in certain spheres; the Ampulembang of Pangala, for instance, might be called the Minister of Health.

Once every moon all the twenty-six Ampulembangs and the three Puangs assemble in Makale with the Controleur and his assistants to deliberate for one or two days. The decisions taken then are communicated to the various complex and village chiefs during the following days, and further assemblies of the lesser chiefs are held before the monthly meetings, so that suggestions and appeals can be received for possible discussion at Makale. The members of the *tongkonan adat* have to sustain duties in the provincial government as well as the routine work of governing their own districts, which comprises a daily round of routine office work, tours of inspection and the administration of justice.

Persons accused of law-breaking are dealt with by village or complex chiefs, the Ampulembang or the Controleur, according to the gravity of the alleged offence. Appeal against an award can be carried up by stages to the highest officers of the administration. Among the honest, biddable Torajas there is not much law-breaking.

Taxation is based, in most areas, on the rice harvest. The *tongkonan adat* decides the sum to be required of each district, and public meetings are held at which the rate of the year's tax in each village is decided. There is often much adjustment of sums. Appeals against tax demands can be carried by stages to the government itself at Makale.

Of one thing I am certain. It would be a disaster if the Torajas were to be granted complete independence at this stage. There is no doubt that the great mass of *kaunans* would get no good out of self-government, and in the districts where the Ampulembang and his fellow-nobles are grasping they would be far worse off. Any withdrawal of the Christian medical mission would obviously be a heavy loss.

The brother-in-law of the Puang of Sangalla, a complex chief, was in Makale Jail while I was in Celebes, convicted of extortion. I am not confident that he would have been imprisoned and deprived of his chieftianship by a *tongkonan adat* which was not prodded by a controleur from time to time.

But if the Dutch withdrew altogether from Celebes it is unlikely that even the nobles would benefit in the end. The Buginese of the coast, who for centuries before the final intervention of the Dutch ceaselessly raided the Torajas for slaves and tribute and resent their lost dominion over the " heathen dogs," would make a strong bid to enslave them. In the unsettled period between the Japanese administration there were massacres of the poor Torajas in the area of Palopo and elsewhere.

A newcomer is puzzled by the mixture of autocracy and democracy he observes among the Torajas. The free-and-easy companionship of masters and slaves, the pleasant name given to the freed slaves—the *to'makaka* or big brothers; the different castes joking and eating together, all this suggests a democracy that shames our own. The impression is true only in a limited sense, for there are contrasts between Toraja rich and poor as great as any in Victorian England.

The rich are so few, however, that their dispossession could help only a very few of the poor. The Torajalands themselves are poor and it seems that little can be done to relieve their poverty. The Controleur's scheme for the afforestation of half a million square kilometres of the barren moors and slopes of Pangala will begin to bring in a little wealth from the outside world in fifteen or twenty years' time in exchange for boxwood, turpentine and cellulose. A little choice coffee is exported, rattan, dammar and snake-skins from the forest, and that is all.

Every Toraja, if he is not a slave, owns land. But his land may be one little rice-field and a small garden and thicket of bamboo near his house; or it may be less than that, merely an area of a wild mountain slope, perhaps mostly rock, or some of the rotting pink soil that is stolen by every rainfall.

Slaves are better off than poor free men. Their food is assured them. I refer to the slaves who continue their service to their masters despite the fact that they have been free from birth if they are less than forty years old. According to Toraja *adat* many prominent citizens are still slaves, and ceremonial tribute or duties may be claimed of them

WHITE STRANGER

on certain occasions. In Sangalla the richest man is the slave of a slave!

Slavery was a misfortune into which almost anybody might fall in the old days. A Toraja gambler, for instance, quite frequently wagered himself into slavery. Losing heavily, he would stake his clothes, his fields, even his bulls. When all was lost he would often stake his person against the return of some substantial part of his losses. If he lost that game he became the slave of the winner.

This happened frequently in the old days, and the wily Buginese " won" thousands of slaves in this way by slick cheating. So honest in payment are the Torajas that a man's friends would not intervene, nor would he struggle, when the Muslim victor put a rope round his neck and led him away.

The gesture of respect observed by punctilious slaves and *kaunans* towards their betters is a bending of the knees and the extension of stiff arms and fingers almost to the ground. It was seldom that anybody did this while passing me, but whenever it did happen it gave me the creeps. I always wanted to exclaim with Lady Bracknell, " Rise, sir, from this semi-recumbent posture! "

It is a more general sign of respect when meeting a person of rank on the road to remove your hat or fillet, whether you are man or woman, and lower your sarong to your waist if you are a man. If you are on horseback you should dismount. A bow is the greeting of respect.

It is considered impolite for a *kaunan* to overtake a noble on the road. I had continually to gesture people forward, and if I rested on a bridge the shyer wayfarers would not pass across unless I signalled leave.

The young people were generally more free and easy, but I saw no sign of the bad manners and insolence charged against the Christianised African.

278

The *to'mina* are not an hereditary caste, but most Torajas consider them their betters. I have called them wizards, because most of their activities consist in the wielding of magic; but I might have called them priests, for they are also the appointed intercessors between the people and the *deata*.

A *to'mina* learns his mysteries by serving an apprenticeship with an old *to'mina*. There is one in most villages and sometimes two. They use in their rituals an esoteric language not understood by the laity, with the exception of certain senior chiefs. They can be asked to make a large variety of sacrifices, to officiate at a number of festivities, to share out the beef of sacrificed bulls at death-feasts, to interpret dreams and to cure illness.

Sapondama, the wizard of Karatuan, was a good old man. He kept a little aloof from me, as though it would be unbecoming of him to betray much interest in a representative of rival systems of belief. He never showed the slightest sign of a feeling of inferiority to the white stranger and his famous medicine chest, and I liked him for that.

Each market day an extraordinary figure minced past our gate on its way to Rantepao. This was the *burakke* of Tokesan, the priest-priestess of the *ma'bugi* feasts, the mysterious vestal of the harvested rice-fields. Slender fingers rested delicately on the ribbon of the large hat, the blouse had the choking-tight short sleeves so loved by Toraja women, the sarong was bunched in a feminine fashion at the waist. At the moment of passing the gate the dark eyes slid sideward for a flashing glimpse of me on the veranda, as did the eyes of most girls who passed.

" Up to here," Kalo'udun informed me one morning, pointing to his navel, " it is a man. Above that it is a woman."

I had a good look at the *burakke* once or twice, however,

and I am sure he was no hermaphrodite, but merely a sexual invert. It is not unusual for persons of that type to fill positions of importance and be held in some respect among preliterate peoples, and somewhat similar priestly pansies are found in other parts of Celebes. In some places they marry men and set up house with them; in others they even bathe in the women's bathing-pool.

I could trace only three surviving *burakke* of that kind. Those in Tikala were genuine women, performing the same priestly duties after the rice harvest. They were also essential to the great *ma'bua* feasts that seem now to have become extinct, but they may not take any part in a death-feast. I was told that at the death-feast of a *burakke* the normal death-dances can on no account be performed, but the *ma'bugi* is danced instead.

One day I said to Massang, " Would you not like to become a *burakke*? " I did not say it entirely as a joke, for though I had noted no signs of sexual noncomformity about the child, he was of a mystical turn of mind, ever conscious of the invisible beings that shared the village with us, and it crossed my mind that such a career, with its considerable tributes of rice, might raise him from the poverty that seemed so inescapably his lot—that is, if belief in the powers of the *burakke* should last his lifetime.

But Massang looked back at me gravely.

" Only the *deata* can make a *burakke*," he said.

Though some villagers were inclined to smile a little when the Tokesan *burakke* was mentioned, it was plain that he was deeply respected. The smiles were the expression of incomprehension. A complex chief who had been his comrade in childhood tittered slightly when I mentioned him.

" We were bull grooms together, Tuan," he said. " When we were first ripe he was my friend. And then he became a *burakke*. I could not understand it, Tuan."

" The *burakke* can walk along tight-ropes when he

280

carries his snakeskin tambourine," said Massang. " He can get into the pot of rice when it is cooking. He does no work; he has a boy to look after him. We do not laugh at him. If we laughed he would be angry. Yes, Tuan, if the *burakke* were angry with me I should be afraid."

The word *guru* has an honoured ancestry. It is Sanskrit and means " grave," but for two millennia it has been the title of the spiritual teachers of the Hindus. Its use has spread far through the East, and to-day it is the universal name for schoolmasters in Malaysia.

The class of schoolmasters wields immense power in the Toraja country. It is hardly too much to call them the new ruling class, for apart from their influence on the younger generation of Torajas they tend more and more to become village chiefs and eventually capture higher positions in the administration. More and more, I suppose, the keener intelligences and more pushing characters among young Torajas tend to become *gurus*. In many cases the youth who forty years ago would have been the tribe's finest warrior is to-day a *guru*, the leading enemy of Toraja culture in his village.

The small class of *gurus* known as *guru injil* are evangelists. Palinggi is one of them. In general, however, *Tuan guru* means the schoolmaster.

I could never overcome a certain distaste for the school-masters; and this despite their many undeniable good qualities. They worked hard. They were honest. Every one of them I met was earnestly convinced that he was improving the children under his care. Sometimes, like the poor young man at Baoo, they made considerable sacrifices to carry on their work. With the gruesome exception of music, they seemed to teach efficiently. Most were re-spected, and some loved, by their pupils. And several of them showed me kindnesses.

None of them (and I speak of the Toraja ones, not the older Menadonese *gurus* who remain from the earlier days of Western education in the Toraja country) was in the least degree conscious of treachery to his own blood. All believed that the Toraja ways were bad and contemptible, and the white man's ways good and necessary. All wore white man's clothes to a large extent, lived in houses that approached the design and structure of white men's houses, sat on chairs and never danced. The cultural anæmia from which they suffered was repulsive.

Of Christian humility they seemed never to have heard, but this vital betrayal of their new faith is not necessarily a charge against the white missions. Converts from simpler cultures the world over are prone to exhibit the extremes of spiritual arrogance and Toraja teachers are no exception.

Not one Western teacher in fifty would tolerate the conditions under which most Toraja schoolmasters do their work. The village schoolhouses are usually large, mud-floored sheds with *atap* roofs and basketwork walls and partitions. They are neat and kept in structural repair by the pupils. Sometimes they are surrounded by gardens with (of course) European flowers. Usually there are three classes and the house is partitioned into two class-rooms with two teachers. But however many class-rooms there may be, there is always one more class than there are rooms, so one class is free at any given time, swimming in the paddy-fields or playing in groups or more often eavesdropping through the basket walls on one of the classes in session.

Most instruction is oral and full-throated, the class reciting in unison after the *guru* or shouting back unison answers to his questions. When both classes are under oral —or choral—instruction, with only a wicker wall between them, the din is formidable. Conditions in the high schools of Makale and Rantepao, however, come closer to European standards.

The chief difference between a Toraja school and any

Western school I ever came across is that Toraja teachers love teaching and Toraja children love learning. The short holidays are not much looked forward to. A walk of four or five miles to school, rising in the dark to be ready for it, is cheerfully accepted as normal by hundreds of pupils. As for the *guru's* influence, it is usually greater than that of any but the most outstanding of English housemasters. They are empowered to inflict as much corporal punishment as they please, and one told me that beating was an aid to learning, though it seemed to me an aid that was seldom resorted to immoderately. Only a minority of the scholars actually become Christians, but allegiance to their own way of life is in every case considerably undermined.

I did my best to overcome my distaste for the *gurus*, recognising that it was partly sentimental—it is not, after all, as if there were any hope for the survival of Toraja culture. But people ashamed of their origins never seem quite wholesome to me, and, besides, I had found so much in those origins that seemed to me good.

XIII

SETTLED IN

THREE months before going to La'bo I wrote in my diary: "It will be a step in the dark, and what comes after won't always be easy. I can't hope to feel at home in a few weeks with people who are separated from me and mine by millennia of time and 10,000 miles of space."

When it came to comparing expectation with realisation my own anticipations proved to have been as misleading as the works of reference I had consulted. In no time at all, and entirely without effort, I had become even more thoroughly at home in La'bo than I was usually aware of.

After only a week or two I lost all consciousness of the main differences between myself and the other villagers. Despite early language difficulties I never found myself up against walls of hopeless spiritual incomprehension as I had sometimes in contacts with Germans and Russians. Even the crude physical differences between us quickly passed from my consciousness; I was nine inches taller than any other man in La'bo, but I was aware of that only for an odd minute in the day or week, and it was *my* face in the shaving-mirror and *my* limbs in the bathing-booth that now and then seemed to me strangely coloured.

The people of La'bo remained a crowd to me no longer than a corresponding white community would have done; maybe not for so long.

Most of my days were spent in gossip. Every evening I wrote up the day in my diary, incorporating a mass of detail picked up at different times during the day and noted on bits of paper. But without scientific training the collection

284

of data on tribal life is a complicated business. By the time I had been three months in La'bo the earlier pages of my diary had become a tangle of deletions and corrections.

Of course, mine was idle, amateur exploration of my neighbours' lives, undertaken just for love. But it was at least serious enough to rouse in me new admiration for those who give us scientific accounts of far-away civilisations. I know now how their informants provide them with conflicting information, how their early deductions have often to be slowly abandoned in the face of new discoveries, and, worst of all, how bewildering it is when they find their informants' practice diverging from their preaching.

Amateurs who try to learn something of an alien way of life in a short time find themselves at sea over a multitude of everyday mysteries. Take, for example, the trouble I had with the Toraja words for "thank you," *kurre sumanga*, which mean literally "call back your soul." Nobody in La'bo offered an acceptable explanation, though they all disdained my theories. I thought I might be on the track the morning a woman from Tambunan whose small child fell down our back steps exclaimed, " *Kurre sumanga!* " The shock of the fall, I reasoned, could have jolted the child's soul from her body, a likely enough mishap for a Toraja soul, and in alarm the mother had uttered the formula to call it back. But why should the words mean " thank you? " Both Kalasuso and Salu, however, insisted that the woman had merely expressed thanks and relief that the child hadn't hurt itself.

Later, when I had learned a little more about the Toraja soul, I decided that the phrase must derive from the individual's constant anxiety to conserve the full quantity of his personal supply of soul. The reluctance of children in the wilder parts to tell me their names reflected, I considered, an old belief that to give me their names was to surrender a fraction of their identity, of their soul. To give away something personal and intimate was to surrender portions of the soul to a possible enemy who could work evil magic with it; therefore, when a well-disposed person received anything from the hands of another he went out of his way to renounce all claim to the fragments of soul that might adhere to the gift. " Call back your soul," he would say.

None of my Toraja friends would agree with this interpretation, but I believe it may be true. At the same time, if I were writing an authoritative work on the Torajas, I can picture the long and exhausting research that would probably be required to authenticate such a theory.

My quest of the Toraja nose-flute provides a somewhat ridiculous illustration of the pitfalls yawning before the amateur investigator.

" The Torajas have a nose-flute, like certain of the Borneo Dyaks," I noted in my diary for February the sixth after a pleasant evening of gossip with Salu, Palimbong and Barra. " Have ordered Salu to fix a command performance, which he says may be difficult. Its use is dying out, I suppose. Its name is *karume*."

Some time later I asked Salu whether he had yet found a *karume* player for me. He laughed and said not yet. Then, one day at Pangala, when Salu was telling me about Toraja humour and particularly the ill-natured *masimba* popular with the smart young men of Sadan who use it to score off simpler tribesmen, he said there was also, of course, the kind of joking called *karume*.

" Like the nose-flute, Tuan," he said, smiling broadly.

That night I had to enter in my diary: " *Karume* (see Feb. 6) is not a nose-flute but a word meaning, roughly, nonsense. It is a form of joke played by old men on children or guileless strangers. Usually anatomical and often sexy. The two nostrils are the bamboos of the nose-flute. A witless form of humour, a little like our old-fashioned riddles." When everybody laughed at me for being caught by Salu's *karume*,

I told them that nose-flutes played by blowing down the nostrils were known in various parts of Indonesia. I am not sure that they believed me.

I had been several weeks in La'bo before I properly realised that Toraja personal names are distinctly odd.

I asked young Siu the Toraja word for " corner."

" *Siu*, Tuan," he said.

" The same as your name? " I asked.

" I was born in a corner, Tuan," he explained.

Without drawing any deductions, I had known that *salu* was the Toraja word for river and that *timbo* was the name of the cup in which palm wine was collected. I was treating an ulcer on the leg of a girl called Dapo, and *dapo* was the name of the ash-covered bench in the cookhouse on which the fires were lit.

" Is everybody here called after just anything, then? " I asked, but between my dog-Malay and Siu's unawareness of any other system of name-giving than his own people's the poor child was at a loss to reply. That evening I got the answer from Salu.

A baby Toraja is, in fact, called after just anything. Though there are a few words more popular as names than others, there are no names that are names and nothing else, and the vast majority of Torajas are called by the names of every object under the sun.

The mat of Siu's mother, on which he had been born, lay in a corner, so there was some sense to his name. But what about Deppa (cake), Koton (wrinkle), Lelang (auction) and Pong' Masa'aga (wicked)? Karrak's mother, they told me, was called Lai' Sapeda (bicycle), and there was a woman in Makale named Lai' Oto (automobile). At Bunt'ao school there was a girl Lai' Balao (rat), and a man was pointed out to me in Rembon market whose name was that of the male reproductive organs. A little girl in Pangala with a sweet

287

voice and the ability to see souls had the name Lai' Linoh (earthquake).

Then there was Sesa. His name is common among Torajas, though his full name, Sesa Ba'i, is rarer. *Sesa* means garbage or refuse; *sesa ba'i* means pig's garbage, rejected by the pigs. Sesa received that name because he was not his parents' firstborn. There had been another boy baby, who had died in his first moon. The *deata* had taken him. So when a second son was born to the young couple they gave him a foul name, hoping that then the gods would be disgusted and not covet him. In the same way the parents of a weakly child will often change its name to something unwholesome in an effort to win it back from the gods' fatal covetousness. That was how Pong' Masa'aga had got his name.

Massang had the best name among the frequenters of the bungalow; it meant " pure." Tu'ugun meant " aloof " or " set apart," Barra meant " rice," nobody seemed to know what Lendu meant, Duna meant " chatter " (a quaint name for that poor tongue-tied one), Sulo meant " torch," Likku meant " deep," Sipa meant " a bow," Kalasuso meant " a gatherer of shells " and Tanga meant " half " (because he was born at midnight, or half-night). Other names I came across were Lightning, Dog, Backwards (a breech delivery child), Chicken, Morning, Market, Bamboo, Rain, Tax, Mountain, Gun, Flower, Rice-Field, Road, Baboon and Night.

Another oddity is that there is no such thing as a boy's name or a girl's name. There are girls called Massang and Salu and Barra, and boys called Likku and Bonga. Properly speaking, each name should have the prefix *Lai* if it belongs to a girl and *So* or *Lasso* if it belongs to a boy.

Some members of the ruling class have pompous names, like the Ampulembang of Ulu Salu (He Who May Not Be Overcome), and the Ampulembang of Tikala (The Builder of Heaven).

Toraja Profile

Manganda Dancer

From time to time the basket bungalow, besides housing me and my train, was used for the purposes for which it had been built. Once or twice, for instance, we had a *suntik*.

It cannot be said that in general the Toraja people are firm believers in Western medicine, but it is doubtful whether any community in the world is so fond of inoculations. If I had killed a hundred pigs at the bungalow the feast would hardly have drawn a larger crowd than did the news that the *mantri* was coming out from Rantepao to do a *suntik*.

Within an hour of sunrise the first small knots of villagers would cluster under the wide eaves. By the time the *mantri's* horse was seen on the brow of the hill there would be several hundreds picknicking round the bungalow in an atmosphere of festival. Babies, some of them old enough to run about, fed from their mothers' breasts; girls, emboldened by numbers, would stand in plastic groups with their lovely arms around each other and chat with me through my window; pairs of young men, squatting breast to breast, would pull out the few fine hairs of each other's beards, using a couple of coins as pincers; children ate cold rice out of little grass-woven wallets; glossy coiffures were searched for intruders; frail ancients and their sturdy sons talked in gentle, seemly tones, spitting scarlet *sireh* juice from time to time or parking their quids of tobacco in front of their upper gums, giving their profiles a revoltingly prognathous bulge. Dozens of great circular hats would hang from the fence, looking like warriors' shields hung up after a victory.

On his first visit the *mantri*, a colleague of Julianus, inoculated more than nine hundred villagers with anti-dysentery vaccine in three hours. At an early stage I found the unhappy youth, who had not Juli's authority, sweating at his work with a dense mass of people round him, constricting his elbows and starving him of air and light. I cleared the veranda for him and posted the playboys, who so seldom did a hand's turn, as chuckers-out in case of any attempts at infiltration when my back was turned. Seeing that the head of the milling queue was composed entirely of able-bodied men and certain women they had smuggled there, I ordered them all back to the stable to wait until the end.

" Women with babies come first," I directed. This revolutionary idea found favour with none but the women concerned, but I stayed to see that it was carried out.

" Now the pregnant women," I ordered. Some mild expostulation followed, for the right of one or two ladies to their place in this group was questioned. I persisted, though, calling up old women next, followed by old men. The *guru* was put out, because when the whole mass of the schoolboys arrived with Bombai in charge insisting on top priority I said they would all have to wait until the old women and men had been treated. They surely, I said, would not wish to push themselves ahead of women.

They would, of course, and Bombai said so, adding that the *guru* would be angry. I said I was angry, too, and astonished that the schoolgirls had not come first.

When the vaccine at last gave out and the exhausted *mantri* drank coffee with me I wondered whether my interference had not done more harm than good. I was a guest, after all, with far less right in the bungalow than any of the villagers, and for me to foist my prejudices on them by a show of authority they hesitated to question was surely insensitive presumption. Particularly was it wrong to involve Bombai and the other children in conflicts of authority.

On subsequent occasions I did not interfere, or rather I confined my interference to ensuring that the *mantri* had space and light for his work. I charged Salu with the task of explaining to the crowd the reasonableness of this, but he sounded a good deal more peremptory than I had intended.

I am one of those who are unable to master their illogical

and humiliating timidity at the approach of the inoculator's needle. Never once have I been able to achieve indifference to this paltry operation. I admired the unblinking eyes and unaffected calm of my neighbours as they offered their arms: not one of the schoolgirls winced and very few of the babies cried, while I could not watch the plunging needle without mental flinching.

No Toraja knows the deep humiliation of surrender to nerves, to which we of the West must bend the knee day after day.

One day we had an election at the bungalow.

The old chief of Tandam Batu village, a frail and almost spectral figure with an exquisite face, had relinquished his authority some months previously. Now six candidates offered themselves as his successor, and the two hundred grown men of Tandam Batu came to the bungalow to choose one of them in the presence of their prince.

They all squatted on the grass in front of the veranda while he spoke to them, enjoining sober responsibility in their choice. An old, old man, a figure of wrinkled matchsticks under a huge hat, wandered about leaning on a staff and heckling. He was mildly mad and everybody tolerated him with the utmost good humour. Then the voting began.

One by one the villagers mounted the veranda by the front steps, whispered the name of their chosen candidate over the table at which the Ampulembang, Lete and Palinggi sat, and retired down the side steps. Lete had a sheet of paper with the names of the candidates heading six columns; as each vote was whispered he added a stroke to the appropriate column.

All the voters removed their fillets and lowered their sarongs from their shoulders as they came forward and many sketched the hands-down gesture of respect as they passed the table. Some went through their performance like bad actors in a melodrama, bending low over the table with brooding frowns and uttering a name in hoarse, conspiratorial whispers. There was a charming lack of sheepishness about the candidates themselves as they recorded their votes at the end. Each of them respectfully approached the table and with solemn face and unwinking eyes said "Me."

Kadang, the agreeable young brother-in-law of Palinggi, was a candidate. He told me beforehand that he did not expect many votes, and it seemed to me that he would be better to wait ten years before offering himself for such responsibilities. When the votes were counted he came third. A second vote was then taken, with only the two leading candidates to choose between. One by one the two hundred filed again across the veranda and Lete covered another sheet of paper with strokes. Two of the voters, I noticed, had extraordinary feet, with the toes set inwards almost at right angles to the axis of the foot.

Slipping out to the cookhouse to see whether coffee for the representatives of the government would be ready on time, I found the ever-exasperating Pong' Rantebambam kneeling on Salu's bed with his eyes glued to interstices in the basket wall, lip-reading the secret votes as the villagers passed the table. Not deigning to address him, I called Salu and ordered him to see the deplorable old man off.

A grave individual, astonishingly like Frederic March, whose name was Pong' Miringan, was elected, polling more than twice his opponent's number of votes. When the result was announced, he squatted at the head of his men to hear the prince charge him with his duties, loyalties and responsibilities. Afterwards he was summoned on to the veranda to hear more confidential advice and offers of help from his superiors. Finally, Lete addressed the tribesmen, his friendly good humour contrasting pleasantly with the Ampulembang's formal, thin-voiced detachment. A great polished locust alighted on the veranda railing between his brown hands as he spoke.

"It's no use any of you telling the Controleur that I cooked the poll and put your votes under the wrong name," he said. "You have got the chief you wanted most, and whether you voted for him or not you must obey him and back him up. So must the candidates who lost."

The new chief's first public act on his people's behalf was to ask me for some malaria medicine for the wife of one of his villagers.

I had a good many outings.

When the Princess Marijke was born, the Controleur sent his car with an invitation to me to join in the festivities in Makale and Rantepao on the following day. That day began with an *aubade* outside the Controleur's bungalow, charmingly sung and played by the school children of Makale, who processed in colourful trains round the lake at sunrise with the flags of the House of Orange surmounted by sprays of the magically powerful *tabang* leaves. Later the Controleur and Commandant took the salute of a detachment of troops of several Indonesian races and in the market place there was dancing. Troupes of impassive-faced girls in high Gothic headdresses danced the *ma'gellu*, Ambonese women in lace jackets, with handkerchiefs and bunches of flowers in either hand, sang and danced a graceful and quintessentially feminine little *entr'acte* and six men with spears and horned helmets performed a war-dance. But a group of small Menadonese children stole the show.

They had distinguished themselves already by their late and noisy arrival for the *aubade*, clad not in their best like all the other children but in dashing fancy dress and bearing a banner inscribed " The Glory of Minahassa." They had interjected a number of untimely cheers, as ill-timed as the Puang of Sangalla's hoarse inquiry after my health as I was saluting the hoisting of the Dutch flag, and showed a tendency to jig a good deal. Now they charmed us all with ingenuous little dances and duels with wooden swords.

In the afternoon the civilians played the military at football in Rantepao, the civilian goalkeeper punting prodigiously with a bare foot. In the evening there was a concert in the Japanese barracks, at which soldiers and their women sang many of the plaintive modern Malay ballads, three Sumatran soldiers did a dance in the dark, each holding a lighted candle in a saucer in either hand, and there was a sketch that ended in the singing of the noble Netherlands national anthem and the pathetically rubbishy Indonesian national hymn, both of which I had heard twenty times that day. Far outclassing the rest, the loveliest spectacle of all Toraja art, I saw the *pa'gellu* danced for the first time.

As four drummers at one great drum started up a rhythm of massive strength and excitement, nine girls from Pangala advanced in three files, swinging their arms and gliding like goddesses towards us. They wore tight-sleeved tunics and skirts of white silk, with diadems of gilded beads the size of walnuts on their sleek black hair. Necklaces of the same gigantic beads rose and fell on bosoms outlined above broad belts into which two gold swords were thrust. From throat to ankle cataracts of tiny beads swung to the dance, and as the dancers slowly turned we saw the small *fichu* of woven beads that fell from every shoulder.

After the first advance the dancers halted, drawn up in echelon, and afterwards did not move out of position. Their arms were raised outwardly and the fluttering movements of their fingers were enchanting. The exquisite delicacy of the dance and the storming, elemental thunder of the drumming fused into a whole of miraculous perfection, like the union of male and female. As the dance approached its end the dancers retreated backwards, swinging their arms amid a tempest of drumming.

That was the first time I saw Loedia, who is one of the finest *pa'gellu* dancers of this generation.

One morning Palimbong came soon after sunrise and suggested a climb of Sarira, the grim, fretted range overlooking the villages of Tandam Batu, Tambunan, Menke'pe and Ke'te. Within the hour we had crossed the valley of flooded fields below his house and entered the hard world of Sarira.

The path by which my friend led me up the cliffs was cruelly ridged with blades and spikes of ash-grey rock. My fingers were soon bleeding from some of the handholds, and mine was not the only blood on the rocks, for even the tough Toraja foot is frequently wounded by the paths of Sarira. At times we could rest from the difficult pitches and walk a little while along gently tilted slabs or through a glade of trees and coarse grasses, with poor little gardens scratched out here and there, and a few leaves still trembling to betray the flight of a mountain man or woman at our approach.

Looking up, we could see Gothic spires and turrets of ash-coloured rock, and there was one tall arch raised spectacularly against the vivid sky. As we watched, a barking of dogs broke out and seven big black baboons came lolloping towards the arch in unhurried flight. A wild brown girl with bare breasts, a garden-keeper, was chasing them off, helped by two white dogs. The baboons squatted insolently to chew the maize-heads they had stolen, waiting till the girl was quite near before they rose and clambered up the rocks beyond the arch, flaunting their crimson bottoms.

"Wicked, Tuan, those animals," said Palimbong. "Tuan should bring up his *pistole* and kill them."

"Do they sleep at night?" I asked.

"Yes, Tuan, like us," he told me. "Good so, otherwise they would starve those poor people with their thieving."

Farther up there was a grove of tall *kani* trees, the shadowed grass beneath them jewelled with their fallen scarlet petals. I found a climbing cream flower that had one petal only, and also clusters of white blossom with spirally set petals looking like normal flowers that had bloomed in tiny whirlwinds.

The human dwellers on Sarira were shyer than the baboons. Every garden ledge we passed, every tiny cabin was deserted, though we knew the garden-keepers and house-wives must be near. Palimbong was the chief of most of them, but few came when he called. He pointed out to me one little garden on a cliff ledge that could only be reached by climbing a tall *banga* palm and leaping from the top across a narrow gulf two hundred feet deep on to the tiny plot.

The few mountaineers we spoke to were pretty dirty, which was not surprising really, for we saw only one spring on the mountain. There were a few pigs almost as lithe as greyhounds and some buffaloes near the richer homestead beside the spring.

Looking down one precipice I saw a narrow ledge on which was laid an ancient wooden coffin shaped like a *prahu*. It was open and the sun and winds had long ago dispersed the remains it had once held. The ledge seemed even more inaccessible than the rock tombs at Ke'te.

" It is the way the People of Before sent their dead ones to paradise," Palimbong told me. " A hundred generations ago, perhaps. We do not know."

From the pinnacled crest we saw the valley of the Sadang to the west, and to the east the maze of little valleys in which our homes were set. A heavy dog-snouted baboon watched us, peering from above hunched shoulders on a leaning grey pillar of rock, as we turned to descend again.

The first time I went to Sangalla was with Dr Goslinga in his shabby little Opel baby car, which he had inherited from the Kempetai, the notorious Japanese secret police. It was market day in Sangalla and he was paying his monthly visit to the rooms used as a clinic. I stayed with him while he treated some of the local sufferers from yaws and trachoma.

Yaws, or frambœsia, is a disease with symptoms similar to those of syphilis. In any but advanced stages it is easy to cure. About fifty sufferers attended, and the contrast between the ugly sore swellings of those not yet treated and the state of others who had received half their series of injections (it was mapharsen, I think) was gratifying. There were other victims of yaws in the district beside those who met us that morning, but a surviving distrust of western medicine and the Toraja shyness of nudity before strangers prevented them from asking for treatment.

For a people with so well balanced an attitude to sex their prudery in this respect is unexpected. It was not only the women who were shy of removing their sarongs; the men were just as timid. It was odd to watch a normally self-assured young yokel, who had lost his virginity before he gained potency and who would have discussed with balance and appreciation the most intimate details of sex technique, averting his eyes and biting his lips as he lowered his shorts centimetre by centimetre in the privacy of the doctor's room. I was reminded of Indian soldiers, who are so prudish that they do not remove their final undergarments when bathing, even in the privacy of their barracks.

The trachoma sufferers looked as though they were weeping. It is a disease of the inner eyelid skin, which contracts so as to draw the lashes into contact with the eyeball, frequently destroying the sight completely. It, too, can be cured without much difficulty though with much pain to the patient. I had never heard a Toraja child cry for pain before, but I did as the drug (nitrate of silver, I think) was painted on the inflamed inner lids.

Later I went to stay in Sangalla, staying with the Ambonese evangelist Pattikayhatu, his kindly wife and their large family. It is a convention to call the wives of Indonesian evangelists *Nyora* or *Ñora*, a word obviously deriving from the sixteenth-century occupation of certain parts of the archipelago by the Portuguese. *Nyora* of Sangalla was a dear, motherly creature, large and patient and infinitely kind. Her adored firstborn, a youth called Elisa, with a reputation as a star footballer in his native Mamasa, accompanied me when I climbed Buntu Bebo, the mountain that dominates the Sangalla landscape.

That was far different from the ascent of Sarira. Some of the grassy slopes were gentle and the paths which spiralled up the steep gradients were not arduous. As we rose, the land to the north was revealed to us, a sunlit map of noble mountains and curving valleys, with the delicate veining of the rice-terraces patterning each valley floor. The sun was fierce that morning and I would not rest until we reached the summit, where martins wheeled in the drowsy breezes, clipping their mandibles as they snatched insects from the warm air currents.

The martins were not the only things that made me feel strangely at home on the peak of Buntu Bebo, for it was crowned by a fine earthen fort that recalled in structure, though not in extent, the Iron Age strongholds of Maiden Castle and Hambledon Hill in Dorset. Two sloping circular ramparts of earth, each about fifteen feet high, covered with grass and set one inside the other, enclosed a bare floor seventy or eighty feet square. The entrance had formerly been a cool, fern-fringed tunnel through the ramparts, but that had partly fallen in.

Dazed a little by the heat and the pace at which we had taken the three-hour climb, I lost grip of actuality for a few minutes. My eyes began to search scars in the ramparts for fragments of pottery as they always do on Dorset hill-forts. Almost at once I found a triangle of thin red ware and picked it up with care before I realised that the slave who had broken that bowl was quite possibly still alive. Only after the coming of the Dutch in 1906 or 1907 had the castle been abandoned. The last lord's rice-barns had been taken down the mountain and I had seen them earlier that morning beside his son's house beneath the eastern slope. Only the stone pedestals of the high roof-pillars remained inside the deserted fort.

We stayed an hour there, Elisa searching the valleys below with my field-glasses and I musing on the old days, a little before my life began, when life on that summit stronghold must have been so like the life of the pre-historic tribesmen who held Hambledon Hill. I felt miraculously at home. In my middle teens the mammoth earthen ramparts of Hambledon Hill had been my spiritual home. With my dog, I climbed them almost every night to enter the world of ingenuous romance I had created there as I lay on the wet turf in passions of imaginative effort, straining to apprehend the scene and mood of the great fort's early days. That high world of hawks and larks and fighting winds seemed very near as I crouched in the cool shade of the tunnel opening and dreamed for a while over the fair valleys of Sangalla beneath. The pattern of the spreading rice terraces was like an Andalusian dancer's petticoats. The noon sky floated great icebergs of white cloud and the sun drew their shadows across the map-like prospect far below.

Then I was hungry and we began the descent.

Throughout my stay I was on bad terms with my English-Malay vocabulary, an unhelpful work even among vocabularies and conversation books, which is saying a good deal.

I never discovered, for instance, why it included English words like *apothecary*, *embrocate* and *tare*, but omitted words like *sell*, *friend* and *perhaps*. Then there were the conversations, expressly included to furnish examples of colloquial English and Malay The colloquial English was not the sort any of my friends use.

An example:

Jackson (at the theatre) : Oh! There she is. What a beautiful lady! What a lovely voice she has! It reminds me of a nice gramophone record.

Brown: Here comes Mr Bouw. He is not only a good singer, but a talented actor. His very appearance on the stage makes the house ring with cheers.

I thought both the Malay and the Toraja languages long-winded at first, because I was thinking only in words. For instance, I contrasted the English " my son " with the Malay *saya punya anak laki-laki* or the English " ninety-nine " with the Toraja *kasera pulonan kasera*, and compared the monosyllabic English language with the Toraja, which does not possess more than three or four monosyllables. But both Malay and Toraja, especially the former, lend themselves to the succinct type of statement exemplified by such an English phrase as " Least said, soonest mended." Indeed, Malay particularly is a supple and subtle language, the cunning and delicate tool-box, so to speak, of peoples who love eloquence.

Malay is the native tongue of only small populations living around Malacca and the region of Sumatra across the Straits from Malacca, but it became the *lingua franca* of sea-going Indonesians in the centuries during which Malacca was the port to which the swarming cargoes of peppers, nutmegs, cloves and other gustatory explosives were brought for sale to the European merchant fleets. The Dutch and English, finding it the widespread language of commerce, made it the language of government and education, so that to-day perhaps a majority of the population of the Malay Archipelago is bilingual. Few white people there find it necessary to learn any other language than Malay.

Thanks to the patient assistance of my retainers and the children, and despite my conversation book, I achieved in my later months enough Malay to understand readily and be readily understood, though never enough to appreciate subtleties or express myself well in anything but everyday matters. It goes without saying that in any Malay words used in these chapters I have used the English romanisation of Malay and not the Dutch. If you write of the *Toradjas*, as the *Encyclopædia Britannica* does, you must also write *Dajak* for *Dyak* and *toean* instead of *tuan*.

I have not hesitated, when it suited me, to make English plurals of Malay or Toraja words (e.g. *koroks*), and I have even improved on the normal English spelling of Malay words (e.g. *tida* for *tidak*—you will no more hear that " k " in Indonesia than you will hear it in the English word *knot*).

It might also be as well to add here that all Toraja words and names in this book and all quotations from Toraja song and verse have been set down as best I could manage, adopting the usual combination of consonants having their English and vowels having their Italian values. Quite apart from the English romanisation, Dr. van der Veen would surely be puzzled by them, for inevitably the division of words will not always be correct. Nor would the author of the Toraja-Dutch dictionary be impressed by my translations, for while some of them are tolerably accurate, others are no more than paraphrases. My excuse for offering these unskilled fragments is that I merely wished to give ordinary readers a phonetic impression of the Toraja language and some slight idea of Toraja verse.

It would seem that the unsentimental Fates that rule our

lives must frown upon love at first sight; for all too often we see it cursed with a sequel of brackish disillusion. For me, though, there had been no such sequel to that May morning on which I had flown into the Torajas' homeland and out again, to fall in love with them between nine and ten o'clock.

The affection and admiration that grew deeper with every moon of my stay had, of course, both an objective and a subjective basis. I loved and esteemed the tribesfolk of La'bo partly because they are what they are, partly because I am what I am. Judged, then, by the personal standard which I venture to apply in the appraisal of a living civilisation, the Torajas were the best people I had known.

For I base such judgments upon one factor, which for me transcends in importance any achievements of genius in the arts or sciences, any codes of law, reforms of government or standards of literacy. I earnestly believe that in a people's domestic life and everyday social intercourse is to be found the crucial evidence upon which a valuation of their civilisation may be based.

My verdict on the Torajas, which I must hope was no more superficial than was inevitable after only a few months' acquaintance, was founded on their ordering of private, family and community life. It amounted in the end to no more than an endorsement of Mr. van Lijf's own judgment, spoken during his visit to me on my first morning in La'bo.

" They are good people," he said.

XIV

LOVE-LIFE ET CETERA

IT might almost seem as though the Torajas had been throughout the centuries so busy erecting their great superstructure of ritual and drama upon death that time and resource were lacking for the evolution of ceremonies to mark the climax of birth or the successive crises of life—circumcision, puberty, marriage and pregnancy. That, as a matter of fact, was my impression until I realised that I was contrasting the full magnificence of the death-rites of highly-born persons with the scanty observances associated with the intimate life-crises of my neighbours, who were nearly all of the *kaunan* class. Even so, the few ceremonies marking the birth or marriage of Toraja nobles are little more elaborate or impressive than the death-rites of the humblest *kaunan*.

Birth in La'bo is not an occasion of fuss. I created a sensation when—I cannot remember in what context—I confessed the fact that I had never seen a baby born. At first nobody would believe me.

" But Tuan has children of his own! " Barra pointed out, as if that automatically refuted my statement.

" I was not at home when they were born," I hedged, cursing, and not for the first time, my mythical progeny.

" Are not Tuan's sisters younger than him? " asked Salu.

" Yes," I told him; " but in England children do not see their brothers and sisters born."

" Why, Tuan? " everybody asked.

" Because it is our *adat*," I said. " We think children would be shy or frightened."

They laughed indulgently.

303

"*Bukan, Tuan!*" they declared. On the contrary! ("Nonsense!" was what they meant.)

Little Tu'ugun counted on his fingers.

"I have seen four babies born," he said.

In La'bo birth and death alike, as two of the events of major importance in family life, are usually witnessed by all the nearer members of the family, with the exception that no mature males other than the father normally gather round for a birth. Sesa, for instance, watched the birth of his adored little sister Mina, but if another sister or brother were to be born now he would be shooed away from the lying-in because he is about fourteen years old and therefore "ripe."

Expectant mothers seem to observe few taboos. Although their ideas of the physiology of conception and gestation are not greatly mistaken, their calculations concerning the duration of pregnancy are frequently at fault. I rather think it is not so much inability to compute as inability to count and note the passing of days and weeks that throws out their calculations. Two main results are (*a*) that the *to'mapakianak*, the old dames who act as midwives, are for ever being called out on false alarms, and (*b*) that a fairly large number of small Torajas first see the light of day at markets, feasts and emergency roadside halts.

For the mother, child-bed is an ordeal less formidable than it is to most present-day white women; but still an ordeal. Within an hour of delivery she walks to the bathing-pool, but except for her morning and evening baths she may confine herself to the house and housework for a week or longer; then she returns to the gardens or fields.

La'bo fathers must bury the afterbirth and umbilical cord somewhere near the house and may not leave the house during the hours of darkness, or move more than a very short distance away in daylight, for three days and nights after the birth. I suppose this might be a modification of *couvade*. When I went to Pangala I reached the rest-house on the day a child was born to the Christian wife of the Ampulembang's Christian clerk, who lived in an annexe. I noticed a little mound protected by a tiny stockade under my window and was told it was the burial place of the cord and placenta. If evil spirits could gain access to them they would have power over the new baby. When I said I supposed the heathen grandfather and not the Christian father had made the burial, there was a confused silence, which I took to mean that many of the Torajas' animistic beliefs are retained by them after their conversion to Christianity —which is not surprising in view of the fact that pre-Christian animist beliefs survive even in England.

One consequence of the birth of a couple's first child is that its father and mother adopt new names. That is because the Torajas are among the peoples who practise teknonymy, the custom of naming parents from their children. The day Isak was born, Salu was addressed by his wife and all his friends as Ambe'na Tato, Father of Tato, and his wife became Indo'na Tato, Mother of Tato. Tato is a provisional name which is given to every male child for the purpose of renaming his parents until such time as a personal name is chosen for him. If the child is a girl, the parents are provisionally renamed Ambe'na Lalai and Indo'na Lalai.

When, after a few weeks, the name Isak had been chosen for the boy, Salu became Ambe'na Isak, and that title is nowadays far oftener used than Salu. His wife was henceforth normally known as Indo'na Isak. Isak was, of course, baptised by a missionary, but for heathen babies there is no name-giving ceremony.

This complication of names goes further. If Salu had cared to, he could have taken instead the name Pong' Lasso Isak. *Pong* is a minor title denoting maturity and paternity, but more frequently the status of grandfather or the assumption of certain responsibilities—those of village chief, for example. *Lasso* is a word denoting maleness; properly it is a prefix to every boy's or man's name, often shortened to *So*. The word is also the popular name for the male organ. Alternatively again, Salu could have called himself Pong' Salu.

The hand-out of new names does not, however, always end there. If Isak had been the first grandchild of either pair of grandparents they would first have become Nene'na Tato and later Nene'na Isak. Or they could both have renamed themselves Ne'asso.

Toraja babies feed from the mother's breast longer than Anglo-Saxon babies, sometimes for more than eighteen months or even two years. Whatever the duration of breast-feeding, it seems to be the natural one, for nobody in La'bo understood what I meant by weaning troubles. From the second or third moon of its life the La'bo baby eats grown-up food as well, a little rice and vegetable mashed up, or sometimes chewed by its mother first like a mother bird.

It is usual for small children to go naked, the girls for four or five years, the boys for six or seven. But however early or late they begin to wear clothes they never wear garments of a kind specially designed for children, as our small citizens do. The little girl wears replicas of her mother's tunic and sarong and the little boy replicas of his father's sarong and shorts, sometimes omitting the shorts. A girl's ear-lobes are usually pierced in infancy and earrings were the only wear of many small La'bo girls. When their hair was long enough it was drawn into a knot on the nape like their mothers'.

By the time they begin to wear clothes the sex lives of La'bo children have begun their candid, unmaimed course.

Folks in La'bo do not think that the flesh is at war with the spirit, or that it ought to be. They do not think of sex as an enemy planted in their bodies that will foul and destroy

them if it is given the least chance. Virginity to them is
merely a perversion.

" A small baby's legs are weak and useless; he cannot
walk. After a year they begin to grow strong; he tries to
walk. When he can walk he walks; when he can run he
runs. A baby's *lasso* is no good because it is weak. It takes
longer to grow than his legs, but slowly it grows strong
and he can use it; not so well as a man, but it gets stronger
as his legs did and he learns better how to use it. It is
the same."

This analogy was Lendu's, and similar arguments were
advanced by friends when the subject of virginity in childhood and adolescence came up. It was one that fascinated
them, this subject of the white people's denial of the flesh.
I had been asked once again whether it was really true that
there were women in Holland who lived not only their
childhood and first years of ripeness, but their whole lives
without enjoying the embrace of a man.

" Yes, truly," I told them. " In England also."

" Why, Tuan?"

" It is our *adat*," I said, falling back on their own
explanation for practices they were not disposed to
explain.

When you take the lid off La'bo sex life there are no
bad smells. They have no humiliating or tormenting shames
to hide. I never encountered there a single example of the
manifold plagues that are considered to derive from sexual
unbalance. No stammerers, no victims of " nerves " or
nervous tics, no obsessions, hysteria, nervous unstability or
deep-seated perversion. No morbid introspection. The
Christian minority, I soon noted, did not take missionary
sex-teaching seriously enough to upset the balance of their
intimate lives. For my neighbours sex was not a bogy or
a bore or an obsession or a problem.

The only subject which produced among them the un-
balanced reaction which is the white puritan's response to

almost any sex activity whatsoever is incest. In the old days those guilty of incest were tied together and drowned. In none of the La'bo villages, I was told with emphasis, was there any record of a single case of incestuous crime. I wondered whether the emphasis did not, in fact, reveal a trace of neurosis in my informants. If so, it was the only hint of such disorder that I ever noted. Incest was, however, undoubtedly considered as sin by the villagers, an unthinkable offence against a law having more than human sanction.

So far as all normal forms of sex activity are concerned, and I include in that the few familiar byways explored by them from time to time, the Toraja man, woman and child know where they stand. It would be no use the moralist telling them sex is holy or the puritan telling them sex is dirty; they know it is neither, and they know at least as much about it as either moralists or puritans. To them it is straightforward, clean and healthy, not to be questioned, fussed over or profitably debated.

Judging, as I did, by results, I must admit that I found much to approve in the way my neighbours ordered their intimate lives. Indeed, my one criticism was provoked by the slackness of their marriage tie, which results too often in what amounts to desertion of their wives and families by young husbands.

But from the remarks of older villagers, the burden of which was, " When we were young such men would have been ashamed to behave so; they would have been driven from the village," I think it possible that the decomposition of tribal morality which follows the impact of white administrators and missionaries upon preliterate communities may be responsible for such bad behaviour. The prestige and power of chiefs and priests is inevitably weakened by the assertion of alien authority and the bad characters of the community come into their own. I believe it may well be what Mr. van Lijf called the New Heathen who shock the more sober tribesmen with these betrayals of their responsibilities.

But a deserted Toraja mother, whether married or unmarried, is far better off than most white women in such circumstances. If she is unmarried she does not undergo the persecution or condescending charity not infrequent even to-day in Christian countries, nor does her child suffer the slightest social disability. Whether married or not, she has the unfailing support and unquestioning affection of her family to sustain her.

Every Toraja is a member of his or her family first and an individual second. To none of the problems and griefs common to human creatures is the forlorn fate of loneliness ever superadded. The family is always there, warm and sheltering, in ever-faithful alliance against all the ills of life. The mateless mother rejoins (if she has ever physically left it) the group of parents, grandparents, brothers, sisters and cousins, and she and her offspring share in the food and labour of the family homestead.

Small Toraja children have a close and matter-of-fact acquaintance with the practices of sex. Kalo'udun and Likku knew more about it than quite a number of Anglo-Saxon married couples. Their curiosity had never been repressed into a burden on their conscience or mocked with talk of bees and flowers. Boys and girls in La'bo play with each other experimentally and look forward with matter-of-fact candour to the time when they can play their parts properly.

At the age of eleven or twelve a La'bo boy decides it is time he was circumcised. He makes an arrangement with a slightly elder friend who has already been cut, or it may be an elder brother, very rarely a grown man, and they go off secretly up the mountain or into the forest. Without any ritual the elder boy performs the operation with a bamboo blade. Properly speaking it is incision, not **circumcision**, for the cut is vertical and nothing is taken away; but when the wound has healed the effect is virtually the same.

Duna told me about his circumcision.

" I asked Sesa to cut me because he was my comrade. We climbed up the cliffs of Buntu Assa where nobody would come, but I was shy and so I kept seeking a safer place in the rocks because I thought perhaps a woman would come up. It did not hurt much when Sesa made the cut. He is good, he has cut other boys. But always it bled. *Wah*, Tuan, the blood! Near noon he cut me, but we could not come down till sunset because the blood would not stop. If I had put on my shorts before the blood stopped it would have stained them, and the women would have seen and I should have been ashamed."

Though a little local poisoning occasionally follows these operations, Dr. Goslinga told me he had not encountered a case of serious after-effect. None of the presumed former ritual attached to the custom survives to-day and Christian boys automatically carry on the practice, which in one form or another is widespread among the Indonesian peoples.

The incision of girls, which is general among the Buginese and Javanese, is never practised by the Torajas.

Though there is no ban on the sex activity of Toraja children, there is neither, on the other hand, any formal provision made for it. No youth clubhouses, as in parts of Melanesia, for instance. And since there is an absolute ban on any kind of sex activity, even down to chatting and the simple holding of hands, in any place where it might be observed (a ban which has given rise to a charming and exciting technique of speaking volumes by the exchange of swift and infinitely subtle glances) opportunities for love-making are not easily come by. When at thirteen or fourteen the boy is ripe and stronger longings than those he has hitherto known begin to haunt him, he is often melancholy over the difficulty of arranging meetings with the girl he favours.

Chance moments alone in the house are snatched. If she is the sister or cousin of a friend he can sometimes spend an evening with the friend and afterwards sleep in the house, daringly finding his way to her sleeping-mat in the darkness. Or impatiently he may brave the ghost-filled darkness of the valley paths at night with a friend and be lucky enough to meet a pair of the raffish little girls who will sometimes venture out to look for love. But only on the freer and easier occasions of death-feasts and harvest festivals is he more or less sure of success.

So the wistful trials of bachelordom are not unknown to the Toraja boy. They are, however, never prolonged enough to endanger his sexual balance. He is far from thinking of girls all the time, and he and his friends console each other in ways that old-fashioned schoolmasters would grieve over. The balance of Toraja sex is too good to give rise to more than a negligible crop of mild abnormalities. Individuals do not get driven up sexual side alleys by unnatural stresses and strains arising from a system of morality in bitter opposition to the course of nature.

Though both sexes speak with total frankness on intimate matters (for of Toraja ladies it may be said, as the first Rajah Brooke said of the ladies of Tempe, far to the south, a hundred years ago, " They talk, often in a very unladylike manner, on unladylike subjects ") yet this frankness conveys an impression of lusty innocence and naïve gusto; there is never a trace of morbid lubricity.

The frankness, of course, contrasts rather strangely with their careful avoidance of full nudity, which is seldom relaxed even among friends of their own sex. When I inquired about this from friends, I gathered from their answers that the precaution was taken not so much as a measure of nervous prudery as in consideration for others, who would rather not see one's nudity fully disclosed. This

311

made it easier to understand the extreme reluctance of even male Torajas to uncover themselves completely for medical examination. If they refrained from exposing themselves in the presence of their friends in consideration for their delicacy, even more would they be likely to shrink from exposing themselves before the white doctor, to whom they were anxious to show all possible respect.

Only rarely do Toraja girls between the ages of thirteen and sixteen or seventeen conceive. This appears to be a general biological rule. Nobody could tell me of more than one La'bo girl who had become pregnant within three or four years of becoming ripe and she had associated with a boy several years older than herself, which is unusual. Dr. Goslinga confirmed the rarity of such incidents.

The love affairs of newly-ripe boys (I had no opportunity of observing young girls) in La'bo are naïve and not psychologically upsetting. Only among boys in their middle and late teens did I come across signs of the emotional upheavals which we call "falling in love." Somehow I had expected to see none of this in La'bo. I had read some nonsense about romantic love having been a white man's invention—the Troubadours, I think. In a vague way I had believed it, and in a vague way perhaps it may be true. I mean that the idea of Western romantic love may be merely a neurotic exaggeration of something that is universal to man. Certainly the elements of lyricism and romance are not absent from Toraja love affairs. They have a few love-songs and they can be what we would call deeply in love. Unhappy sufferers from unrequited love have been known to commit suicide.

At the same time sustained intensity of focus upon one particular individual is not characteristic of most sex life in La'bo. I have seen a love-crossed youth, with whose forlorn misery I had sympathised, make a spectacular recovery in a week or two. Toraja lovers keep their feet on the ground, but for that very reason they are possibly more vividly aware than most Western lovers, whose heads tend to be in the clouds, of the flowers that grow round their feet. I mean that the lyricism of the flesh and its blossoming in love, the miracle that neither imagination nor intellect avails to apprehend, is something that may be more fully revealed to Toraja lovers than to the great majority of whites.

I would say that there is nothing to strike the average Anglo-Saxon as outlandish in the Toraja ideals of human beauty. Whenever I found general agreement that a certain girl in La'bo was beautiful I found myself endorsing the opinion of my neighbours. What I could not endorse was the general opinion among the other races of Celebes and the whites in the island that the Torajas are a plain people.

I would agree with that judgment in that I know of no race, not even the Balinese, the vast majority of the members of which are not plain. Who on earth would claim that more than five per cent of the women of England, the United States, Holland, France, Germany or Austria are beautiful? Nobody, surely, with good eyesight. In the village of Karatuan there were, I believe, about fifty girls between the ages of fourteen and nineteen, the ages at which Torajas consider feminine beauty is at its height. Believe me, I could show you many more than two or three beauties among them.

Only Kalasuso contributed anything vivid to the list of features in the catalogue of female beauty which I compiled from the interrogation of several young men. The general preferences, now and then rhapsodically volunteered, were for a low voice, an " easy-coming smile," hair straight or very slightly waving, a pale complexion, a sweet-smelling skin, large eyes with a slight tilt, arched brows, a small but not flat nose and full lips, small, even teeth, a round face

and rounded arms (" arms like music that is dreamed "—
Oberammergau), small hands and high, rounded breasts,
rather wide hips and curved legs (" not like bamboos "—
Masak). The figure should be rounded and not like a man's.
I would say that the fragrant skin and shapely arms were
demanded with most insistence.

When I asked Kalasuso to detail the features of a Toraja
beauty he can have had no difficulty, for he had merely to
describe his wife, a beautiful girl set in an aura of sweet
serenity like a goddess in a shrine. He hesitated when I
asked " Figure? " and sketched an outline in the air with
his hands.

" *Like a guitar!* " he said, with shining eyes.

In point of fact, though all my friends seemed to dream
of the universal male preference, plenty of convexity, Toraja
women's dress tends to disguise their curves—like our
fashion magazines with their repellent illustrations of models
from whom clumsy photographic retouchers have amputated
the hips.

I got little help from Loedia in formulating the Toraja
ideal of male comeliness. A strong voice and a " tall "
figure seemed to be important. Unlike Anglo-Saxon males,
however, Toraja men seem well aware of the ins and outs of
masculine beauty and gave me a picture easily enough which
particularised strong, thick hair, pale-brown skin, a round
face, strong eyes, even teeth, broad build, heavy muscles, no
body hair, massive legs, a graceful deportment and a
courteous manner.

Variations on these two pictures, then, are the images
best calculated to rouse the passion of Toraja youth. Nothing
distasteful or even very strange to Anglo-Saxon tastes. Nor
is there anything very alien or at all grotesque by our
standards about the techniques of Toraja lovers. The kiss
of passion, although not unknown, is far less important to
Toraja sweethearts than to European lovers. Their favourite
preliminary endearments consist of a series of facial

pressures ranging from the subtle and tender to the mildly sadistic, all accompanied by the sensuous inhalation of the natural fragrance of youthful flesh. If this is dubbed " rubbing noses " it will sound grotesque to us, but in fact it is in no way repugnant or unrewarding to people with white skins; kissing, after all, would sound as coarse if described as unsymathetically.

Certain white men who do not even admit that the Colonel's lady and Judy O'Grady are sisters under their skins, much less that women with golden skins are sisters to their own paler women, profess to find in the use of coconut oil as a cosmetic and hair-dressing evidence against æsthetic sensibility. I cannot agree. I like everything about the coconut palm and its fruit. The oil has a delicate fragrance, and girls anointed with it compare favourably, to say the least of it, with white girls who smoke and whose hair all too often smells like an overcrowded compartment in a workmen's train.

For the rest, Toraja love-making follows courses not strange to the West. Their range of positions for the climactic act are familiar to Anglo-Saxons, though the one that tends to be the stand-by of unenterprising whites is least of all favoured by them because of its denial of equal partnership to the woman.

The men and women of La'bo seem to be as free from marital maladjustments, frigidities and impaired delight, as their children are from what we call the problems of adolescence. The only form of birth control known to them is abortion. A number of old women can induce this by manipulation, but what information I secured suggested that it is not frequently resorted to.

The virility of Torajas is a legend among the other races of Celebes and is by white standards remarkable.

A young slave who sometimes visited the bungalow was called Pesangpulo. The obvious connection with *sangpulo*, the Toraja word for " ten," suggested to me that he was

315

perhaps a tenth child. However, I noticed that at times he was called by another name, and when I remarked on this, I was told that Pesangpulo was only a nickname. It meant " ten times," and celebrated his performance in the lists of love during a night of a death-feast the previous year. He appeared to be about seventeen years old.

I naturally took this to be a generous exaggeration. Nicknames often have a basis of exaggeration, and in any case the subject is one on which young men tend to boast. But I realised later that the circumstances of such entertainment on the occasions of death-feasts make false claims difficult, for the young lady or ladies concerned are not the only corroborative witnesses. I was still unconvinced when Salu, a little prim as usual when such subjects were discussed, explained that the feat had only been celebrated by a nickname in view of the lad's youth; older men often surpassed him by fifty per cent.

Though I still have some difficulty in crediting all the details I was told of such exploits, I must add that I received confirmatory evidence from a large number of patently honest witnesses. Certainly the sex appetite of white men is accounted unbelievably weak by young Torajas. The normal programme of an average married Western couple is considered by them consistent only with sickness or senility.

Naturally it was in the holiday atmosphere of death-feasts and harvest festivals that these marathon performances were achieved by young people making the most of such not very frequent opportunities. . . .

The Torajas are in agreement with Byron that the night was made for loving. Not the day. Love-making and its preliminaries, kept severely to darkness and the hours of darkness, could not be allowed to spill into the hours of daylight without grave impropriety.

I found it a wholesome arrangement.

How do they get married?

It couldn't be easier. Proposing is the only difficult part, so difficult that few young Torajas ever do it in person. They ask their father, or perhaps a trusted friend, to put the question. If both boy and girl have been to school, he may write his proposal in Malay and send it by hand of a little boy.

Once the girl has agreed, and she has full liberty in making her decision, the rest is simplicity itself. A day is fixed, for which the girl and her kinswomen prepare a small feast. Accompanied by a band of his male friends, the bridegroom goes to the girl's house. The feast is eaten in a holiday atmosphere, and when bedtime comes the boy shares her sleeping-mat.

"They are shy, though, because the house is full with guests who tease and listen. Sometimes all night the boy and his wife do not play. They are shy." Thus Barra, who ought to know. He thinks he is twenty-four, looks twenty and has been married four times.

If after a year or two the couple are happy together, and especially if there is a child or expectation of one, a ceremony called *di'parampo* may be held at which the wizard sacrifices a pig and entreats the *deata* to prolong the pair's happiness and bless the union with children and prosperity. It is then considered a " real " marriage and divorce rarely ensues.

The couple do not necessarily live in the house of the girl's family; it is just as often the boy's. Only in the case of rich families would they have a house of their own.

Upper-class couples go through a little more ceremony. When Palinggi fell in love with Lai' Rora and wanted to marry her he confided in his father. Shortly afterwards his father visited Lai' Rora's father at Terampak, where I was so often entertained. After due preparations the question of marriage was broached. Lai' Rora was called into the presence of the guest, who offered her *sireh* from a silver box. She thanked him and accepted some, leaving them shortly afterwards. Palinggi's name was never mentioned, nor was the subject of marriage, but her acceptance of the *sireh* had been her formal acceptance of Palinggi's suit.

Plural wives are allowed by the *adat* of most districts, but only a small proportion of nobles and priests, and virtually no lesser men, took advantage of the permission. I met one man only who had three wives.

Divorce for common folk is even easier than marriage. A divorce takes place when the boy stops sharing his sleeping-mat with his wife. If he has been living in her family's house he merely leaves; if she has come to his family's house, his withdrawal from her mat is the hint for her to go. In the case of well-to-do couples, the man must pay an indemnity in pigs or even buffaloes.

Theoretically the wife can do the same if the marriage ceases to please her. In practice, too, she quite often does, but divorce by the wife is in fact less easy and less frequent. Often when it happens it is not because of an emotional or physical breakdown of marriage, but because the boy has failed to bring home food for her and the children—that is, has failed to find employment regularly enough.

Infidelity is not uncommon, more frequently on the part of the husband. In the old days the discovery of a wife's unfaithfulness was held to justify murder of the poacher, and even of the wife, but this rarely happens to-day.

I formed the impression that rather more than half the marriages between couples over twenty years of age were permanent; but the estimate is extremely tentative. What is beyond doubt is that there are plenty of happy marriages. It would be hard, for instance, to imagine a happier family in the world than Sesa's. His parents are poor. His mother has lost her looks and his father begins to grow old. Never once did I see a kiss, an embrace, a handclasp between them or hear a tender word. Between Sesa and his mother there could never be the remotest demonstration of affection. Only little Mina was small enough to be held between her father's

thighs or to take Sesa's hand as she walked up the slippery
path to their poor cabin.

But the radiance of pure and unaffected love that
illuminated the family group on all occasions, the sweetness
and content of their home, was supremely enviable.

XV

TORAJA MILLIONAIRE

AT the death-feast for Palinggi's father I had taken photographs, by request, of Pong' Masa'aga's brother-in-law. Rombelayu was his name, but he was more often spoken of as *Siambe di Nanggala*, the Old Man of Nanggala, and I heard many stories of his wealth. The Ampulembang of Nanggala, who was both his nephew and his son-in-law, I knew to be the richest of all the princes.

An invitation to visit the old gentleman's seat at Kawasik was extended through Palinggi and later repeated. One radiant morning, then, accompanied by Palinggi and attended by Duna, I set off along the path that led east-nor'-east across the mountains to the rich valleys of Nanggala.

It was hot on the climb, but I was too proud to tell Palinggi that the pace he set was murdering me, for despite his boyish looks he was an older man than I. But his foot was on his native heath, whereas I was not yet in training after seven years of army service during which very little walking and no climbing had been possible. For a couple of hours we climbed, passing two crudely painted corpse-houses. Palinggi and Duna spat as they approached them, as Easterners usually do when they encounter a bad smell or think of one. The corpses inside were not recent, however, for I went close to examine the decoration and noticed nothing offensive.

The hill-tops were desolate, with only a few lonely boys tending buffaloes amid expanses of rotting shaly soil that opened in a great wound wherever the smallest streamlet flowed. In mid-afternoon we descended into a valley of the richest, deepest rice-fields I had seen. Reflecting the glory of the sky, the depths of blue and the white alps of cloud, they also reflected their owner's wealth, of which they were the foundation.

The village of Kawasik is like a posy floating upon the valley waters. A toy village, so pretty and clean and neat that it never looks quite real. There is a long, level ribbon of clean-swept red soil on an airy ledge, with on one side of it a row of houses, Rombelayu's own being the finest, and on the other an array of no less than seventeen rice-barns. Fruit trees and coconut palms shade the "street," and handsome red *tabangs* and hedges of crimson hibiscus fringe the bluff behind the barns. And once again the irresistible impression is of being among a small fleet of craft at anchor, so suggestive are those high-peaked golden roofs.

We found the old noble and his lady taking their ease on the platform of one of the barns. Surrounded by members of their family and favourite slaves, they sat chewing *sireh* and spitting frequent crimson jets into individual spittoons. Siambe, who is crippled with something resembling rheumatism, could not rise to greet us, but invited us to sit on the fine mat at his side.

If you jib at envisaging graciousness and dignity in association with a lot of spitting, it shows that you cannot have travelled in Indonesia. Old Rombelayu and his consort can be counted on to display more dignity in their most informal moments than we on our best behaviour. Neither is handsome, but the old chief holds his deeply-lined face high, and, despite the slight scowl that belies her good-heartedness, his lady, *Siindo di Nanggala*—the Old Woman of Nanggala—moves with the calm authority and some of the grace of a medieval *châtelaine*. Indeed, the Controleur of Makale's description of Rombelayu as a feudal baron is nearer fact than fancy.

Drinking the water of a young coconut through the delicate lipped hole cut deftly in the shell by a slave, I leaned against the stout pillar of the rice-barn and feasted

my eyes upon the scene of content and plenty that Rombelayu's home provided. A woman slave, having obtained a
great key from the bunch hanging at Siindo's waist, climbed
up to the door of a barn and drew out several golden sheaves.
A congregation of handsome cocks and hens collected
beneath her to glean the few grains that fell as she brought
them down and followed her when she turned away with
the sheaves in her shoulder-basket. On a mat before the
chief's house the rice was spread to dry in the sun under the
eye of a tiny little girl armed with a cane to keep off the
thieving hens.

A boy humming a drowsy chant rode a big bull up the
" street," calling down a greeting to the young girl slave
who sat spinning cotton under a crimson *tabang*, the sun
glorifying her exquisite arms and bosom. A flute melody
drifted down from the hill beyond the copse of giant bamboos. The sunshine that had been an ordeal on the mountain-
top was a blessing there.

That was one of the moments when I wished I had been
born a Toraja.

A few alien details from the Western world flawed the
perfection of Kawasik. The space beneath the chief's own
house, traditionally empty between the piles, had been
pavilioned and a white-latticed veranda room and certain
inner rooms introduced. It did not look too bad.

Inside this room, to which we retired at sunset, a collection
of shoddy Western treasures contrasted violently with the
grace and magnificence outside. There was a horrible wall
clock that didn't go, a huge framed certificate recording the
award to Rombelayu of the Bronze Star by the Governor-
General, a dreadful photo-portrait of the chief's late father,
and a spirited battle-piece of the school of Lady Butler
showing what I took to be some kind of Balkan infantry
withstanding a Turkish cavalry charge. A number of

chairs and a table stood unsteadily on the uneven earth floor.

As I took a seat of honour at the table, with Duna squatting close behind me, a number of Rombelayu's kinsmen and guests crowded in to fill the room, an all-male company from small boys nursing glossy cocks to ancients tottering with staffs. Among the young men I saw Palimbong's heir, a kinsman of Siindo. The old chief sat upright, a favourite grandson in his arms, and asked questions which Palinggi had usually to interpret, for like most older Torajas the Old Man of Nanggala cannot speak Malay.

He spoke chiefly as a landowner and farmer, listening with grave attention to my answers concerning English crops, seasons and domesticated animals. Siindo, herself a considerable landowner, leaving her supervision of the cooking of our supper, came and leant her elbows on the table and made earnest requests for a consignment of English grain to plant experimentally in her fields. " But you will send me some, Tuan," she coaxed when I insisted that wheat would not grow in her flooded fields under the strong equatorial sun. " Just a little, Tuan." When she wheedled she had some of the charm often wielded with such effect by elderly French women. The lamplight shone softly on her white hair and gleamed on the heavy magnificence of her gold bracelets.

It was a good meal she had ordered for us. Rice was served in a huge Western enamel colander, a utensil appreciated by Torajas of substance, for they rightly hate muggy rice; the colander allows the steam to escape and the grains remain separate and dry. There was a dish of fried chicken, a mess of green vegetables and a stew of chicken and young bamboo in coconut milk.

Slaves squatted behind their masters with bowls of rice, and received, from time to time, scraps of meat from their masters' hands. When I found in my portion of stew the blanched head of a cock, complete with beak and comb, I passed that on to Duna, with a leg of chicken as well in case he felt the same way about the head as I had.

A noble pipe of *tuak* was brought in and served by a slave who had to stand two yards behind me to fill my glass, so long was the pipe. The process had alarmed me in early days, when suddenly a great pipe would be thrust over my shoulder noisily glugging and plopping like an early oil bomb falling until at last a delicate stream of wine, filtered by aromatic leaves stuffed into the mouth of the bamboo, fell into my cup. Every time I myself tried to pour, a long pause in which nothing happened was followed by an uncontrolled torrent of wine and leaves falling as much as a yard beyond the receptacle aimed at.

I had by now discovered the complicated method of obtaining palm wine. It is, in fact, sap taken from the stem of the fruit cluster of the sugar palm, which the Torajas call *induk*. Every few months the palm, with its huge, dark green metallic fronds and untidy, black-haired trunk, brings forth a great cluster of round, dark fruit. As the fruit approaches maturity a man climbs the palm every third morning for a whole moon and beats the stout stem of the cluster for an hour with a club. At the end of the moon he pierces the stem close to the fruit; if *tuak* flows from the wound the cluster is cut off, and the receptacle after which our friend Timbo was named is hung to catch the dripping from the amputated stump. Between a pint and a quart of wine is collected from the *timbo* at sunset each day, a little always being left in the bottom, or the following day's yield would be unpleasantly sweet. The man who collects the daily pint always cuts a very thin slice from the stump before replacing the *timbo*.

The palm is strangely sensitive. The flow of wine will stop if the trunk is struck or if the man who cuts the stump ever washes his hands with soap. A thirsty wayfarer may climb any *induk* tree and refresh himself from the *timbo*, though nowadays, unlike the easier former *adat*, he is expected to leave a coin on the edge of the pot.

As a rule *tuak* looks like water you have washed your hands in. When newly collected it is, as the Torajas say, boiling, with the suds working up and down. Its flavour varies very considerably. From twenty to forty hours is the normal age for drinking. It is then what Norman Douglas would call " young, but not altogether innocent."

The vintage served at Rombalayu's table was the pink Nanggala *tuak*, which looks a little like champagne rosé. It was the best I had tasted, and the old chief, abetted by a coy Siindo, declared he would make me drunk on it. Every time I set down my cup a grinning slave poked the pipe over my shoulder and replenished it to the brim. But the liquor is even less intoxicating than post-war beer, and something like two quarts induced no more than a slight preliminary warmth round the heart (which is, however, all said and done, the best part of intoxication). From the mutterings of the company and the expectant faces of the girl slaves round the inner doorway I gathered that a more spectacular reaction was looked for. It seemed no more than a fair return for hospitality not to disappoint, so I made a point of swaying slightly on my seat, stammered once or twice and took my cue from Palinggi, who was by now quite tipsy. I was so successful that when I rose to leave the room for a moment a youth sprang forward to support me and remained with me outside lest I should collapse in the fresh air.

The main entertainment of the evening, however, was provided by a delightful wizard called Nemani, whom Rombelayu had summoned from far Pangala to perform certain strong magic on his behalf. Nemani was a lean, active elderly man with a distinguished profile and eyes that sparkled with a torrential zest for living. Seldom do I remember being so taken by storm by a brilliant personality.

For most of the evening he talked of the old days, when

he was a head-hunter of renown and later a fighter under the warrior hero Pong' Tiku in the Torajas' last stand against the Dutch. When I started to draw him out on these subjects he was obviously delighted. One is accustomed to old people's mild and melancholy nostalgia for the past, but the light that came into Nemani's fine eyes as he described his early days and the intensity of his deep voice was true love, if ever I met it.

Alas, he spoke no Malay and almost all our conversation had to be passed through Palinggi. You might consider a tipsy evangelist a tragically unsuitable interpreter for a talk on the good old days of heathenism, but you would be wrong. My friend is still enough of a Toraja to thrill to the story of his people's past whenever the puritan gags of his new religion do not press too stiflingly upon him. That night he was off the leash.

What follows here is necessarily a most imperfect paraphrase of some of what Nemani told me that night. To taste anything at all of the flavour of his discourse you must picture the setting—the narrow dark room with its dim oil lamp gently lighting the proud set of Rombelayu's head and the gold buttons on his tunic, and at his side the lithe and splendid magician, a blue and white head-cloth rising above his brow to twin peaks, his tongue, his eyes, his hands, his shoulders all vivid with eloquence. Siindo stands by the door of the inner room, her white hair shining, and behind her perhaps a dozen whispering kinswomen and girl slaves. Around the shadows of the floor are as many kinsmen and male slaves, revealed as a tangle of stalwart limbs when the lightning flashes glint through cracks in the shutters. There is a smell of paraffin and pungent *sireh*. The slave with the *tuak* pipe watches my cup steadily and Nemani speaks. . . .

It was good, Tuan, how we lived in that former time. Sometimes when I sleep my soul travels to paradise and I meet my friends of that time, and I am happy. These boys here will never be truly men as we were. Tuan, hear! As soon as I was circumcised, every day I asked my brother to take me on a war, and as soon as I was truly ripe I went on my first war. I carried my brother's blowpipe and arrows for him. He had a gun, no lie, but when he must be silent he used his blowpipe. To the valley of Bituang we went. They would not let me seek a head, but I carried my brother's blowpipe and part of the way back I carried a head. The head's blood smeared my leg and I did not wash it off until I was home and the women saw it.

I was afraid in those nights. We were in the country of our enemies and there were many ghosts of those people in the forest. One night I lost the men in the forest. When I knew I was alone in that darkness I called my brother's name aloud and he came back and cursed me. He said to me, "You are truly a girl-baby." He was ashamed because the other men were angry that I had made noises in the forest. I stole a bull calf from those people, but he wept, and my brother said, "He is like you. Your twin he is. Let him go!"

Four nights we made that war. Two captives, a young man and an old one, we took from those people and one man my brother killed with his sword. His head we brought back. The captives were for a chief's death-feast. On the *rante* their heads were cut off and carried on long bamboos. While the heads cooked the warriors feasted on a pig, and I with them, for I had been on that war. I was happy because boys who had been cut many moons before me were saying, "He is small, but he is more a man than we. He went on a war."

Tuan has been on big wars. Tuan knows a young man's joy is to be afraid and brave together, and go forward in wars. So it was for our people in that former time. I cannot truly remember how many wars I went on. Many, Tuan. More than ten. Day wars and night wars, many.

I will tell you, Tuan. Day war we made thus. There were young men in our village and some of them had newly become men. Always they wanted a war. From the day we stopped feeding from our mothers we had all wanted it. Then our chief chose a day and asked his wizard was that day good. The wizard split a standing *biang* branch and the half on his right hand fell with its round, outer side to the ground, so he knew the day was good. Thirty-two men we were on that war. Before we set out a boar was cut and we ate the flesh. If his heart had been black then we should have set out with joy, because blackness was success. But the heart was red and we swallowed our pork in trouble.

But young men do not stay troubled for long. Besides, we had a strong wizard with us. The chief and his brother climbed horses and we went singing away. Guns we had, and spears and swords. For me and my cousin it was our first day war. We were many and strong, so we had no fear as we went forward in the direction of Rembon. We did not kill men we saw on the way, though truly it was few that we saw because all feared us and hid. When we came near the enemy chief's fort we set fire to two houses and we saw his braves running with their spears into his fort. We all shouted together and danced our war-dance, and our wizard made strong magic on our bodies and weapons. Truly I remember it well.

The boar's red heart had said it would be hard. Six days it was before we could enter the fort. With our spears ten of us made a tunnel through the earthwork round the camp in the night. When it opened inside the fort much earth and stones fell and one of our men was killed under the earth. But we beat the men in the fort. I with my spear opened the belly of one of the chief's sons and he danced and bit a hole in his arm as he died. Two of that chief's sons we killed, but the chief escaped with many of his men. Four altogether we killed, and they killed two of us.

See this my leg, Tuan. The hole of an arrow that day.

But my cousin sucked it and the wizard made good magic and in six days it was sound. Their old women and children we did not touch, nor their rice, but some of the girls our young men enjoyed there in the daylight in our victory, but not I for I was shy. More than twenty bulls and cows we drove away with us and we took swine and chicken for food. I carried only the head of the chief's son I had killed, because I was lame with my wound.

That head I have still. It is hidden.

There was a feast and dancing when we returned. Always in Pangala we had the best dancers. I will tell you, Tuan, the girls were mad for us then! Even the ugly ones would not take the men who had not been on the wars. Tuan, hear. In my good days there was no girl in my village who would not open her arms to me. Ah, Tuan, I could tell you till the sun rises of my good sport in those former nights. In one night five girls . . .

(Siindo, who had listened so far with a smile as rapt as those on the faces of Nemani's two wives and the household females who massed the doorway behind her, began to frown at the disclosures which followed and ordered her hand-maidens back to the kitchens, upbraiding her lord for permitting talk shocking to a high-born guest. It is a pity that I must omit Nemani's entertaining erotic reminiscences, which he confided in a lowered voice, with mischievous relish lighting his vivid eyes. Palinggi wouldn't translate all of them.)

Ah, Tuan knows our old ways. Yes, truly, many things were *pemali* to our women while we were away on a war. They might not bathe till we returned, or the blood would flow from our bodies even as the water flowed from theirs. They might not give away anything at all, or our lives would be surrendered so. And indeed, as Tuan says, they might not play with men, we being away, but (this with bland complacency) truly they would not wish to. For us they waited.

Night war was otherwise. Not so many men. Not so many days. Night war was to find heads for a chief's death-feast so that he might have slaves in the Land of Souls. Maybe twenty for a great chief. Or one man might go to avenge a kinsman taken by an enemy in a night war. Night wars were silence always and creeping. We ambushed men to take them silently, alive, and we took them back to be sacrificed on the field of the death-feast. Even women or children could be taken so. And I will tell you, Tuan, if a chief had not enough braves to capture heads for his feast his family would buy slaves and sacrifice them. Not in Pangala, though. In Pangala warriors were always many.

Tuan knows the name of Pong' Tiku. I was a soldier of Pong' Tiku when all the other Toraja chiefs had fallen to the Company. I was with him at the end in the rock fort at Barupu. But truly we could not hold back the Company when they brought up their giant guns that shook the mountains. We were all afraid when a bullet from such a gun tore the tripes out of a man and shook the eyes from his head. At the end we had no more bullets for our rifles and when we fired our arrows at the Company soldiers—*Wah!* they only caught in their uniforms and they picked them out and laughed.

One time, Tuan, the Company soldiers made a high ladder and set it against the top precipice of our fort. But we saw them, and when many soldiers were climbing up we seized the top of the ladder and hurled it back. *Doi!* The soldiers wept and kicked in the air and died down on the rocks. See this my breast; through that small hole one of their bullets entered. Where it came out you may see here in my shoulder. When our chief yielded I was lying wounded. Him they shot, but me they only beat.

We fought best and last of all the Torajas, who were all fighters then. Now our young people forget those former days, as if they had not been good. They are wrong and

330

all their lives they are children still. Who would take the young men of this time on a war? Babies they are!

He laid a gently contemptuous hand on the shoulder of a slim schoolboy wearing a European shirt under his sarong. "Boy, thou wilt never be a man as thy grandfathers were." But he sighed as he said it, for he knew—and so did the boy—how far better it is to be a young sparrow than an old Bird of Paradise.

The guest-chamber allotted to me was a coffin-like tank of eternal darkness, for the low door was its only opening, and that had to be shut as it gave upon an apartment slept in by certain members of the household. There was a mattress on the floor upon which lay the bolster known as a Dutch wife, and a canopy or mosquito net of thick linen. Duna, tuned to the feudal atmosphere, perhaps, declared that he would sleep across the threshold and undertook to wake me before sunrise. Owing either to the failure of the faintest glimmer of day to penetrate the sealed room or else to the cup of *tuak* I had given him before retiring, or to both, the arrangement failed to work and day started in the room with the following colloquy:

"Ah, Duna, it is morning."

"No, Tuan, it is night."

"It is day. I ask you to open the door."

After some fumbling the door flew open to admit floods of light in which my incredibly dishevelled retainer knelt blinking and scratching his head. From a brief excursion outside he returned with the news that my bath was not yet ready.

"Do they, then, cook water for my bath?" I inquired.

"No, Tuan, but they hang mats by the place of bathing so that the women may not see you and make you ashamed."

This solicitation for my modesty caused delay. At last Palimbong's son came to tell me I might bathe with propriety and guided me through the elaborate curtaining erected round the pool. It was only admission that was difficult; views of the bather were obtainable from many angles.

Palinggi was occupied with a slight hangover during breakfast. Nemani greeted me with marks of affection and begged a photograph of himself with his wives. I was very full of chicken, rice and banana when a slave came in and displayed the biggest goldfish I had ever seen—a five-pounder, I should say. Slightly at a loss, I smiled approval and he withdrew towards the kitchens, infecting me with a spasm of panic in which I pictured the fish being killed and cooked for a final breakfast course. But it didn't happen.

The young Ampulembang was away from home on government business, but his wife sent a servant to invite me to drink coffee with her. An hour after breakfast Palinggi and Duna and I climbed the steep hill at the far end of the village to visit the prince's home. He has two homes. One, his ancestral seat, is magnificently situated on a narrow hill-top, a huge old house of traditional design with finely carved and painted walls from which views of great beauty to north, south, east and west could be enjoyed. There are fine rice-barns and a smaller house with an ancient stone for offerings of food to the gods.

The prince does not live there. The splendid crag-top home is empty. The wealthiest Toraja lives in a small and hideously ugly bungalow of dark basket-work in " European " style, set about with high camellia bushes and stone paths. The little lounge, in which the charming and hand-some daughter of Rombelayu received us, was a horror, a place of massed and pathetic ugliness.

" Fish," muttered Palinggi as I greeted her. I wondered whether he had recovered complete sobriety.

We sat on cane chairs, and my eyes roamed with morbid fascination from the faded mauve *portière* to the fret-work bric-a-brac, from tasselled table-centre to the terrifying woollen flowers embroidered on to canvas squares that shared wall space with plants in glass jars held in ornamental wirework pockets hanging from the wall and reaching fleshy leaves and greedy tendrils towards the framed photographs and highly-coloured copies of advertisement pictures.

" The lady has beautiful flowers," I said, quite unable to compliment anything in the room with a straight face. " What is the Toraja name for such flowers?"

" Fish," said Palinggi softly.

" We have no name for them because they do not grow themselves here," the princess said. " We call them by the Malay name, *katcha piring* (literally " glass plate ")."

" Is the little boy better now?" I asked then, having heard from Siindo that the pale heir who greeted us had been ill.

" He is half better," she said, and left the room to order refreshment.

" Tuan hasn't thanked her for her *fish*," Palinggi burst out in a hoarse undertone as soon as she was gone. Only then did I understand that the noble goldfish displayed to me at breakfast had been the gift of the Ampulembang's wife. My friend was keeping very earnestly his promise to me to guard me against inadvertent discourtesy arising from my ignorance of local custom and language. I had time to prepare a phrase of thanks before the princess returned.

What a room that was! On a sort of high, three-legged table, of the type that support potted ferns in Skegness boarding-houses, an old portable typewriter was displayed as though it were an *objet d'art*. The table on which our coffee was set had tormented and warty legs and a top of imitation alabaster. Over one of the *four* remaining tables a white calico cloth had been draped so as to display a stamped trade mark and the recommendation, EXCELLENT QUALITY NO. 1,000. Caught in the obscene grip of the crawling plants were several amateur pencil drawings of European girls—the sort of thing soldiers sometimes make

333

with tracing paper from movie magazines. A place of
honour had been given to a ticket or label of the kind fixed
to cheap ready-made garments. It gave certain bust and
hip sizes and the declaration, MADE IN ITALY. Some poor art-
lost eye and hand had combined to curl a livid tentacle of
creeper to form a setting for this trophy.

And up the hill, deserted and disdained, the lovely
mansion of the past stood empty in the blue winds.

When I had taken photographs of my host and hostess,
and also of Nemani and his two wives, one his own age and
inclined to scold and the other a pretty young piece, it
began to rain. The elements had been working themselves
up into a state of hysteria and now thunderstorm, cloud-
burst and whirlwind fell together on the village. Lightning
flashes blazed on the ruddy scales of my goldfish as a boy
killed and gutted it. To clean it he held it under one of the
raging spouts of rainwater shooting down from the roof.
The flood shot through the fish's hollow belly and he leapt
back as a stream ran up his arm.

Nemani came up to me.

"What makes the thunder, Tuan?" he asked me.
"What is your belief?"

I told him the white man's theory in so far as I knew it.

He nodded. He and Palinggi then resumed an argument
that went on for more than an hour, and was, in manner, a
model for all disputants. The new Toraja was arguing with
the old. The new arrogant, chromium-plated, sterilised,
clever, anonymous, self-righteous, mass-produced ideas
against the old ideas, hand-wrought, individual, naïve,
blood-warm, the long-loved ways of a humble people of
whom the world has never heard.

Yes, that is sentimental and not quite just, I know; but
it is as it seemed to me then. For I had seen too much of
the evil that attends those triumphant new ideas and I felt

tenderness for the wild beauty of the people's own way of
life that was dying now of a thousand wounds.

I took no part in the argument and could not, indeed,
follow it in more than broad outline, for the wizard and the
evangelist spoke their own tongue. But I took a sustained
delight in the grace and graciousness, the humour and good
humour, with which the dispute was conducted, for all its
vivid animation.

Rombelayu rested during the afternoon, but he rejoined
us for the evening, still wearing the Bronze Star he had
brought out when he posed for my camera. He called a
slave to bring the contents of his armoury for me to see—a
handsome collection. Shotguns with rich silverwork, heavy
swords, slender spears and a fine blowpipe. The blowpipe
was seven feet long, of polished dark wood with an ivory
mouthpiece and fine rattan binding at the far end. The
arrows were very light, with staggered barbs. There was a
remote smile on the old chief's heavily-lined face as we
handled his sleeping weapons. Nemani was not the only
one there with an affection for his people's past.

The young men of the house, seeing these rusted trophies
brought out of their darkness, began to bring to light other
treasures. There were old ivory dice and an ancient pack
of painted playing-cards that unhappily could not tell their
story. The gramophone, too, was antique, as gramophones
go. Its one record was of Buginese songs, which sounded
faintly and absurdly through the harsh mechanical background rasping, like a lullaby crooned during the passing
of an armoured division.

An old man handed me a heavy bag from which I drew a
handful of fine old silver coins—crowns and crusados,
Portugese escudos and Mexican dollars and many Dutch
florins or crowns, all bearing the busts of long-dead
sovereigns. I was in no way surprised to find such treasure
in Siambe's possession; for centuries the Toraja nobles have
collected and hoarded coins. Before white men even knew

of the existence of the Torajas, a traffic in white man's money was going on between those valleys and the outside world through Palopo. Rich Torajas still possess hoards of silver coin. Some of them have chests full of Western money.

"Don't go away to-morrow, Tuan," Rombelayu said as he rose to hobble off to his early bed. "Stay a moon with us. It is good here."

Yes, it was good there, but next morning I was on the road again, the road for Rantepao, where I had an appointment with Dr. Goslinga. With an air of importance a small boy insisted on leading me off the track down a narrow, slippery path to a glade in which a grey old house stood. He pointed up to the place under the gable where normally a long-necked cock stands out from the decorated wall.

But this was an old *tongkonan*, a tribal house, the temple which enshrined the ancestral spirits of Rombelayu's clan. And instead of a cock there was a staring human skull.

Green lichen had overgrown some of the white bone. Some of the teeth had fallen out. But the sacrificed warrior's head still bore the supreme emblem of courage and virtue— the horns, wide and resplendent, of a sacrificed bull.

Welcome at Pangala

Back View at Buffalo Inoculation

XVI

MOVING HOUSE

MY Toraja diary records only nine morning rains during the whole of my stay. Five of these fell on the five days upon which I moved house.

"Tuan travels, morning rain." Massang and the rest evolved this catchword and chanted it as porters lounged among piles of roped baggage, staring out into the grey, gauzy rain. It was like that the morning I moved to Tikala, the district north of Rantepao, where the *baruga* of Bori had been placed at my disposal for a fortnight.

Before noon the rain ceased and we set off—Salu, Barra, Lendu, Sesa, Massang and Timbo, seven porters and myself. The journey was only twelve miles, but I spent most of the day in Rantepao, and sunset was not far off when Timbo and I turned northwards on to the long, narrow rice-plain of Tikala. Our path took us first across the plain to its western wall, winding between expanses of high-standing green rice. The cliffs of various little mountains and eventually the foothills of Sesian himself comprised the western wall, and soon our way became the narrow grassy track at the base of those cliffs, passing over many thatched bridges and beneath many small cliff villages. From one of these eyries we were hailed by Lendu and Barra, who were staying the night in some congenial company they had found on their way back to La'bo after helping Salu to move in at Bori.

"Tuan will have far to walk for his bath," called Barra in answer to inquiries about the house, "and the dirty Nippons have written all over the cookhouse wall."

Timbo was a good walking companion. He had a word

for everybody we met and usually some comment to make on them after they had passed. " Hoho, done to a turn! " he shouted at a startled old woman who was bending over a fire in a cabin. " Ho, stay! " he called to two girls who darted away from a bathing-pool at our approach. " The Tuan wants you both to-night! " He carried my Hounsfield bed and wore the big straw labourer's sombrero I sometimes wore on horseback.

Salu, fearing that we had lost our way, lit outside the house a great beacon fire that we saw for miles across the silent fields. Later the moon rose and showed us the tombs in the boulders at the roadside. The mask of the bull had been incised and painted on each of the small square doors, and on some the dead person's hat and *sireh* bag were still hanging. We came suddenly on a roadside *rante* in the moonlight that was crowded with megaliths ten and twelve feet high of a kind I had not seen before. They had all been worked to smooth, rounded surfaces and slender, column-like proportions with the exception of one, which was an obelisk. They were so closely crowded that they gave the impression of a temple that had lost its roof.

The *baruga* was a handsome little place on top of a bluff with a shingled roof, grilled windows and floors of *banga* bark so springy as to alarm. Its front door commanded a superb view of Tikala plain and its enclosing mountains. Golden orioles whistled in the tall trees at the back and huge banana leaves flapped resoundingly with every rising of the wind. But it was lonely after La'bo. The grass track past the windows was usually empty of wayfarers, and after the social hurly-burly of La'bo, the Bori bungalow, with its high, barred windows, was almost as solitary as a prison cell. Only the County called—the agreeable old *kepala bua* and his sons, one of them agricultural adviser to the area.

I don't think Bori was less friendly than La'bo, in fact; but I was there only a short time and was, moreover, busy with a disagreeable task connected with the world I had left behind; so I did not set about getting to know my neighbours. I left without knowing more than two or three of them, apart from a handful of children.

White men are curiosities still in Bori, so I was not surprised when all the small buffalo grooms made the discovery that the platform of thin grass directly outside my window offered the best grazing in the neighbourhood. The parish buffaloes grew very tired of that halting-place and demurred, gently but in vain, at spending so long there acting as grand stand seats from which their grooms could watch the exotic pageantry of my daily life.

One of the smallest of these admirers was a shaven-headed scrap of rapt humanity who wore a small tunic of pineapple fibre cloth but nothing below the waist. His cow became almost a fixture beneath my barred window, and for a week or so he smiled seraphically whenever I looked up, but never ventured a word. One early morning when he reined up his patient beast in her usual station he spoke at last.

" *Tuang Neneh!* " he said, in a cooing tone.

Neneh, or *nenek*, means grandfather, but though most white people look far older than their years to Torajas, it did not necessarily mean that he imagined me elderly. Quite often humble Torajas addressed me as *Siambe*, or " Old Man," out of respect. A young prince is often so addressed.

Later that morning, when I gave Salu some *golla-golla* for the children, I said, " Ask the name of him who has the grey cow, the small child who is always there. The very good little boy."

Gravely Salu returned, and said, " His name is Nefarious."

" Nefarious? " I queried.

" That is his name," said Salu. And so it was. My small admirer was another whose parents had feared the gods might take him away, so they called him So' Kedanking, which means " abominable " or " nefarious."

339

In return for the sweets Nefarious brought me shortly afterwards a small, feathery nest with four baby birds in it. We took it back to the hairy trunk of a sugar palm and he went off to find an alternative gift in the rice-fields below the bungalow. After an hour he climbed up to my window with three speckled eggs, smaller than pigeons' eggs, which he had found and sunk in the warm water to test their freshness. Fried, they made three delicious mouthfuls.

One day a buffalo inoculation was held close by the bungalow, a large-scale event at which the cattle of nine villages were protected against anthrax. Along the edge of the bluff a skeleton tunnel of stout bamboo had been erected at great speed, the villages concerned co-operating in the work as they co-operated to provide wood for the fires in which the branding-irons were heated and on which water for the sterilisation of the instruments was boiled. The beasts arrived at well-spaced intervals and generally the event was a good example of quiet organisation and joint effort, varied only by an old man with some small grievance who seized on the opportunity for eloquence to state his case to all and sundry with the passion and fine music of a great actor in the later scenes of *Lear*.

On his arrival the Toraja *mantri* came to greet me, took off his shoes and stowed them carefully in the cookhouse, and went off barefoot in the mud to superintend his assistant's preparations. The inoculating syringe was gruesomely large.

The buffaloes, usually so docile, became aware that something abnormal was imminent, and many of them distrusted the narrow entry into the tunnel. It was an exhausting day for the grooms. Even the mild cow I knew best there, she in the charge of little Nefarious, took sudden fright and bolted, with Nefarious hanging on to her rope while his tiny heels drew stubborn and unavailing grooves in the thick mud.

Ten beasts could be accommodated at a time in the

340

tunnel, each held in place by cross-bars. The grooms swarmed over the scaffolding, quelling or comforting their charges while the *mantri* went down the outside of the tunnel, leaping up ten times to plunge the great needle with a lunge of his arm deep into an animal's shoulder. Then the cross-pieces were whipped out, the beasts plunged forward, and there were scenes of confusion before the child grooms regained control.

Ta'ropu! was the curse most frequently shrilled at the restive buffaloes. " May you have the anthrax! "

Massang and Timbo were dismissed the day after our arrival in Bori, but three days later they came back saying they wished to stay with me until I departed for my own country. Despite Massang's dreadful desultory whistling, the bungalow became livelier with their return and Salu was particularly pleased to have our clown back. *Tuak* was very cheap in Bori, and half a cupful each sunset stimulated Timbo to new extremes of foolery.

The two boys, whose lives had hitherto been spent close to a road along which hundreds of people passed daily and even an automobile once a week or a fortnight, conducted themselves like boulevardiers exiled to the provinces. Bori, they gave me to understand, was a wild and primitive place by comparison with La'bo.

It certainly seemed so on the day I set off past the school-house where Mr. van der Loosdrecht had suffered his inadvertent martyrdom and climbed for more than an hour into the hills to attend the preliminary death-feast for a small chief who had died a week or two previously. The feast-field was the sort of place you hardly believe the moment you have left it—suspended in mist so thick that the tops of the surrounding trees were out of sight and echoing with the tragic cries of birds that perched invisibly above our heads. The longstones were thickly crowded, very tall and

341

pillar-like, leaning as though from weariness. There were echoes, as though the whole place had been inside a great cavern. The moment I reached the edge of the field an old madman came at me, mouthing and waving thin arms.

The mourners sat like people who had missed a train at a country junction, in the shade of a high bell built of *induk* fronds and overhung with dripping pennons of purple silk. Six buffaloes were slaughtered and a heap made of their dismembered limbs, organs and tripes from which boys kept stealing scraps. They would sidle up to the heap, passing like shadows from the shelter of one grey megalith after another, and suddenly whip out a knife and tear off a strip of warm flesh. If the wizard who was orating beside the meat-pile saw them he would shout angrily, or even throw a stick, but nobody moved to punish the children or take back the filched shreds of meat.

They were all avid for meat, reminding me almost of tobacco smokers in England during cigarette shortages, for meat was something they tasted perhaps only once a year. Everybody, young and old, got a share, including me. The wizard, mounted on a large flat stone instead of the *balaka'an* platform, threw hundreds of joints towards the ring of guests, calling a name each time he threw. The squelching collapse with which some of the not-so-choice cuts landed in the wet grass was extremely unattractive.

The people were, for Torajas, tall and slim, moving with delicacy and seeming always to be listening. Wild people. But their sudden answering smiles were Toraja smiles, warm and guileless. A four-year-old who was picking the marrow from a bone and eating it raw offered me some as soon as he saw me watching. A man with an axe sliced up the six buffalo heads, detaching the horns. A little girl took one bloody head on to her lap and carefully drew the brains out through a hole in the forehead.

I sat with a chief under an awning and drank *tuak* while the old madman, who was treated with rough kindness, squatted by a longstone and stared at me through gummy eyelids. Youths danced in a circle, chanting on three stark notes. I stayed three hours there, very content without really knowing why.

The Builder of Heaven paid me two visits at Bori. He, the Ampulembang of Tikala, was an agreeable visitor, nicely spoken for an ampulembang. A pleasing change from the colourless miser of Kesu. In European clothes he and his younger sons might be taken for handsome Frenchmen. His hair is white but his face is youthful and his eyes a little calculating, I always thought.

After one of our talks I realised more regretfully than ever what a meagre fraction of the treasury of Toraja ceremony I had been able to glimpse. " It is little you have seen, Tuan, of our big feasts," the prince said. There were, he told me, the *ma'bua* feasts, for instance, feasts that may now be extinct, for none has been held in the past few years. In them *burakkes* or wizards prayed day and night in the tops of little towers from which hung ribbons held by dancers like maypole dancers in England. It may be, too, that the *maro* rituals will soon be extinct. None of them was held during my stay in Celebes. Their purpose is to plead with the *deata* for the recovery of a sick person, or perhaps a community of sick persons during an epidemic, and also to promote recovery by magical practices.

Salu, who has attended many, told me about them.

" After sunset they start, Tuan, and do not stop until past midnight for many nights, perhaps a whole moon. Much bamboo is collected for torches and it is lighter than day and warm from all the torches. The sick person is in a little pavilion and a circle of dancers dance the *ma'gellu* round him. They dance a long time. Two hours, perhaps. Then the wizard cuts his tongue with his sword and rubs his blood over the sick person's body. The dancers sit in their circle, watching, and asking the *deata* to heal the sick person. The wizard makes *tabang* leaves hot and rubs them over the sick person because they are strong (the village people think they are strong; we Christians do not). And the wizard takes a spear and pushes it into the sick person's arms and back and belly and legs, especially where he is sick, because the spear is strong and will give the sick person strength (that is what those village people believe; we not). The singers ask the *deata* not to let the spear cut the sick person's flesh. And perhaps the wizard presses the blade of a sword into the sick person's body and the singers sing prayers that it may not cut him. Sometimes they light a fire under the sick person, with strong leaves burning, so that he may get strength from the smoke.

" After that they carry the sick man home, it may be four hours past sunset, and the dance begins again. It gets harder and harder until one of the dancers, or perhaps more than one, Tuan, gets strong in his soul. He does not know what he does. He is *ma'deata*. The gods are holding him. He jumps into the middle of the circle and whirls round for a long time, seeing stars and wonders, and then he calls for a spear or a sword or a high bamboo. All those things are near, because truly it is known that some persons will be *ma'deata*. If it is a sword he wants he will cut his head with it and cover his face with blood, but feeling no pain. If a spear he will sit on it and whirl round. If a bamboo he will climb up it and sit on the top playing a flute.

" When a woman is *ma'deata* she will not climb a bamboo, but she may cry out for a ladder of swords. There will be a ladder of swords ready, each step a blade, and she will climb it singing and her feet will not be cut. Or she may dance, whirling like one mad, while a man standing behind her holds a sword-blade round her waist. After they have been *ma'deata* persons are weak and sleep long. Then the dance will start again and when it gets hard more dancers

344

will be held by the gods. And thus every night, perhaps for one moon."

I would have given much to see a *maro* feast, but I did not even see the much smaller and rather similarly named *merok* feast which is held at a *tongkonan* and attended only by the higher castes. It is a ceremony held for the welfare of the tribal house, with much feasting on pigs and music played by virtuosi on *poni-ponis*. Nor had I any chance to see a *mangrara banua*, the festival of dedication performed in a new house.

" It is a little you have seen, Tuan, of our feasts," sighed the Builder of Heaven, and I, too, sighed again for the excitement and colour and vitality that is falling away from Toraja life, to become for a short time the glowing memories of the old men and women and then to drown in oblivion.

There was morning rain on the day we moved to Pangala.

That was a hard day's trek, up for hours along a path through the foothills of Sesian and the coffee groves of Tondoklitak, again and again crossing the spectacular Alpine road that climbs from Rantepao to Pangala. A dozen porters, climbing in pairs, carried our belongings slung on poles resting on their shoulders. Up through the clouds over a high pass and down into the upland valleys of Pangala, where every morning the coconut cooking oil was " dead," or congealed by the cold, and my thermometer recorded sunrise temperatures below 60 degrees Fahrenheit.

The moon we spent in Pangala was a major adventure for Timbo and Massang, who had never dreamed of travelling so far from their homes. Halting near the top of the pass and gazing back through a rent in the mist across the mountains of Tikala, Timbo said wryly, " There is the last of our country," and they turned and went on like old Christians crossing the frontier of Turkey, plunging down hair-raising short-cuts between the tight, steep bends of

345

the path, for no Toraja seems able to resist a short-cut in
the hills, however close to the vertical it may be. Unfortunately, the boys were not among those who can enjoy
the real pleasures of travel, for they believed that their own
ways were the best and all alien custom was the object of
either their scorn or their patronising tolerance.

On my first evening in La'bo I had been told of the
formidable and malignant sorcery commanded by the men
of Pangala. The two young slaves took no chances with this
and never had anything to do with the people there. They
would not go out alone and they delighted in telling me
tales of the barbarous habits of the Pangala people, their
coarse speech, their unreliability and their folly. " What
a lot of cigarettes the *parenge* smoked! " remarked Timbo,
usually respectful to his superiors, removing a loaded ashtray after the prince's first visit to our bungalow. That
fine piece of building, however, compelled their reluctant
admiration. " They are clever at building, these bad men."
" It is a good prince they have got here," Salu said, with
shrewd head-noddings. " He sees that all is done well."

Tondon, the village capital of Sarungu, the Ampulembang, bears witness to his energy and resource. The word
Pangala means " forest," and his district, unlike Kesu, grows
a good deal of hardwood. Moreover, he has a body of
builders, carpenters and other craftsmen in wood who are
unrivalled in the Torajalands. Instead of the basket-walled
schools of Kesu, thrown up in a day or two and easily kept
in repair by the young schoolboys, Pangala has schools of
whitewashed wooden walls and shingled roofs. There is a
handsome district office in the same style. Besides the very
large rest-house that was my home in Tondon there are fine
barugas in Barupu and Awan that put the humble lodges of
other districts in the shade. The prince has built an avenued
approach to his district office, which is the terminus of the
240-mile road from Makassar. (There is no road linking
South Celebes with the northern half of the island.)

346

Our house, with its large rooms and many windows, commanded a magnificent prospect through a screen of tall *lomben* trees across to the mountains of the west. The front faced a near mountain called Buntu Assa, like the crag that faced the front of the bungalow in La'bo. Some of the warriors who made an unavailing stand there under Pong' Tiku before retiring to the fortress at Barupu for their final stand, still live on the high slopes of the mountain. One of them had his cabin and garden on the very summit, so that the smoke from his little fire gave Buntu Assa the appearance of a feeble volcano.

Between the house and the *lomben* trees was a stretch of levelled turf grazed by the Ampulembang's horses and used as a playground by the school children. On one glittering morning it was the stage for a charming ceremony of welcome, when the *pa'gellu* dancers came and danced to me below the house. There was a lively breeze and the girls' white silk dresses and cataracts of beads fluttered with other rhythms than those of the dance. The sun shone on smooth black hair and gilded beads and swords. The four men crouching round the old brown drum filled the air with sudden drama.

It is sad that dances cannot be adequately described in words. The grace and shining beauty of the *pa'gellu* is unforgettable, more delightful than anything I saw in Java or Bali or Europe. The most astonishing thing about it is the harmony between the flower-like delicacy of the dancers in their beauty and the tempestuous uproar of the drum—a harmony as perfect as it is enigmatic.

As long as I live I shall remember that morning; the shining clouds in a gentian sky, the distant cloud-frilled peaks, the pale trunks and limbs of the *lombens*, the golden bloom on perfect brown arms and fluttering fingertips, the tranced faces under diadems of barbaric gold beads, the sheen of snowy silk, gold-sheathed swords rising and falling on full young breasts, slim figures turning slow circles in perfect unison and the earthquaking echoes of the drum. . . .

Another greeting, just as welcome but less lovely, came from the village school children, who serenaded me one morning with song and orchestra. The girls and a few boys played recorders and flutes while the older boys had instruments that were quaint bamboo caricatures of cornets and trombones and tubas. Each child had made his or her own instrument.

There was charm about their performance of the rubbishy bits of rum-tee-tum fairground music they had been taught. The tone of every instrument was mellow and the dissonances, due to limitations of the lower instruments, rather improved the compositions. Surmounting the prodigious bass *pompangs*, played by grave senior boys, were large tin horns like those seen on early phonographs.

A few days previously the choir had won first place in a music festival in Rantepao, and certainly their singing was better than any I had heard in Kesu. They sang like little automata, frowning eyes fixed on the Menadonese *guru's* rigid, mechanical beat. All the notes were right. But the Western hymns were as wrong and alien on their lips as Chinese songs would be on the lips of children in Manchester. I knew better, though, than to ask for any Toraja music. That would have shocked the *guru*.

It was sad that I had to be so insincere with my praise. I was delighted at their visit and grateful to them and the *guru* for thinking of me. I was touched by the purity of the young voices, but angry that they had been torn and lured away from the music and the song that was their birthright.

The landscape of Pangala was a contrast to that of Kesu, twenty-five miles away and 1,500 feet nearer sea level. The soil of the uplands was of a brilliant rose madder and shockingly vulnerable. A small gash would widen in the next storm to a great rosy wound with a rivulet of what looked like tomato soup flowing from it. That was the soil of the barren moors, wastes of horned bracken which the children wore like tiaras. The rice-fields were deep and rich, set in narrow valleys enclosed by steep cliffs of soft sandstone. The rice ripens early there and the first fields were harvested before the first green ears had appeared in La'bo. On the banks of many fields I saw small stone platforms with columns at their side, places for offering food to the gods, and there were a few fertility symbols of sandstone ten or fifteen feet high.

The waterways of Pangala were swifter and noisier than the little whispering rivulets and falls of La'bo. Most of them were confined in deep, square-bedded courses easily carved in the soft sandstone, but they were so turbulent that those who used the paths running beside them got their legs splashed. There were fewer buffaloes and few coconut palms; what palms there were, were barren because of the cold. In the highland village of Tondoklitak, the stopping-place on the formidable path to Rantepao, it was colder still and I shivered under my two blankets.

It was in Tondoklitak, which was the home of Lai' Lebok, that I photographed the *manganda* dancer. Knowing that the dance, in which headdresses of prodigious size and weight are worn, could not be performed during the growing of the rice, I had not asked to see it, but I told the Ambulembang I would like a dancer to pose for my camera in the headdress. He told me later that he had been unable to arrange this, since all the dancers feared that the rice crop would suffer if the sacred helmet were worn even for a moment while the rice stood in the fields. I asked the prince to explain that I had made the request out of ignorance.

Up in Tondoklitak, however, they were less conscientious and representations made through Lai' Lebok resulted in a man agreeing to wear the helmet for a moment so long as he was not asked to dance. He was tall for a

349

Toraja, only three inches short of six feet, with a grave face pitted with smallpox, and strong; for only strong men can bear the crushing weight of the *manganda* helmet, and then only for two minutes at a time. Each dancer is partnered by a fellow-dancer, who takes over the wearing of the helmet every two minutes or so.

I will not estimate the weight of this fantastic headdress, but I had to make a real effort to lift it from the ground. The main feature was a pair of immense bull horns and between them were ranged rows of hundreds of large silver coins, among them an old English crown. Plumes surmounted it and *batik* cloths fell in a train from the back. I was not surprised to hear that the dance was " very slow."

What else do I remember Pangala for?

The arm-chairs in the bungalow, certainly. Eight of them, expertly made from the rattan gathered in the forest close by. " Lazy chairs " the young slaves called them, and when they cleaned the room they always arranged them with their backs to the centre, like seats in a picture gallery.

The spider in the lavatory that was so big I could hear his footsteps. To walk into one of his webs was to recoil sharply, as when one collides with a wire.

The tomb on a high cliff-ledge of the man who had beheaded his wife and then committed suicide. The two *tao-taos* sat side by side, staring at us with white, tranced eyes. Realistic crimson lines had been drawn round the wooden throats.

The grave of the warrior chief Pong' Tiku, protected by a swarm of wild bees that live inside it. The grim, lonely falcons that perched on the dead cliff-top branches. The fluting of the rice-stalk pipes, the *poni-ponis*, made by the children. The blind man who came day after day to sit and listen to Salu's talk of me, turning his saintly, uplifted face in my direction whenever I spoke, like a poet listening to the nightingale. The musical cries of the school children, enraptured by such simple games as blindman's-buff in the field below the bungalow (the girls never playing in the same game as the boys).

Then there was the steep rise in housekeeping costs as chicken prices rocketed owing to the heavy demand for birds to sacrifice at the harvesting of each field. The lively, shrewd conversation of the admirable prince. The little girl whose foot I healed so successfully and whose name was Cockroach. The grim Christian funeral of the poor woman who had died in child-bed, the silent mourners and the black coffin. The morning when the *guru* taught the senior class the " Marseillaise " in slow-march time. . . .

Best of all, I remember the chorus of evening rice-pounding, the whirling rhythm of that ringing music echoing from every surrounding slope. For the time of the rice harvest is the only time when there are no hungry Torajas.

XVII

SWAN TO MAMASA

WHEN my last Toraja moon was born, lying on its back and kicking like a baby in the evening sky, and I knew that before it had waned I should be far away, I decided on one last fling, a last wide look round the fair region for which I should one day be homesick in my own homeland. A seven-days' wander through the hill country. What in an armoured division we had called a " swan; " the free, swift advance of the armour through enemy-held country after a break-through.

" Let us go to Mamasa, Tuan," said Salu.

" For one week's journey Mamasa is best," declared the Ampulembang of Pangala. " Stay till the harvest is over and I will come with Tuan."

Massang did not fail to impress upon me the formidable nature of the magical powers commanded by the people of Mamasa. Some of their wizards could raise the dead.

" It is a beautiful journey to Mamasa," said Dr. Goslinga. "As beautiful as our *patroli* to Baoo and Simbuang." He had arrived at Pangala for a night, having combined business with pleasure in a short swan to Balokkan and over the hills with his family. They came over the high moors and mountains, the flaxen-haired boys marching barefoot along the hard upland tracks, Mevrouw Goslinga frequently stopping her horse to study or gather the small tropical flowers she knows so well.

On a morning which, though it followed eight rainless days, we had known beforehand would surely bring one of the rare morning rains, we set off in a fine, cool downpour, I and Salu and Massang and Timbo and two porters from

Lai'Lebok

Horse and Horseboy

the village. I was mounted on the small bay stallion which had kindly been placed at my disposal by the Ampulembang, a useful little beast who, however, was less of a character than Ronni and seldom seemed entirely at ease with me.

" What is his name? " I had asked the horse-boy who first brought him to me.

" He has no name, Tuan," the boy said, adding the question: " Have horses names in Tuan's country? "

" Always," I told him.

His next question I took to mean, " What is the word for horse in Tuan's country? " so I answered " Horse."

He and those around laughed and began to talk to the stallion, addressing him as " Horse." In fact, he had asked me for an example of a name given to a horse in England. From that day my mount's personal name was Horse and, for all I know, still is. He carried me now along paths between deep paddy-fields, the wealth of rice standing in level forests of gold under high sandstone cliffs in which children had carved miniature make-believe tombs. As soon as we were up on the wild moors of diadem bracken the rain left us. There were many chestnut cuckoos up there, but though Massang kept a sharp lookout, fortunately none was seen to fly across our path. I do not think I could have persuaded Massang to advance that day along a path which he had seen the bird of ill omen crossing.

Then down into a valley that was more like an immense gorge, with Horse picking his way in the most finicking manner round the giddy succession of hairpin bends and gazing earnestly into the smallest puddle of water before venturing to plant one unshod hoof into it. He climbed with gaiety, though, picking up speed whenever the ground rose again, his long tail sweeping the rocky path. My feet almost swept the path as well, for even at their full extension the stirrup leathers were too short to accommodate my long legs in comfort except over short distances.

I was lucky in my companions. Unless they were dead

tired they kept up an inconsequent flow of chatter and comment, all in Malay so that I should not feel out of it. Timbo was never dull, for his drollness was largely in his manner and appearance. I had never been able to afford a private jester before and the small expense of his keep was abundantly justified. Like Sterne with La Fleur, I was " hourly recompensed by the festivity of his temper."

Later that day I wished I had met him earlier. He all at once stopped and declared he could hear an aircraft. I could hear nothing and an aircraft over those mountains seemed more than unlikely; but a moment later Salu and Massang could hear it and Timbo could see it. Still I could not hear it. After twenty seconds or so I heard-it, and though I found it with my field-glasses, flying at something like 25,000 feet, it remained out of sight of my naked eye.

I told them we should have been glad of them as spotters on our Portland ack-ack gun site in 1940. They would have liked that, the young slaves said, after I had described what would have been their duties and some of their experiences. I dug out of my mental war diary the story and picture of the battle on that hot July afternoon when in a few minutes more than forty enemy aircraft had been brought down over the harbour.

" *Bagus!* " cried Timbo. Lovely! But Massang frowned. I think he was calculating the gigantic power of the magical forces that must have been deployed on such an occasion.

That was the first aeroplane I had seen for five months. I could still do very well without them. It was better to turn my glasses on to a fine falcon with a back of arctic grey and snowy underparts that hovered above the valley for whole minutes together.

" We say that he pleasures the wind," said Salu. It struck me as an earthy fancy of some charm.

Up, up above the village of Awan, which means " Cloud," and along a bald ridge for miles to the coffee estate of Rante Karua. Salu had at one time worked up here among the bushes of scarlet berries and we were obliged to stop and accept the hospitality of a village chief who was a friend of those days.

At Rante Karua is the end of one of the few Toraja roads, the road to Balokkan, Bituang and Makale. It is a wide, grass-grown track, falling in serpentine curves and darkened by the thick orchid forests on either side, a little like a drive between rhododendron woods in the grounds of an English country house. For more than an hour I saw no house and met only three men, tall and rather handsome mountain men wearing loincloths and basketwork back-shields to protect them while working in the noon sun.

Ahead of the others at one point, I went into the forest to pick some orchids. I found it in that state of chaotic dilapidation characteristic of Celebesian forests; on all sides dead and rotting trees leaned in the toils of choking creepers, unable to fall into their graves. Every footstep sank into soft, yielding layers of decay. There was a smell of fermentation and one of those delightful birds, still tantalisingly unseen, that sang " Dee-lullulla-lulla " chromatically down from E to B.

I do not know whether there is a season when the orchids of those forests burst into concerted bloom or whether the different varieties maintain a small but steady output of blossom over the year. In May, at all events, there is not a great deal of flower. I saw orchid plants sprouting and drooping from nearly every branch, but it was a moment or two before I spotted the first spray of primrose and beech-green blossom on an old stump. As I gathered it, rather a large tree fell down quite close to me and I withdrew to the road, wondering wheter hI may have been disturbing the balance of nature.

While waiting for the others I lay down in a patch of dead yellow grass, but this was another unfortunate intrusion. After a moment I became aware of a subdued hissing or rustling about me, and turning to look among the dry reedy stems I discovered that I had invaded a dragonfly dormitory.

These fragile creatures retire to rest as soon as the sinking sun ceases to glitter on their jewelled bodies. Upon that eastward-facing slope the sunshine was lost more than an hour before sunset and already a company of some hundreds of them had folded themselves in amity among the stems of the tall, scorched grass. I now saw that in my intrusion I had crushed scores of them. Their dazzling bodies, ruby, gold, carmine and sapphire, trembled in ruin where I had lain, while the survivors fluttered in drowsy alarm, their frail wings rustling like thin paper being crumpled. With awkward compunction I moved away and sat on a rock.

The neat, white-walled *baruga* at Balokkan is really a *passanggrahan*, for there is a staff in charge to cook and serve meals, as well as beds and oil lamps. That evening there was a fragrant wood fire besides, almost a necessity in the low, fresh temperature, and before it sat a young controleur from South Celebes and his wife. They were enjoying a short change in that quiet spot after the tension of the recent outbreak of terrorism in the south of the island, now happily past. For a controleur during that time survival had been no more than a fifty-fifty chance.

We talked rather drowsily for an hour. I was asked where I had been during the war and gave my account. Then, and I am afraid it may have been with a trace of condescension as from a belligerent to an enforced non-belligerent, I asked the Controleur where he had been.

"For the last two years, in Buchenwald," he said.

It was downhill for several miles next morning, down into the radiant valley which Nemani, then a newly ripe boy, had invaded fifty years ago on his first war, the valley of Bituang. To our left as we descended we saw through screens of pampas grass a valley that flashed with a thousand mirrors, for there the rice had been planted no more than a month and the plants merely stippled the water surfaces. The morning sun blazed on the faces of many outcrop hills of

chalk that were crowned with copses and homesteads. In a
large rice-field stood a rock fertility symbol perhaps fifteen
feet high. The village of Bituang lay hidden in woods on
the far side, and the western mountains beyond, over which
our path to Mamasa lay, were hooded in cloud.

I remember the high hedges of marigolds, too, splendid
blossoms of gold standing taller than myself; and there was
a gruesome scarecrow—or scareboar, rather—a caricature of
a hairy man brilliantly devised out of a huge *banga* leaf and
hanging by the neck from a tall bamboo, pirouetting horribly
in a morning breeze.

Bituang was a village with a mosque, a small one roofed
with thin grey shingles that looked like slate. Then we were
off the high road and on the path for Mamasa. Like all paths,
tracks and lanes, it was nicer than any road or highway in
the world.

The climb up into the orchid forest was long and gruelling
under a sun that seemed to pierce the flesh and scorch the
bones; but in the forest the coolness was delicious. Our path
became curiously blind there, and we could see none of the
waterfalls that thundered near and far. After landscapes so
vast that the curvature of the horizon was almost manifest,
it was strange suddenly to be shut in a dark little coffin of
space, bounded by narrow green walls of foliage and the
last turn in the path and the next.

It was virgin forest, a congested and ant-ridden world of
a thousand different greens, almost explosive with the uprush of its vitality. Orchids abounded, several of them
disturbingly fragrant. Indeed, the trees themselves were
only a background, mere rows of display-stands for vast
assemblages of orchids and other epiphytes and parasitic
plants.

The polymorphous diversity of these hangers-on was
overwhelming. One step into the forest and you were
surrounded by them, by creepers and streamers and veils
of them, by plumes and fountains and fishbones of them,

357

cockades and rosettes, climbing or winding, falling or sprouting, usurping the *lebensraum* of honest plants having their roots in the soil. I didn't like them very much.

The steep track down from the path is so narrow on certain stretches that two wayfarers cannot pass each other without ado. Not that the situation arises very often; when it does, seeing the lonely, tiny figure amid the immensities of slopes and skies, one is reminded of T. E. Lawrence's words, " The essence of the desert was the lonely moving individual, the son of the road, apart from the world as in a grave." On the descents I was always well ahead of the others, because I had no patience with Horse's painful caution at such times and left him behind with them. (I had begun to think that it was not so much nervousness that made him crawl as a search for discarded banana skins. Whenever he found one he halted and ate it with lingering relish.)

Losing my way for a few minutes down by the side of a headlong river, I came upon a scene of arcadian fascination. Four girls, about to bathe or having bathed, were playing together among the rapids in a diamond storm of sunlit waterdrops. They did not see me and I focused the scene, framed in dark folliage, on the reflex viewfinder of my camera, watching the unmeaning system of blurs resolve themselves into points of sunlight on hair, teeth and water-glistening breasts and limbs. It was the only time I saw Toraja girls nude in the open without adopting the graceful and deft series of poses and hand movements with which they avoid full exposure.

Then I recollected myself with a twinge of shame. I was being too Anglo-Saxon altogether. Toraja men did not spy on unclothed women and they despised the Australian soldiers who had. So I closed my camera, merely filing the scene in memory for possible revival in elderly daydreams, and turned away with a guilty glance over my shoulder in case Salu should be standing there in shocked dismay.

But Horse and his attendants were still far behind, snailing down the steep path. Soon I was lost again, or thought I was. For more than a mile I walked, hot and tired, looking for the *baruga* at Belaoo, where I had said we would halt for the midday hour. I saw two ancient death-houses, but the only dwellings of the living in sight were on the other side of the river. I could see a path there and wondered whether I should have crossed where the girls had been bathing. A very old woman who came up the path fled in terror when she saw me, crying out, " No, no! " to my despairing plea to be directed to Belaoo, her thin legs stumping wildly in a frenzy of primitive fear. I am sure there were others like her, whom I never saw, who hid in the forest or among the rocks when they saw me coming.

A more helpful encounter rewarded me a little farther on, where the path turned and plunged into the river, a torrent four feet deep with a number of boulders here and there just under the surface. I was saved from the tiresome necessity of stripping off clothes and field-boots by the arrival of a magnificent man in a fringed loincloth and a fine sword who, taking my right hand in his left and holding his sword aloft with his right, plunged in and led me across like a conductor leading in a *prima donna*. The picture became even more absurd in midstream when I slipped off one of the submerged boulders and saved my cameras from total immersion only by throwing my arms round his neck. Grinning indulgently, he took the weight, restored my balance and led me safely to the other side.

The delightful little rest-hut of Belaoo was by then in sight. Waiting in its shade for Salu to come down and make coffee, I fell sound asleep amid the roar of the waters that pass in tumult on either side of it.

In the uplands above Belaoo the rice was almost ripe and

the war on the little finchy birds that flock to rob the ears was in full swing.

The Torajas display much ingenuity in the armament they have devised against these greedy marauders. There are bunches of coconut shells hanging from posts and attached by long strings of rattan to the tiny headquarter huts of the field-guards, where their ends are tied to the big toes of the small boys on duty who jerk them at intervals and rouse the drowsy sky with their clatter. Then there are edifices like windmills twenty feet high, with plumed sails that flap and creak and waver in a breeze. There are balanced bamboo containers under slow trickles of irrigated water which the moment they are full depress levers and release trip-wires controlling intricate systems of dry bamboo poles geared to clatter alarmingly on receipt of an impulse. Then there are baffle-boards suspended in waterfalls; their swinging and buffeting is communicated by wires stretched across several fields to rattles and clap-boards, the tortured, ever-writhing wires tufted at intervals with bunches of feathers.

We passed through the smiling fields to an accompaniment of this percussion chorus, rattling, clapping, groaning, whirring and grinding. At a corner we were ambushed by a party of schoolboys, all quite naked, their leader as fierce and ugly as the rest were cherubic and gazelle-eyed. They gave a melodramatic performance of the usual greeting.

Leader (subito feroce): *Satu, dua, tiga. . . .*

Chorus (sostenuto dolcissimo): *Ta-a-a-be, Tuan!*

Their schoolmaster, down in the valley of the Masupu, came to invite me to stay the night at his house. He was a pleasant young man, obviously longing for a stranger's company, and I was so tired I should have been glad to stay; but it had to be Tandung that night. Even at that to-morrow would be a hard twenty miles over the high pass to Mamasa.

360

"It is ten kilos to Tandung, Tuan," he said earnestly, catching at Horse's bridle, "and rain is coming."

Both proved to be understatements, but I declined the invitation and rode on. Soon the rain came thundering down and I reached the half-dozen houses of Tandung in the state of feeble bad temper that near-exhaustion inspires. The rest-hut was dirty and had been sited at some distance from a spring. After pronouncing a formal curse on the man who had built it there I began to take a bath in the downpour, walking naked into the raining-roaring darkness with a cake of soap in my hand. By the time I was well soaped the rain had abruptly abated to a mere trickle.

It was a sombre evening. Even Timbo failed to raise our spirits with his clowning, but instead asked plaintively for aspirin. The thirst that affected me was unassuagable, though I drank kettlefuls of water almost as soon as they had boiled. Aspirin all round restored the spirits of my suite to some extent and they listened with animation to my lecture on the combined wedding and funeral of the male praying mantis. One of these unattractive creatures had flown out of the darkness to perch on my potato bowl. I asked its Toraja name.

"*Somba-somba*, Tuan," Salu told me.

The insect is rare in that region and none of them knew of the ungrateful habit of the female *somba-somba*, who turns round and begins to eat her partner during their mating embrace. They were suitably shocked. The tall Pangala porter killed the intruder, and Timbo worked out that whatever its sex this action had saved at least one male praying mantis from a *liebestod*.

Two pints of water and a pint of coffee failed to quench my terrible thirst. Our small water-pot was kept constantly on the fire, but my polydipsia remained with me and I lay in bed wondering whether I was not really ill, a prey to humiliating night fears.

Or was the little bungalow still haunted by the suffering

of a friend who had passed a night of torment there only a
few hours earlier?

There can be few things in the world harder to learn than
the warning given in mountaineering guides for novices:
*Remember that the summits are always farther off than they
seem.* Time and again that next day I underestimated the
summit of the pass we had to cross. I prepared myself for
a hard day when we started soon after first light: twenty
miles of ascent and descent in tropical sunshine, with a pass
6,300 feet high to cross, a day like that would have been no
trifle in my livelier days; and though sleep had refreshed me,
I was saddle-sore, and, in fact, walked fifteen of the twenty
miles in preference to using Horse.

But that makes the day sound like no more than an ordeal.
It was a lot better than that. The first hours of the steady
uphill plod in the mild early sunshine were delightful. The
roar of the wild Masupu, which there plunged on its
maniacal course amid gigantic boulders twenty miles from
the point at which we had camped beside it at Baoo, faded
from a thundering to a murmur as our path rose higher above
it. In all that long valley there was not enough level ground
to make a tennis court, for the slopes of grass and naked
rock plunged unbrokenly to the river's edge. There were
small purple terrestrial orchids in the poor grass and the
strange carnivorous pitcher-plants into which insects are
lured to their death. Raising the lid of a pitcher, you can
see various drowned flies and beetles half digested in the
long pouches that contain a tablespoonful of pepsin each (or,
according to Massang, ghosts' urine). Gruesome things.

The only wonder in the valley is the herd of cows
belonging to a Menadonese married to a local lady. The
gentle beasts looked absurdly miscast in their wild setting,
like farmyard ducks in mid-Atlantic.

I climbed hard for the first two hours, well ahead of my

party, trying to reach the dark forest before the sun began his persecutions. The path, narrower with every mile, kept looping deeply to cross little streams that had cut gullies for themselves in the mountain-sides. I reached the forest and climbed a thousand feet in its shade, two thousand, and still no glimpse of the head of the pass. The slopes before me soared steeply into cloud. At the top of a very steep stretch I waited almost an hour for the others to overtake me and we moved on together, the only travellers on the path. I prayed that it might never fork, for by now I had hardly any idea of our position or direction and my map was only a bad joke. But the narrow path was everywhere well marked and did not fork until the desolate heights were left behind.

Two fellow-wayfarers, a few small bronze lizards, a lonely bird or two and occasional small butterflies—they were the only creatures encountered in five hours of mountain journeying. The final 500 feet of the climb was through close white mist that afflicted us with a discomfort I can only describe as visual suffocation. It was as though another world hung a few yards above our heads, muffling and choking us.

When a patch of the broad-leaved grass which Horse especially liked was found we halted for a midday snack. While Horse ate steadily through his little pasture, with Massang and the tall porter hanging round him in the intimate, unsentimental kinship with the beasts which most Torajas seem so strongly aware of, Salu and Timbo made coffee and macaroons. The forest was murmurous with the dripping of mist-drops, spider webs were spangled, great gulfs of white mist hung below the path, and the tops of the trees under which we built our fire were hidden in the soffocating whiteness that made us screw up our eyes as if full noon had been blazing.

The forest was incredibly shabby. Every plant seemed to be a weed and the sickly white orchids looked like some kind

363

of floral vermin. Hundreds of branches were festooned with a creeper like dingy green whiskers; I named it *Clarksonia* and recommend it to actors playing Macbeth's witches.

Considerably refreshed, we trudged on half a mile up a gentle, turfy path, and then it turned left and descended suddenly. In three minutes we were out of the mist. The steep path, cruelly gashed and cliffed by the violence of a million downpours, was a sad trial to Horse, who had almost to be lifted down to gentler levels. The summit chill receded, and with the hot sunshine came the factory uproar mass-produced by an army of stridulating cicadas.

" *Banyak ribut*," said Timbo. Very noisy.

Down and down. There was a village suddenly in a little clearing. A hamlet of half a dozen very long, shabby houses in which, so Salu found out, the population of more than two hundred lived. Two men with pack-horses were gossiping with one of the villagers and Salu joined them as I passed with a greeting. Possibly explaining me a little, I thought, but then I heard them talking about a death, as Torajas always will when they get the chance, like shopgirls at home talking about weddings and engagements. But when Salu came hurrying after me I could see that he had news of more than ordinary urgency.

" *Nyora* of Sangalla is dead, Tuan," he said gravely.

I had not even heard that our kindly hostess at Sangalla was ill and I couldn't understand why the bad news should reach us in that far-distant hamlet. Then I remembered that her home had been near Mamasa, so I concluded that news of her death had reached kinsmen there by letter.

But that was not the way of it.

" She died here, Tuan," Salu told me. " In the forest. Yesterday. The *pandita* and his family came over the pass yesterday. They left Sangalla to come back to their home here. *Nyora* was sick and men carried her through the mountains. Much pain, Tuan. She died beside the path outside this village."

I thought at once, and I have thought many times since, of the morphia I have always carried with me since the Normandy landing. The celluloid-protected needle, the strong mercy in the tiny tube, the blessing that the clumsiest operator can bring to a sufferer in a few moments. If only we had set off one day earlier!

Walking alone ahead of the others down into the vale of Mamasa, I remembered the placid gentleness of the big, motherly woman, the innocence of her smile, the serene friendliness of the large family she had brought into the world. I remembered her especial tenderness for the idiot child, the girl of perhaps eight years who still cried and murmured unintelligibly like a baby, whose dank hair she had tied with a silk ribbon and whose blank face and vaguely clawing limbs she had tried so hard to coax into something less grotesque while I took their family group portrait by request. There on the mountain-path I experienced again the resentful feeling, so familiar in the battles of Normandy and Nijmegen, that some cruel god of death chose the best among us for his sacrifices.

Tired limbs had somehow persuaded me that Mamasa must lie at the bottom of the descent, just where the path reached the valley floor. When a boy told me we still had twelve kilometres to go I put it down to Toraja ignorance of distance measurement, and even went so far as to compare his appearance and intelligence unfavourably with the South Toraja children. A sick or tired traveller is often an unreliable witness.

We left the marigold hedges and the gated hill gardens behind. The path levelled out to skirt paddy-fields, indifferently planted by the standards of Kesu or Tikala.

"Ignorant people here, Tuan," said Timbo, spitting contemptuously. "They don't know how to plant rice. Dogs would plant it as well."

365

Salu, mounted now upon Horse, pressed forward to tell me that sugar, 50 cents a half kilo in Rantepao market, was 150 cents in Mamasa. He had been gossiping with a man who had his pack-horse laden with sugar from Makale market on which he would realise 200 per cent profit.

"Hear, Tuan!" interrupted Massang. "These people don't make *tuak*. They are not able. Truly fools, these people." On the strength of the occasional half mug of *tuak* I gave him, which sufficed to produce hours of mild tipsiness, he glanced round him with the disdain of a *bon vivant* forced to stay at a temperance hotel.

We saw men bathing at a hot spring and in one place a large children's band that was practising as we passed struck up a spirited march to restore our flagging step. Soon it rained and by the time we reached the small rest-house I was soaked. Our porters had fallen behind, so when I took off my wet clothes and bathed I had no dry ones to change into. As I sat wrapped in a blanket in a rattan chair Elisa came to me, walking softly and his eyes very wide, and told me about his mother's death. He sank on his knees beside me and cried.

"We could not help her," he said. "We could not help at all. We carried her in a litter and we could not help jolting it on the rough path, and it made her cry. So much pain, Tuan. She died of pain. When we rested in the forest yesterday, because we were very tired, she said, 'No, take me on; I must see my sister,' but then she said, 'No, I won't see her because I am dying here.' With so much pain a person must die, Tuan, and we could not help her." He was a little boy again, understanding nothing beyond love and loss, no more the star Toraja footballer or the vain youth who had taken an hour to dress for his portrait at Sangalla.

Later the *pandita* came, his little nondescript figure and unshaven face inadequate for the tragic rôle thrust upon him. There had been nothing embarrassing about poor

366

Elisa's grief, it was so like a child's, but his father embarrassed as well as moved me by the unreserve of his sorrow. The favour he asked before leaving was an embarrassing one too.

" When they told me Tuan had come to Mamasa to-day I saw that it was God's hand which had brought Tuan here. Two moons ago *Nyora* was alive and happy far away, and Tuan took her *portret* with me and our children. Now she is dead and now Tuan comes here, and I ask Tuan to take a photograph of her coffin with me and our children beside it before the funeral."

I agreed, of course. I had already decided to stay for the funeral, and not merely as a gesture likely to please the dead lady's family.

When the young doctor-missionary called on me he told me that it was cancer that had killed *Nyora*. I could only be thankful that the disease had been so mercifully swift; but I shall always regret those twenty hours and that great mountain which came between me and a friend in need, whose final ordeal of suffering I could so easily have spared her.

Mamasa is the capital village of the South-West Torajas. This group of tribes is not numerous, no more than 40,000 altogether, which is little more than the population of the single district of Tikala in the South Torajalands. They are fairly closely related to the Sadang tribes, but on the whole seem poorer physical types and to possess, or to have retained, a less impressive culture.

I found Mamasa more adulterated than Makale by alien blood and faith. Bugis people, with their mosque and goats, were everywhere. Many local Torajas, too, have been converted to Islam; one in every ten Torajas in the province is a Muslim now. Of the other nine, two are Christian and seven heathen.

The village lies in a fair valley encircled by handsome mountains. It is bigger than Makale and there are even little streets of small wooden houses with roofs of shingles, modern houses of mass-produced hen-house design. There are hedges of frail pink European roses. A church with two spires stands on a steep hillside and a magnificent roofed bridge spans the swift river. There is a hospital and more than one school. The office of the Controleur is also in Toraja style; its walls and the beautifully painted gables of the bridge are the only examples of traditional Toraja building I could find in the village.

Their market, we found, was far smaller than Rantepao's or even Makale's. The prices were different and some of the goods were different. Many wild forest-dwellers were there selling dammar in cylindrical baskets nearly five feet deep. The stuff looks like chunks of quartz and is a resin collected from certain forest trees. It is an important constituent of varnish. Chinese dealers were buying it for transport to Makassar and the world market.

" Salt is cheap here," Salu informed me, " and rice is not so dear as in Rantepao. But sugar—*Wah!* "

All day the mist never rose from the mountain-tops, and by the time Elisa came to fetch me to his mother's funeral the rainclouds were assembling over the valley. *Nyora's* black coffin lay among flowers in the veranda room of a kinsman's house; her husband and children stood round it weeping, and fifty relatives and friends sat near, among them Tammu, who had been my servant in Sangalla. The acting Controleur and the doctor-missionary, the only white men in the province, occupied two chairs set centrally and I was led to a third beside them.

There were prayers and hymns, one of them a fine old Dutch chorale beaten to death by the brutal slogging of the mechanical beat that passes among the Torajas for good Protestant hymn-singing. Then, after an address in Malay from the doctor, I was invited forward with my camera.

Seldom have I felt more miserably shy. The silence was broken only by the unrestrained sobbing of the bereaved family; the sky was grey with heavy rainclouds and the press of mourners excluded most of the fading light from the black coffin with its roses and orchids, and the apprehension that I should not be able to produce the brilliant enlargement expected of me further diminished my self-confidence.

The ordeal was repeated at the graveside, after the church service. It rained as we stood round the grave, but that did not cut short the addresses which several mourners delivered there. One of them was Tammu, and he powerfully reinforced my high opinion of the Torajas as orators.

Eloquence is a gift found in abundance among the Indonesian peoples, and I had seen how ready Torajas were to speak in public and how appreciative they were of a graceful turn of phrase. Now here was the rough, humble Tammu standing like a fine romantic actor on the mound of sandy soil beside the grave and sending a shiver of thrill down my spine with the authentic accents of oratory.

" My words are poor," he began, " for I never went to school. But I speak for the people of Sangalla."

Nor was his any perfunctory tribute, much less the mere egotistical seizure of an opportunity to hold forth. There were tears in his eyes and he was able, as not one working-class Englishman in a million would be able, to express in a noble voice and moving language his salute to a lost friend.

I rose in darkness for the long trek back to Tandung with the unease that follows nightmare oppressing me. It hadn't been a vivid nightmare, not like the one in which I had once performed at length all but the final detail of a suicide pact with a friend, cutting her throat in patient despair with a safety-razor blade and then starting on the equally long-drawn-out task of cutting my own. This had been no more than a dream of vague fear—fear of torture and death in the dark forest.

It seemed to me quite possible that morning, though it does not now, that the bed or the pillow was haunted by the nightmare of some other recent sleeper. And what more natural than that one of the junior administrators from the south who had lately been there for a short rest after the outbreak of terrorism should have nightmares of ambush, torture and death in the jungle?

As I tugged on my field boots I was remembering the horrible bodies and parts of bodies of the victims of Javanese nationalists which had been seen from time to time in the canals of Batavia. The obscene pulped faces, the swollen dismembered trunks, the mutilated sex parts, one young man crucified on two boards. At times as I flew over Java in storms I had wondered what would be my fate if the plane were forced down. One R.A.F. crew had been mutilated and murdered. A Dutchman who had faced such danger for weeks together might easily fall victim to such a nightmare as I had dreamed, and could not the pillow retain the imprint of his fear and communicate it to a subsequent sleeper? No, of course not; but on that morning I thought it might. . . .

It was good to be on the mountain-path again. The climb up through the coffee thickets and *taro* gardens was tough and it got steeper and tougher the higher we went. Timbo emerged from the forest at one point dragging two branches or creepers of lemon and white orchids two yards long. I carried them for a time and pretended to forget them when we left our midday halting-place. I was more pleased by my discovery of two frail heliotrope violets with a trace of the authentic perfume.

The steady descent was pleasant. I was always excited to see the Masupu River again. We came first in view of it on a spur two thousand feet above it. We saw how the broad, stealthy stream crept in unrippled silence towards a fork in the gigantic valleys below us. It glided silently to the turn and then the deep, calm, drowsy giant woke and pounced in a lashing fury of high-flung spray and a roar of splendid anger. For ten miles down the long valley it raged through labyrinths of rocks the size of cottages and a succession of falls and rapids. A prince of rivers.

Our arrival at the rather squalid *baruga* at Tandung was happier this time, in evening sunshine with the young *guru* meeting us with a bowl of refreshing *langsas* and asking about *Nyora's* funeral. But next morning there was an alarm.

Returning from my bath, I paused for a moment to dwell upon the consummate beauty of the western earth and sky, the picture which I supposed I should never again behold in all the mornings of my life. Suddenly I cursed and looked down at the grass by my naked foot. I expected to see a large snake there, for the attack on my heel had been violent and the sudden pain convulsed every nerve in my body.

There was nothing to be seen in the grass, but already a swelling the size of an egg had distorted the side of my foot and filaments of crimson ran from it up across my ankle and instep. I hobbled in ridiculous agony to the veranda step and collapsed there. When Salu came I could not speak for some moments. He ordered Timbo to bring the morphia tin and they all gathered round with shocked faces.

With one of the plastic-coned morphia tubes in my hand I hesitated. Only three in the box—they might not be enough. I faced the thought of death there. In the confusion of my pain I thought only of the inaccessibility of Dr. Goslinga, two hard days' journey away, and forgot the doctor at Mamasa, ten hours away.

"We must sacrifice the chicken." That was Massang, of course, eager to save me by propitiation and magic. They began to talk quietly together in Toraja, and I was afraid they might already have seen some sure and well-known sign of doom on me. The foot was now an obscene object, hideously swollen and covered with radiating filaments of crimson and purple. When I turned with awful difficulty on to my side I could see the centre of the poisoned area. It showed a single red dot.

"I think it wasn't a snake," I said. "A snake has two teeth. I would have seen a snake."

They made no reply. Through my mind a crowd of rushing thoughts stampeded, out of all control. Ought I to cut out the centre area of the swelling with a razor blade? Wasn't it too late for that, anyway? Or perhaps it was really negligible. Perhaps it happened every day and they were shocked at the fuss I was making. Pencil and notebook— if I was going to die I would have to leave a message. It was a good place to die, and I was in good company. . . .

Timbo was wiping the streaming sweat from my face and chest with a towel. "I'm completely miscast for this sort of rôle," I thought to myself. "Surely I'm not going to die in a mess up here. This is just shock and panic." I began to feel the resentment at this sordid assault on my dignity, which had been so familiar a reaction in difficult moments in action during the war and which is, I suppose, a sustaining influence on such occasions. At all events, from that moment I no longer considered a fatal ending to my swan. The pain was still driving me to the edge of endurance, but the shock was abating.

And that's all. After an hour the swelling began to subside. Within three hours both pain and swelling were sufficiently manageable to allow of putting on my boot and soon after noon I left Tandung on foot, having the idea that exercise would be good for it. It was, too, for by the time I reached Belaoo, perhaps thirteen miles away, an uncomfortable numbness was all that troubled me. I never knew what had bitten me. A giant centipede was suspected, but it seemed that its sting was less agonising and the pain never lasted less than twelve hours, according to Salu.

The tiny *baruga* of Belaoo is three-parts surrounded by

streams of a rushing river. The local *parenge* sent me fodder
for Horse and a necklace of eggs for myself by the hand of
his *mata-mata* (literally " eyes "), his policeman, a young
man with prodigiously wide shoulders, waving hair and a
periwinkle skirt.

Salu smiled in his fatherly way when we said good night.
" Tuan was afraid this morning," he said.

" Yes," I said, " I was much afraid."

" When I was a boy," he told me, " a green snake bit me.
I kicked and I beat it with a stick, but it still bit my foot.
Another boy pulled it off. It was not a wicked snake. It
gave me no poison."

" Good night, Salu," I said.

" Good night, Tuan," he answered, and I was sorry at
the thought that soon we should be together no longer, I
and the Toraja I knew best and liked best.

Naturally enough, the excitement of the swan tailed off
towards the end, returning as we did in our old tracks. But
it was still satisfying. Back we trudged, over the high pass
crowned with orchid forest, cool and dark, where I called
a greeting into the olive depths to a man who was axing a
tree. He called back, and I stared for minutes into the dark
maze of sullen greens and greys, seeking him. Three times
he answered my call and evidently he could see me, for he
laughed at my baffled peering in his direction, but I never
saw him. A landslide had carried away fifty yards of the
path since we had passed four days before; Horse had a
bad time crossing the scree there. In Bituang I saw a
pleasant example of sympathetic magic, a rough iron rat-trap
in the form of a cat. I also saw a small spider that could
hop like a flea.

The porters travelled faster as their loads grew lighter.
There was no rice left, and the last of the chicken that had
travelled with such complacency in the globular open-work

basket had escaped the sacrificial knife to spare my life at
Tandung only to be fried at Belaoo for my supper. The big
porter looked somehow one-sided without the spherical
basket with the birds murmuring contentedly inside it like
babies being taken for a walk. (And what an absurd phrase
that is, to describe an activity which the baby undertakes
lying down or sitting up. Almost as absurd as " rising to
one's feet.")

At one point I remember remonstrating with Timbo, who
sang for a whole mile the same dreary song.

" I forgot, Tuan," he apologised. " We had to sing that
in school when the Nippons were here. It's a song about
their rajah."

Up, down, up the wide grass road to Rante Karua, with
greetings from the tall, loin-clothed men working at the
ditches; over the bridge where their woven envelopes of rice
hung from the rails; along the upland path beyond the
coffee groves, pausing to greet another friend of Salu's;
down into the vale of Awan and up on to the high moors of
diadem bracken where we met groups of school children on
their way home; down to a river from which men emerged
after bathing, combing out their long hair in the yellow
sunshine; up and down for five hours with " our " house
at the end of the last up.

I was in time for the earthquake.

It was my first. I was sitting outside with a mug of coffee,
and when my arm-chair swayed I said, " Hallo, Horse! "
for he would sometimes come up and rub against my chair.
Dust was falling from the eaves and a shutter slammed.
Perhaps thirty seconds of the gentle rocking and unsteady
focus, and then all was still again. An earth-tremor rather
than a quake.

A sudden chorus of rice-pounding echoed across the
valley as housewives ran to the rice-trough and beat out
fortissimo tattoos to quiet the earth and protect the rice.
In La'bo, Salu told me, all our friends would circumambulate

the fields, striking gongs and improvised percussion instruments to ward off the peril to the rice; in Pangala that is not customary.

I did not leave Celebes for two more weeks, but the end of the swan was in a sense the end of my stay. It was all packing and good-byes after that, and the painful return to the Western obsession with the details of Time, calculating the lengths of the journey back to Kesu for a final farewell to friends in La'bo, then to Makale and finally down-country to Makassar, the sailing dates of boats, the arrangements for a stay in Singapore, the passage to England.

Paradise lost.

XVIII

GOOD-BYE

MY sixth Toraja moon was ripe and it was time for me to go. Time to say good-bye and time, perhaps, for a short backward glance over the experience, its motives and its value.

Mainly, of course, it had been simple self-indulgence, the realisation of a romantic ambition that had been with me in essence since childhood. A holiday. A holiday, far from deserved, for the war and its seedy aftermath in the East had not tried me hard.

What else? Well, I had travelled a little at last, and travelled in the way I had always longed to travel, out of my world and century, tasting the refreshment of alien custom, sharing the fellowship of far-distant hearths, seeing life in a few swift flashes through the strange brilliance of quite other eyes. That is the sort of adventure and exploration I care for.

Yes, and I had found a possible shape for my next years. I wanted to return to the Indies, to mature my acquaintance with the Torajas and some of their kin among the folk of Island India. If in books and photographs I could find a way of sharing with those unable ever to go there the refreshment and colour of such journeys, then enough money might come in to make a succession of them possible. It may still happen.

No more? There was one other discovery, yes, or more strictly an impression, that I was to bring away; for as time went on one of the strongest impulses that had driven me up into those highlands became apparent to me.

Some years ago I asked a psychiatrist friend why I should

so frequently dream of my childhood. His offhand reply was that it might indicate a longing for innocence, since in the popular mind innocence and childhood tended to be identified. I suppose he might interpret my impulse to seek a temporary home among neighbours only now emerging from the childhood of man as confirmatory evidence of that longing. And I think he would perhaps be right.

For I would give much to know whether man, so pitifully bemused to-day amid the fair world which his clever wickedness has reduced to a slum, was in his youth a sweeter and more wholesome creature. It came to me in my Toraja days and nights that indeed he had been. In an earlier day, and even to-day in a few remote, unregarded valleys, he had fallen less far from grace and his crystal eyes were still untarnished by blood and soot.

So it seemed to me.

And so, at last, the day came.

When I rose and went out to see my last sunrise over the shoulder of Buntu Sanik there was no mountain to be seen, and only a blur of faded primrose in the lavender cloud banks. A little later the soft *uran allo* began to fall, as we had known it would.

Friends began to arrive to say good-bye before I had finished my informal breakfast of two boiled eggs and three double whiskies, the latter so that a little boy from Tandung should have the bottle which, so he reminded me in a wide-eyed, reproachful whisper, I had promised him many markets since. I was feeling little older than he, for the familiar relapse into the lost inadequacy of a twelve-year-old had overtaken me again, as it always does when I am deeply moved.

Soon the basket bungalow was crowded. The porters who were lashing my remaining goods to shoulder-poles protested repeatedly as the bark ropes became entangled in crowded ankles. Lendu and Barra were again two of the porters.

It seemed to me then that my life had been nothing but a succession of losses, and I had little left to lose. Time and time again barriers rose between me and those I most liked—death, and the war, and the Iron Curtain—and now ten thousand miles of sea, a daunting barrier for a poor man in these times. I did not know then that on my return to England rare mornings would be cheered by a letter from Salu or Palinggi, stiff and a little remote, it is true, on account of the florid prolixities characteristic of Malay correspondence, but how warmly welcome! Nor did I for a moment dream when I gave young Isak my despised English-Malay Vocabulary, knowing that he loved to handle it and try his hand at pronouncing English words, that I should one day be the first man ever to receive a letter in English from a Toraja.

This historic document ran as follows:

" Good day.

" With a letter this I send to the Master, reason the letters of the Master we already get. We very restful, reason the Master are in the condition which healthy and safe and also the familys of the Master.

" I here are also in the condition which healthy and safe, and my father and my mother and my brothers and my friends in La'bo.

" And the photos of the Master my father already get in post office Rantepao. One my photo, four photos of my father, one photo of our house in La'bo, six photos of Lady Loedia which my father to give her and three photos of Lady Lai'Lebok. It is we recite thank you to the Master.

" Here every day I go at school learn. And also I already say to my friends in La'bo who go at school Rantepao (Sesa and Siu and Sulo) I was get a letter of the

Mr. Colonel and he write when I come back I kill a swine and we all feast. And they very glad heard it. And also I say to the children which at the market Rantepao, Timbo and Lelang and Massang and Duna and Lindung and Sipa, the words of the Master. And they say thank God, reason the Master is in the condition which safe and the Master not forgets to us here. And also I say to the children the Master comes again of one year or one and one half year. And Timbo say Yet too long.

" We already very hanker to the Master, but we hope so that us find once again. My goodday to the Master, the Mrs. and the children of the Master. Indeed this my words and neatlys not perfect but I hope the Master get understan. And also many which faults.

" Enough before here!
" Goodday of me
" ISAK "

Good-bye, then.

Though all was not yet ready I could not endure the heavy waiting for the moment of departure. The grey skies and the strangely silent crowd of well-wishers oppressed my already sunken spirits.

For the second time Timbo failed me. I needed him, our hired clown, that morning to ease my heaviness, but he did nothing to animate us. For two days he had forsaken his japing and taken to sitting quietly near me, still and silent like a good child in church; and earlier that morning he had astonished me with a glimpse of sentimentality, a vice of which I had believed every Toraja completely free. When the rain had started to fall and everybody had remarked that it was always so when Tuan took to the road, Timbo looked up and said with a hint of defiance, " The *deata* are weeping."

This flight of fancy embarrassed us all and efforts were

made to provoke him into some of his popular antics; but he remained silent at my side, turning the jack-knife I had given him over and over in his hand.

A crowd rose to its feet as I strode out on to the veranda, putting on my hat. Palimbong came to my side and was the first with his unaffected, generous farewell. Then there was Palinggi's wife and Deppa, Poi' Bunga and the glum chief of Tandung, Pong' Masa'aga's sons (for the old man was still sick and could only send a message), Sesa's nice father, Masak and Manga, Palimbong's writer and Oberammergau, Kadang with his little son in his arms and many others. I thanked them all for their kindness, shook hands and told them I hoped to come back some day. Then I turned to the children.

There were not many of them, for school was in. Dear Mina had already taken her leave, twinkling off on her tiny legs with two yards of blue muslin, my parting gift, strained to her bosom. Lelang, the time-expired outlaw, had wished me good-bye the night before, because though no longer in danger of pursuit he still preferred not to visit the bungalow when the *guru* might be there. And Tu'ugun had just passed the gate mounted on Saleko, rising on to his knees on the great beast's back and hammering his Adam's apple with his fist as he yelled his last greeting.

" Good-bye, Kalo'udun," I said. " Good-bye, Ma' Salu. Good-bye, Sipa, and thank you for all the mud bulls. Good-bye, Koton; salute Duna for me when he comes back. Good-bye, Dapo. Good-bye, Lindung; don't forget me." (Lindung hung his head and folded his small hands.) " Good-bye, Sampekanan. Good-bye, Lepeh and Nimpa and Torri. . . ."

Down the steps for the last time, leaving my last footprint among the crowded naked prints in the mud by the gate. And then a great shout as the school doors filled and children raced in single file along the narrow path between the fields of rice. I waited at the gate while fifty of them, girls and boys, came crowding up the lane, setsquares and pencil-cases rattling and swinging, the first-comers crying on the panting stragglers. Black Bombai marshalled them into five ranks in the roadway, frowned and for the last time shouted his introductory *satu, dua, tiga. . . .*

" *Tabe, Tuan! Selamat jalan, Tuan!* "

With Palinggi at my side, I stood hesitating in the light rain for a little while. I am not equal to such moments. There must be many who would scorn an adult European whose heart knew no better than to ache at parting from a crowd of savage urchins with vermin in their hair, and I envy such people their detachment. For me it was a moment of pain as I looked along the rows of guileless brown eyes, of flat-backed, shaven heads and heads with tiny buns of black hair, of wild brown bodies frail and sturdy, of pitiful mended rags and bare, plucky feet and smiles of glorious teeth. With helpless regret I wished again that it had been in my power to ease the too-hard poverty that was the lot of so many of them. It was hard to be able to make no return for the joy their friendship and the sweetness of their presence had given me.

" *Selamet tinggal, pia-pia,* " I greeted them, mixing the languages. The ranks broke up and Likku and the boys clustered round me, the other little girls too shy to the last to venture very near. I stayed only a half-minute with them and then went off up the hill with Palinggi, glad for once of the stiff pace he set. When we came to the top of the hill I would not look back.

We walked as far as Ke'te in silence, my mind full of things I could not speak. My real farewell to my neighbours in La'bo I never spoke till I climbed a crag above Makale next day and turned on the summit towards the valley which Sarira hid from me. It did not seem excessively sentimental then to utter aloud in the blue silence the words first spoken by another lonely one in my own Dorset valley. *If ever I forget your name let me forget home and heaven. . . .*

The sun came out as I shook hands with Palinggi and said good-bye to Lendu and Barra. The three friends, Massang, Timbo and Sesa, had also followed me as far as the truck.

"*Selamat jalan, Tuan*," said Sesa and Massang, the Malay greeting to one who departs. "Peace on your journey."

"*Selamat tinggal*," I said. "Peace on you, remaining."

Timbo the clown, silent for an hour, had decided on his own way of saying good-bye.

"In Tuan's country, what do men say for *selamat jalan*?" he asked, his head hung down and the sun blazing on his furry black hair.

I answered, "'God bless you,' Timbo."

"God bless you, Tuan," he said, very carefully.

An old man from Marante had halted respectfully, his great hat in his hand.

"*Umbara miola, Tuang?*" he asked, with the gentle candour I was so soon to miss. "Where are you going?"

"To England, Old Man," I answered, and wished with all my heart that it need not be so.

POSTSCRIPT

TIME for good-bye was time to remember once more the volume of good will, encouragement and practical help that had made the venture possible. Because I myself usually skip a list of acknowledgments at the beginning of a book I hesitated to record my thanks there. They cannot, however, be left unsaid, so I have set them here. Readers who have come with me to the end may have decided I was worth helping, and so care to read my formal thanks to those who helped me.

At the best of times a traveller must be a nuisance to the various officials whose help he is bound to ask; but that was truer than ever in my case, for the times were not at their best. Again and again I was ashamed to be worrying, with my holiday affairs, busy Dutch officials, some of them on duty continuously since their release from inhuman Japanese internment camps and coping with situations of crisis. Under such conditions attentions which might have been matters of normal courtesy in easier times became personal kindnesses.

First, then, my grateful thanks to the Dutch authorities in Batavia who authorised my visit at a time when odd whites with no serious business to justify their presence could hardly have been welcome. I am particularly grateful to Dr. van Mook, at that time the Lieutenant Governor-General, and Dr. Guyt, head of the Department of Immigration.

In Celebes the Resident of Makassar showed me kindness. For protection on the journey up-country I am indebted to the Military Commander of Borneo and the Great East.

For help in planning and liaison work I have to thank my kind friends and hosts of the British-American Tobacco

383

Company (Java); also Arthur Lovell of Austin Motors, and Bertie McShane, then of Michael Stephens, Ltd., Makassar. I remember, too, the delightful friendship in Makassar of Ruby McShane, who has not lived to see these pages.

My warm thanks are due to Mr. J. M. van Lijf, Controleur of Makale, for generous and valuable advice, as well as much practical help; and to Dr. J. J. J. Goslinga for very many kindnesses and much information. To the wives of both these gentlemen I owe thanks for welcome hospitality. I am also indebted to Dr. and Mevrouw van Dijk for assistance early in my stay. Major Brengen, commanding the troops in Makale and Rantepao, showed me many favours, and I am grateful for a long talk with Dr. H. van der Veen.

I shall never forget the constant help and friendship of Palinggi. As for Salu, I cannot imagine what the enterprise would have been without him. To these two good Toraja friends I owe the heartiest thanks of all.

For much kindness and hospitality I am grateful to Kalasuso, Prince of Bunt'ao, to the Ampulembang of Pangala, to Siambe and Siindo di Nanggala, Pandita Pattikayhatu and his family, the Puang of Sangalla and Palimbong, Chief of Menke'pe. But it is impracticable to name here the many Toraja folk whose help and generosity deserves to be recorded. To all of them, and especially to the children, my thanks and blessing.

Some other Oxford Paperbacks for readers interested in Central Asia, China and South-East Asia, past and present

CAMBODIA

GEORGE COEDÈS
Angkor

MALCOLM MacDONALD
Angkor and the Khmers*

CENTRAL ASIA

PETER FLEMING
Bayonets to Lhasa

ANDRÉ GUIBAUT
Tibetan Venture

LADY MACARTNEY
An English Lady in Chinese
Turkestan

DIANA SHIPTON
The Antique Land

C.P. SKRINE AND
PAMELA NIGHTINGALE
Macartney at Kashgar*

ERIC TEICHMAN
Journey to Turkistan

ALBERT VON LE COQ
Buried Treasures of Chinese
Turkestan

AITCHEN K. WU
Turkistan Tumult

CHINA

All About Shanghai: A Standard
Guide

HAROLD ACTON
Peonies and Ponies

VICKI BAUM
Shanghai '37

ERNEST BRAMAH
Kai Lung's Golden Hours*

ERNEST BRAMAH
The Wallet of Kai Lung*

ANN BRIDGE
The Ginger Griffin

CHANG HSIN-HAI
The Fabulous Concubine*

CARL CROW
Handbook for China

PETER FLEMING
The Siege at Peking

MARY HOOKER
Behind the Scenes in Peking

NEALE HUNTER
Shanghai Journal*

GEORGE N. KATES
The Years that Were Fat

CORRINNE LAMB
The Chinese Festive Board

W. SOMERSET
MAUGHAM
On a Chinese Screen*

G.E. MORRISON
An Australian in China

DESMOND NEILL
Elegant Flower

PETER QUENNELL
Superficial Journey through
Tokyo and Peking

OSBERT SITWELL
Escape with Me! An Oriental
Sketch-book

J.A. TURNER
Kwang Tung or Five Years in
South China

HONG KONG AND MACAU

AUSTIN COATES
City of Broken Promises

AUSTIN COATES
A Macao Narrative

AUSTIN COATES
Myself a Mandarin

AUSTIN COATES
The Road

The Hong Kong Guide 1893

INDONESIA

DAVID ATTENBOROUGH
Zoo Quest for a Dragon*

VICKI BAUM
A Tale from Bali*

'BENGAL CIVILIAN'
Rambles in Java and the Straits
in 1852

MIGUEL COVARRUBIAS
Island of Bali*

AUGUSTA DE WIT
Java: Facts and Fancies

JACQUES DUMARÇAY
Borobudur

JACQUES DUMARÇAY
The Temples of Java

ANNA FORBES
Unbeaten Tracks in Islands of the
Far East

GEOFFREY GORER
Bali and Angkor

JENNIFER LINDSAY
Javanese Gamelan

EDWIN M. LOEB
Sumatra: Its History and People

MOCHTAR LUBIS
The Outlaw and Other Stories

MOCHTAR LUBIS
Twilight in Djakarta

MADELON H. LULOFS
Coolie*

MADELON H. LULOFS
Rubber

COLIN McPHEE
A House in Bali*

ERIC MJÖBERG
Forest Life and Adventures in the
Malay Archipelago

HICKMAN POWELL
The Last Paradise

E.R. SCIDMORE
Java, The Garden of the East

MICHAEL SMITHIES
Yogyakarta: Cultural Heart of
Indonesia

F.M. SCHNITGER
Forgotten Kingdoms in Sumatra

LADISLAO SZÉKELY
Tropic Fever: The Adventures of
a Planter in Sumatra

EDWARD C. VAN NESS
AND SHITA
PRAWIROHARDJO
Javanese Wayang Kulit

MALAYSIA

ISABELLA L. BIRD
The Golden Chersonese: Travels
in Malaya in 1879

MARGARET BROOKE
THE RANEE OF
SARAWAK
My Life in Sarawak

HENRI FAUCONNIER
The Soul of Malaya

W.R. GEDDES
Nine Dayak Nights

C.W. HARRISON
Illustrated Guide to the Federated
Malay States (1923)

BARBARA HARRISSON
Orang-Utan

TOM HARRISSON
Borneo Jungle

TOM HARRISSON
World Within: A Borneo Story

CHARLES HOSE
The Field-Book of a Jungle-Wallah

CHARLES HOSE
Natural Man

W. SOMERSET
MAUGHAM
Ah King and Other Stories*

W. SOMERSET
MAUGHAM
The Casuarina Tree*

MARY McMINNIES
The Flying Fox*

ROBERT PAYNE
The White Rajahs of Sarawak

OWEN RUTTER
The Pagans of North Borneo

OWEN RUTTER
The Pirate Wind

ROBERT W. SHELFORD
A Naturalist in Borneo

CARVETH WELLS
Six Years in the Malay Jungle

SINGAPORE

RUSSELL GRENFELL
Main Fleet to Singapore

R.W.E. HARPER AND
HARRY MILLER
Singapore Mutiny

MASANOBU TSUJI
Singapore 1941–1942

G.M. REITH
Handbook to Singapore (1907)

C.E. WURTZBURG
Raffles of the Eastern Isles

THAILAND

CARL BOCK
Temples and Elephants

REGINALD CAMPBELL
Teak-Wallah

ANNA LEONOWENS
The English Governess at the
Siamese Court

MALCOLM SMITH
A Physician at the Court of Siam

ERNEST YOUNG
The Kingdom of the Yellow Robe

Titles marked with an asterisk have restricted rights.